EXPLAINING *the* UNEXPLAINED

Mysteries of the paranormal

EXPLAINING *the* UNEXPLAINED

Mysteries of the paranormal

Hans J. Eysenck & Carl Sargent

PRION

This edition first published in the United Kingdom 1993 by
PRION, an imprint of Multimedia Books Limited,
32–34 Gordon House Road, London NW5 1LP

Exclusive distribution in the USA by
AVERY PUBLISHING GROUP INC.
120 Old Broadway, Garden City Park, NY 11040

Editor Anne Cope
Design, graphs, diagrams Kelly j Maskall
Production Hugh Allan
Picture research Julia Hanson

A catalogue record for this book is available from the British Library.

ISBN 1-85375-104-9 hardback
ISBN 1-85375-120-0 paperback

10 9 8 7 6 5 4 3 2 1

Colour separation by J Film Process Ltd, Thailand
Printed in Singapore by Imago

Contents

Preface

Surveys of 'ordinary' people show that a majority believe in ESP (extra-sensory perception) Most believe they have experienced telepathy personally. Many believe in 'dreams that come true'. Interest in 'the paranormal' is perennial — a steady outpouring of films, magazine articles, and books shows this to be the case. Yet 'catalogs' of miraculous and extraordinary events are deeply unsatisfying. People want explanations, not lists. 'Why do these things happen? How do they happen?' they ask. These are essentially scientific questions, questions that seek deeper, more meaningful knowledge. Curiosity and the desire to explore, measure, and understand are in us all.

Surveys of scientists, however, show that only a minority accept the existence of ESP, although, encouragingly, fewer and fewer are prepared to rule it out as an impossibility. Is this because the research that would enable them to suspend their disbelief, or at least admit the possibility of ESP, has not been done? Or do they, with all the confidence of prejudice, refuse to look at the evidence?

We consider that there is a wealth of evidence suggesting that 'paranormal' human abilities are real. These abilities range through telepathy, clairvoyance, and precognition (all aspects of ESP) to psychokinesis (PK for short). We also consider that these abilities are as much a part, albeit an elusive part, of human nature as intelligence or personality, and that they are of practical importance. The evidence surveyed in this book shows lawfulness, order, and meaningful pattern. We are not dealing with 'empty anomalies'. The evidence makes sense. The findings are coherent and repeatable.

However, *Explaining the Unexplained* is not solely concerned with scientific studies of the paranormal, although as scientists this is our major area of interest. After all, if people did not repeatedly report paranormal experiences in everyday life there would be nothing to investigate scientifically. In fact some of the most successful ESP experiments have been attempts to capture something of the psychological conditions which favor 'spontaneous' ESP (real-life, 'out of the blue' paranormal experiences). Experience and experiment should inform each other.

It is eleven years since we compiled the first edition of this book. Since then there have been many high-quality experiments and studies — particularly in the areas of machine-PK, faith healing, reincarnation, and near-death experiences — and also some genuine breakthroughs (a term we studiously avoided eleven years ago), especially in the statistical evaluation of past and ongoing research findings. Much has happened to maintain our interest and excitement.

As this book was being prepared for press we learned with great sadness of the death of Charles Honorton, arguably the most distinguished parapsychologist of the last 25 years. Honorton's work was of the highest calibre, and his friendly generosity towards us in reviewing recent research advances for inclusion in this new edition was much appreciated. His friends will miss him greatly, and the loss to parapsychology is incalculable.

Eleven years ago we wrote: 'There is no reason to think that the coming years will not show us more and more of the picture.' It is gratifying to see just how much more of the scenery has become visible and to have the opportunity of sharing that expanded knowledge with our readers.

Hans Eysenck and Carl Sargent
December 1992

What is paranormal?

Science is a powerful tool for investigating the Universe. The extraordinary scientific advances of the twentieth century have furnished us with profound insights into the fundamental processes of life and matter. These advances have certainly made the world a more dangerous place — the atomic bomb is the most obvious symbol of that — but they have also brought great freedoms, from disease, from hunger, from total dependence on a particular environment (ask any Canadian with a central heating system in midwinter). These freedoms allow the possibility of a vastly enriched life for ordinary individuals, but they also give the illusion that science is a process of discovery leading smoothly towards a set of fixed and final answers. Nothing could be further from the truth.

Since this book is greatly concerned with parapsychology as a science, it is important to establish what science is. The most accurate description of science is to say that, at any given time, it consists of a network of theories and models of how the Universe is organized and how it works and of an army of researchers busy formulating and testing those theories and models. There are, of course, certain rules which govern the development and testing of theories and models against experimental evidence. A theory or model should explain why people, or objects, or particles behave in the way they do, and predict how they will behave in the future. If it does not adequately or reliably do this, then it is replaced by other theories or models. That is the picture which many scientists and philosophers of science have of science. In fact, matters are much less clear-cut. In different areas of science, different levels of theory and different criteria for testing them are employed. What works in physics will may not apply to psychology, for example.

Likewise, there are rules governing the conduct of experiments. There are good ways to do experiments and bad ways. It is generally thought that, for the the results of an experiment to be accepted, it should be possible for other experimenters to repeat the results of the original experiment. This is fine in theory, but in practice it may not work out so easily, as we shall see.

The true nature of science

Science is a growing, not a static, method of acquiring knowledge and understanding. It often makes mistakes. Practice often doesn't fit theory. Since this book is all about parapsychology, about the scientific investigation of anomalous events often referred to as 'paranormal', we would do well to remember that science is not an infallible, wholly objective march towards ultimate understanding.

Many scientists feel that phenomena such as ESP (extrasensory perception) are impossible because they contradict fundamental laws of physics. This is not a viable point of view. In the eighteenth century, following the pronouncement of the great French chemist Antoine Lavoisier that there were no stones in heaven and that none could therefore fall to earth, museums removed meteorites from their exhibits. In a gesture which seems ludicrous now, reality was simply arbitrated out of existence. In 1850 the German physiologist Johannes Müller stated that science would never discover the speed of the nervous impulse; two years later Hermann von Helmholtz did. When Ernest Rutherford, the physicist who split the atom, was an undergraduate his tutor told him not to bother taking up physics because scientists had a complete picture of the nature of matter and

Opposite: The Voyager II flyby of Saturn in 1981, one of a series of highly successful NASA unmanned missions, discovered 11 new moons and dozens of new rings. The triumphs of science and technology are sometimes spectacular, but progress is often painful. Wrong turnings, red herrings, setbacks, and hiccups are common in science.

only the final details remained to be settled! It is interesting to speculate on the consequences for science if Rutherford had accepted that advice. The growing ozone hole over Antarctica was not initially detected by American scientists because their computers were programmed to eliminate the data, the 'anomalous', out-of-place data, that showed that the hole exists. Darwinian evolutionary theory (and its neo-Darwinist derivative) is now under devastating attack from biologist Soren Lovtrup.

Examples of imperfections and about-turns in science could be multiplied over and over again. In the realm of the social sciences, the problems become even greater. In economics, it is now widely accepted that classical economic theories cannot explain the combination of simultaneously rising inflation and unemployment that plagued the Western industrial nations in the 1980s, nor do they explain chronically high levels of unemployment in the same economies in the last decade. In psychology, despite claims made during the 1970s that the neural basis of Mind would be understood within 20 years, advances in that direction have been, frankly, negligible.

The notion that science is a dynamic and powerful tool for investigating the Universe is not wrong, but like all human enterprises science is capable of many mistakes and biases which may persist for lengthy periods of time. In particular, science does not deal well with genuine anomalies that challenge established views. This is a key point for parapsychology, since such anomalies are the very stuff of parapsychology. What is not acceptable to the authors or to parapsychologists in general is the viewpoint often encounted within science which says: 'ESP contradicts physics, therefore it cannot exist.' This is simply Lavoisier telling us that stones don't fall from heaven again.

That unfortunate mindset is often presented as 'skepticism'. It is anything but. Skepticism is the attitude of the researcher who, faced with an anomaly (such as ESP appears to be), says: 'Well, what's going on here? Let's take a look at it.' It is not the attitude of the armchair critic who simply *knows* it's all nonsense and can't be bothered to address the evidence offered to him. Indeed, those who are placed in the position of challenging the status quo are often the true skeptics, because they do not accept conventional wisdom and are prepared to take an objective look at the evidence.

ESP and PK: the best candidates for investigation

Throughout history there have been reports of events that were not explainable in terms of the accepted scientific theories of the day. These are the kind of events that tend to get lumped together as 'the paranormal', an unfortunate term perhaps, but a familiar one, so we will stick with its use here. There is no doubt that 'the paranormal' is a ragbag of highly varied material. Depending on which popular book or magazine you read, the paranormal includes ESP (extrasensory perception) and PK (psychokinesis), astrology, the Loch Ness monster, 'earth energies', people being abducted by space-hopping aliens in UFOs, faith healing, astral planing, reincarnation, and a hundred and one other weird and wonderful phenomena.

There is little reason to suppose that most, or even many, of these different phenomena involve similar underlying causes and mechanisms. But in order to investigate the paranormal scientifically, it makes good sense to concentrate on phenomena that can be studied easily and on phenomena that seem to have some linking principle.

Two apparently paranormal human abilities stand out as being the best candidates for investigation. The first is ESP, extrasensory perception. This is often subdivided into three categories: *telepathy* (person-to-person ESP), *clairvoyance* (detection of information about objects or events by ESP), and *precognition* (ESP used to detect information about future events). The second is PK, psychokinesis, mind over matter, the apparent ability to influence other people, or events or objects, by an effort of will. Both ESP and PK have been with us, as reported events, since antiquity, and surveys show that most people

'PARANORMAL' PHENOMENA: A CHALLENGE TO SCIENCE

This display of phenomena as yet unexplained by science is not exhaustive. Science has always had a problem explaining anomalies. Some of these may be genuine, but others may be illusions or hoaxes. So far, parapsychology has tended to concentrate on those areas easiest to investigate: ESP and PK.

ESP (extrasensory perception)

The reported ability to gain information about people, events, or objects at some distant place and/or time by means as yet unknown to science.

Fortune telling in medieval times.

PK (psychokinesis)

The reported ability to influence other people, objects, or events, by act of will and not involving any known physical force.

Uri Geller demonstrates spoon-bending at a children's party. PK seems to influence the molecular structure of metal in a manner not reproducible by any other means.

Astrology

The claimed influence of the sun, moon, planets, and stars on human personality and behavior, mediated by means unknown to science.

A star map from the tomb of the Egyptian pharoah Seti I (ruled 1312-1298 BC). The constellations of Leo, Taurus, and Sagittarius can be clearly seen. The Ancient Egyptians had no doubt whatsoever that celestial events influenced human affairs.

UFOs (unidentified flying objects)

Reports of aerial objects and events said to unexplainable in terms of known phenomena (clouds, weather, balloons, aircraft, etc.)

A scene from the film Close Encounters Of The Third Kind.

OBEs (out-of-body experiences)

Claimed separations of 'mind' and 'body', variously categorized as autoscopic ESP, near-death experiences, astral travelling, apparitions, mental mediumship, reincarnation, etc.

Out-of-body experiences touch on the greatest mystery of all: Is there life after death?

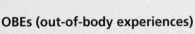

believe that they have had personal experience of one or the other (especially telepathy).

Scientists and lay people alike realize that if 'ESP information' does not arrive through the ordinary channels of our five senses (that is part of the definition of ESP) then some other mode of gaining information must be involved. Extrasensory perception is in some ways an unfortunate term, because it implies that ESP is 'other than', fundamentally different from, alien in some way to the normal function of our everyday senses. It also tends to imply that, because of that different nature in principle, investigating it is somehow beyond the bounds of science. But recent research has confirmed that human beings operate on more than five sensory levels.

It appears that many people are more or less sensitive to the magnetic field that surrounds the Earth and can therefore orient themselves in accordance with their position within that field. This long-suspected ability constitutes an extra sense comparable with, but of course much weaker than, sight or hearing or touch or smell or taste. There is nothing paranormal about it. Indeed it can be neutralized quite simply. Just as vision can be neutralized by a blindfold, so fitting a small electromagnet to a person's head blocks his or her direction-finding ability; the strong local field produced by the magnet obscures the much weaker field of the Earth. Near power lines or large electrical complexes, the weak lines of force of the Earth's magnetic field are disrupted and therefore cannot be detected and used for the purposes of orientation. Frank Brown, at Northwestern University in the United States, has shown that fluctuations in the Earth's magnetic field affect many natural processes, including the metabolism of sea creatures and the respiration of plants (his work was laughed at or ignored by the scientific establishment for decades, but that did not stop him being right).

So although ESP may be unlike our other senses, we can still study it scientifically. Human magnetic sense research give us an example, possibly an analogy, of how new findings might be integrated with what we already know in science.

Spontaneous ESP and PK

Now let us take a closer look at reported cases of ESP and PK. What sort of events suggest that these abilities exist?

One of the strangest types of reported ESP is *precognition*. The word means 'foreknowledge', knowledge of future events not obtained by sensory means or by logical working-out (reasoned prediction). For millennia people have believed that particular individuals have the gift of prophesy. This belief lent tremendous authority to ancient oracles such as that at Delphi in Greece. Prophets, seers, soothsayers, diviners, and readers of omens have influenced the spiritual and political lives of many peoples and cultures.

Ancient oracles are one thing, but what of our own century? Two dramatic British examples of precognition will serve our purpose here. In 1966 an appalling disaster occurred in the mining village of Aberfan in South Wales. In the course of a few moments 128 children and 16 adults died in a cataclysm described by one newspaper as 'the greatest single disaster that has ever hit our people in peace time.' Here is one description of events.

'First, I saw an old school house nestling in a valley, then a Welsh miner, then an avalanche of coal hurtling down a mountainside. At the bottom of this mountain of hurtling coal was a little boy with a long fringe looking absolutely terrified to death. Then for quite a while I saw rescue operations taking place. I had an impression that the little boy was left behind and saved. He looked so grief-stricken. I could never forget him, and also with him was one of the rescuers wearing an unusual peaked cap.'

Eye-witness testimony? Of a sort. The coal tip at Aberfan slid down the mountainside at 9:15 a.m. on 21 October. But the woman who wrote the account just quoted 'saw' the events she reported in the form of a vision at a Spiritualist church in Plymouth, 200 miles south of Aberfan, on the evening of 20 October. Moreover, there were six witnesses present at the time. The woman also told a neighbor about her vision at 8:30 on the morning of the disaster.

At 4:53 p.m. on 1 June, 1974, a massive explosion at the Nypro (UK) chemical plant at Flixborough, South Humberside, virtually demolished the 60-acre complex. The sudden

OTHER REPORTED PRECOGNITIONS OF THE ABERFAN DISASTER

Do terrible events cast a shadow before them? Here are three more reports of precognitive experiences connected with Aberfan.

'She was an attractive, dependable child, not given to imagination. The day before the disaster she said to her mother: "No, Mummy, you must listen. I dreamt I went to school and there was no school there! Something black had come down all over it!"'

Source: Child victim of Aberfan
Time of dream: 14 days before the disaster
Confirmed by both parents and a local church minister

Rescue workers search for survivors at Aberfan, South Wales. The community still bears the scars of the terrible events of the morning of 21 October, 1966.

'I had a horrible vivid dream of a terrible disaster in a coal-mining village. It was in a valley, with a big building filled with children. Mountains of coal and water were rushing down the valley, burying the building. The screams of the children were so vivid that I screamed myself.'

Source: Woman in Sidcup, Kent
Time of dream: 7 days before the disaster
Confirmed by two friends, one of whom confirmed in writing that this dream had been related to her four days before the disaster

'In the evening of 19 October I had a terrible dream that I was being smothered in deep blackness. I kept saying "I must wake up...". On the evening of 20 October I went to the Aylesbury Spiritualist Hall...the medium at the meeting said as he came to me that...he had to go to Wales and asked me if I knew anyone who had been killed in a pit disaster. I did, but this was 30 years ago, but he insisted it was Wales over and over again.'

Source: Woman in Aylesbury, Buckinghamshire
Time of dream: 2 days before the disaster
Time of church meeting: night before the disaster
Confirmation of both dream and meeting by a friend

Aftermath of the explosion at Flixborough, South Humberside, in 1974.

and totally unexpected disaster claimed the lives of 28 people and injured hundreds more. Nearly 2,000 buildings were damaged by the blast. At noon the same day a young woman watching television in Cleethorpes (some 23 miles away from Flixborough) 'saw' a news flash in which a male announcer gave news of an explosion at Flixborough in which several lives had been lost. She mentioned it to a couple staying in her home, so again there were witnesses to the event before it actually happened.

At this point we are not offering these reports as evidence for the existence of precognition, merely giving examples of the kind of account which is difficult to dismiss.

There are equally remarkable examples of telepathy. Stepping back a century in time, here is part of a report published by the British Society for Psychical Research: 'In 1967 my only sister...died suddenly of cholera.... A year or so after her death [I] became a commercial traveller and it was in 1876...that the event occurred. The hour was high noon, and the sun was shining cheerfully into my room. I suddenly became conscious that someone was sitting on my left.... I turned and distinctly saw the form of my dear sister.... Now comes the most remarkable *confirmation* of my statement...'. The man went on to explain that the apparition of his sister had a bright red scratch on her cheek. When he told his parents of his experience, his mother became very distressed, for no living person, other than herself, knew that she had accidentally scratched the face of the corpse during preparation for burial. She had never mentioned the incident to anyone.

Was this telepathy between mother and son? Or was it communication between the living and the dead, between a mind inside a body and a mind freed from one? Reports like this are too arresting to be ignored.

A more common type of possible telepathy is that experienced by one of the authors. One evening he felt impelled to pay a visit to a female friend he did not know especially well, even though the hour was late and not one for casual social calls. On arrival, he found her very distressed and in tears after a row with her boyfriend, who had become violent and struck her. The author's arrival turned out to be greatly comforting. Was this telepathic detection of a 'distress signal'? Many people report similar experiences.

The distinction between telepathy and clairvoyance is a hazy one. Since information about events and objects must exist in the mind of someone somewhere, might not 'clairvoyance' be telepathy? However, tales of recovery of lost objects, of objects lost for many lifetimes in some cases, and of the exploits of so-called 'psychic detectives' are less easy to categorize at telepathy.

What about mind-over-matter events? Very few people have not heard of the famous (or infamous) Uri Geller whose metal-bending feats may or may not involve PK. Metal-bending is a fairly recent addition to the canon of reported PK events, which have traditionally involved inexplicable movements of objects, levitations of people, and so on. In one recorded case of ostensible telepathy *and* PK, a woman saw an apparition (ghostly figure) of someone who had died at a distant place, and at exactly the time the apparition appeared a clock in the same room stopped.

PSI PHENOMENA: FOUR VARIATIONS ON A THEME?

Psychical abilities

ESP (extrasensory perception)

PK (psychokinesis)

Telepathy

Acquisition of information about another person, at a distance, by means not involving the known senses or logical inference

Influence of the human mind, by direct action of will, on another person, object, or event, not mediated by any physical force yet known

Clairvoyance

As above, but this time the acquisition of information about objects or events

Precognition

Acquisition, again by means unknown, of information which will only exist in the future

These four phenomena — precognition, telepathy, clairvoyance, and PK — are the core of the paranormal so far as allegedly mysterious human abilities are concerned. They should not necessarily be thought of as different processes, although people often think of them as separate. Very often it is difficult to distinguish ESP from PK, and especially one type of ESP from another. That is why the term 'psi' (short for psychic, or psychical) is often used instead, because it denotes a whole range of possibilities. In this book we will use the terms ESP and PK most of the time, particularly when describing experiments specifically designed to test one or the other, and also when use of the term 'psi' would be rather pedantic.

Problems for investigators of spontaneous psi

Do reports of the kind mentioned above, which come into the category of 'spontaneous' psi (because unwilled and occurring 'out of the blue'), prove the existence of ESP and/or PK, or at least that something genuinely anomalous is going on? Are such reports reliable accounts of true perceptions? Are the facts, as recounted, trustworthy?

The need for caution on the part of the investigator can easily be illustrated. In 1964 a British TV station, Anglia Television, broadcast an interview with the researcher Tony Cornell, filmed outside an allegedly haunted house. After the broadcast five people wrote in to say that they had seen an apparition looking over Cornell's shoulder. So the program was broadcast again and viewers were invited to write in if they saw anything strange. This time 27 people wrote in saying they had seen a ghost (which goes to show that people are more likely to 'see' something if they are led to believe they might). Since, in this case, the 'evidence' is on film, we can examine it for ourselves. Behind Cornell is a grainy, mullioned window from which, with a fertile imagination, it is possible to see Cornell's shadow turned into a 'ghost'. Incidentally, the 30 or so people who wrote in all saw a different type of ghost!

What are we to conclude from this? First, that our senses are not wholly reliable; we see things which just aren't there. Second, human beings are suggestible. Even first-hand, eye-witness testimony is notoriously unreliable. Obviously, concern about the fallibility of our senses applies more strongly to some cases than others. Going back to the man who saw an apparition of his dead sister, the crucial element in the tale is the scratch; whether he actually saw the figure exactly as he described is not relevant.

Human memory is also fallible. Psychologists have found that the form and content of remembered events change with time. Our recollections tend to become more simplified, more clear-cut and definite, and sometimes more dramatic and interesting than the original events. This is true of events remembered at first hand, and even more true of information passed from person to person. Second- or third-hand testimony collected long after the event may be so degraded and distorted as to be completely worthless.

Ideally, what we need from people who have cases of possible spontaneous psi to report is a written (or taped) account of events made as soon as possible after the events took place. Obviously, we rarely encounter such a state of affairs. Few individuals are in a position to contact a parapsychologist who might be interested in their experiences, for one thing. For another, especially in the case of distressing events, people are not sufficiently cool and detached to realize the importance of such a permanent record of events. Also, many people with possible precognitions may not realize their significance until the sensed future event takes place, by which time it is too late to make a record uncontaminated by knowledge of the event. Only first-hand recorded accounts made before the event constitute strong evidence to a rational researcher.

Nevertheless witnesses can strengthen the value of a spontaneous case. The Plymouth woman's 'vision' of the Aberfan disaster was confirmed by six independent witnesses. Witnesses minimize the possibility of fraud.

While fraud is highly unlikely from ordinary people who report possible psi experiences, in other cases it is a genuine problem. 'Psychic' Tamara's Rand's precognition of the shooting of President Ronald Reagan turned out to be a hoax cooked up between Rand and certain members of a TV station which broadcast her 'revelation'. Film of her 'prophesy' was shown to have been recorded *after* the attempted assassination.

The predictability of allegedly ESP-sensed events must also be taken into account when weighing the evidence. Imagine a person waking up and seeing an apparition of his uncle at the bottom the bed. The uncle, who lives on the other side of the world, turns out to have died that very night! Is this telepathy? Possibly, if the uncle was a reasonably young man who had previously enjoyed the best of health. Possibly not, if he was 85 years old and bedridden with terminal cancer. The more predictable an event is, the less 'special' ESP cognition of it becomes. Unfortunately, it is often extremely difficult to say just how predictable something actually is.

Even more difficult to assess is the strength of the evidence in the light of the personality of the alleged telepathic receiver, or percipient. Suppose that a mother dreams of the death of her healthy son, who is by profession a bank clerk (hardly a dangerous profession). The target event, the son's death, is unlikely. But what if the mother is a chronic neurotic with a fixation about her son? What if she dreams most nights of something awful happening to him? Ideally we should investigate the personality and integrity of alleged telepathic receivers, but this can be a difficult, embarrassing, and highly subjective business.

Such problems are no excuse for abandoning the investigation of spontaneous cases of claimed psi — scientific investigation of any naturally occuring phenomenon is fraught with difficulties. The problems merely oblige us to find better, more reliable, and more informative ways of investigating whether ESP and PK do, in fact, exist.

Designing psi experiments

How are we to track down psi scientifically? Clearly we need to conduct experiments in which the problems we have identified so far — sensory fallibility, suggestibility, predictability, personality influences — are eliminated or properly allowed for. And the design of such experiments should be such that they can be repeated by other researchers and their results verified (repeatability, which we will discuss in more detail later, is central to scientific parapsychology). Above all, we need to be able to calculate the likelihood of chance and coincidence giving us false or confusing results (with over 5,000 million people in the world, 1 million to 1 coincidences should be trivial everyday events).

Parapsychology began as a science in the 1930s, simply, with card-guessing experiments. Obviously these lack the richness, complexity, and emotional content of spontaneous psi experiences, but they demonstrate some of the fundamental principles of psi testing. Later in this book we will look at more subtle, complex, and intuitively appealing tests.

Excluding the conventional senses is the first requirement of ESP testing. The tester must make sure that his subjects cannot gain information, about symbols on cards or any other 'targets', by using their ordinary senses. In a telepathy test, the possibility of either party hearing, seeing, touching, or communicating in any ordinary way with the other must be excluded. In a clairvoyance test, in order to rule out the possibility of telepathy, the target information must not be in the mind of the tester; in a card-guessing test, this requirement would be satisfied by asking subjects to guess the order of cards in a sealed pack inside a sealed box.

Excluding fraud is the second requirement of ESP testing — there must be no possibility of collusion between subjects themselves, or between subjects and investigators, or between investigators.

Eliminating problems of memory and testimony is the third requirement. In practice this means making sure that the results of experiments are recorded objectively, at the time, and under good conditions. In a card-guessing test this would mean writing down the percipients' guesses without knowing what the 'targets' (cards) are, recording the targets separately (ideally someone who has no idea what the percipients' guesses are should do this), comparing both sets of information, then double-checking the match-up between them.

If all of these requirements are satisfied, then it should be possible to measure any ESP effect that might be operating.

Using statistical methods to measure psi

The simple five-card deck shown right was developed for ESP testing by Joseph Banks ('J.B.') Rhine, the founding father of experimental parapsychology. Rhine's work at Duke University, North Carolina, during the 1930s, using these simple cards, triggered an intense controversy within science and put parapsychology firmly on the academic map.

Rhine's original test methods required his subjects to guess the sequence of cards in series of packs of 25. The packs were thoroughly shuffled to ensure that the cards were in random (completely unpredictable) order. This eliminated the possibility of his subjects using logical inference as a means of guessing them correctly, and also made it possible to assess how many of their guesses were just guesses and nothing more. The important point here is that *with a truly random sequence of targets, it is possible to work out exactly what the average number of correct guesses should be if chance is the only factor at work.*

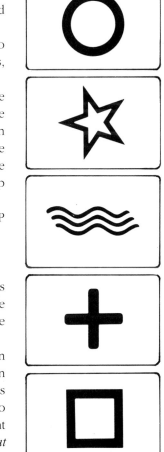

J.B. Rhine's famous ESP cards, invented in the 1930s. Researchers still use them today, although machine-generated targets are preferred for reasons of time, money, and minimizing error.

In order to measure test results parapsychologists make use of a simple statistical notion called a *chance average* (chance 'mean' is the correct term, but the more familiar term 'average' will be used here). This means working out, for any given test situation, what level of success is likely to be obtained by chance alone, with no ESP occurring.

Let us return to Rhine's ESP cards. There are 25 cards in each pack, in random sequence. Each card is equally likely to be any one of five possibilities, so each guess has a 1-in-5 chance of being correct. With 25 guesses and a 1-in-5 chance of being correct each

A simple 'clairvoyance' experiment using ESP cards. The subject points to the card she thinks is being dealt by the tester on the other side of the screen.

Opposite page: Predicting how likely something is to happen by chance is an essential first step in any controlled psi experiment. The diagram opposite shows the 16 possible outcomes of tossing four identical coins. If the four coins are tossed often enough, on average 6 in every 16 throws should result in two heads and two tails, if only chance is operating. The chance average of two heads and two tails is therefore 37%. Test yourself to see if you score significantly above or below that chance average.

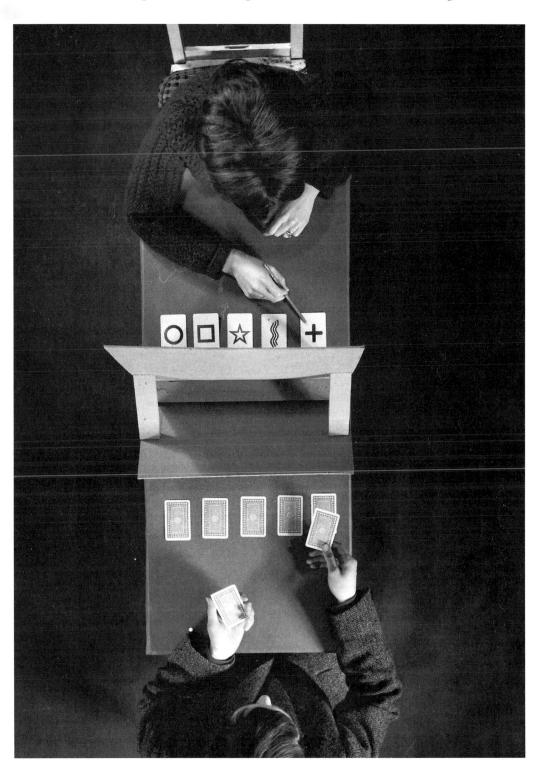

time, the *chance average* for the whole pack is 5 correct guesses (25 x ⅕ = 5). Note that the laws of chance do not predict that *every* test will give 5 correct guesses. Sometimes one would expect 4, and sometimes 6; less often 3 or 7; less frequently still, 2 or 8; even more rarely, 1 or 9; and so on. In other words, there will be *scatter* around the chance average. Nevertheless if we do the same experiment ten times the chance average should be around 50 correct guesses (5 x 10 = 50). If the subject scores 50 correct guesses when we match his guesses against the order of the cards, we can be reasonably sure that nothing out of the ordinary is happening. He has scored at chance, exactly as the laws of chance predict. But if he scores 60, or 80, or 100 (or 40, or 30, or 20, for that matter), we are entitled to say: 'It looks as if something other than chance is operating here.'

There are certain arbitrary but conventional rules in science by which an experimental result is agreed not to be due to chance alone. In the social sciences, the rule is as follows. If a researcher obtains an experimental result which is so different from the chance average that it would be expected to happen only once in 20 similar experiments, or even less often, he accepts that it is not due to chance. Something else is responsible. In truth, there are no pressing logical or empirical reasons for this criterion; it is simply an accepted convention. The smaller the probability, though, the more confident the experimenter feels, and that is the most important point. A probability of 1 in 20 (a 5% chance, often put in the form 'probability of .05') is acceptable, but 1 in 100 (a 1% chance, or a 'probability of .01') is clearly more satisfying.

Let us return to our ESP test, in which we collected 250 guesses from our subject and he scored 50 correct guesses or hits. Or was it 60, 70, 80, 100? If it was 50 hits, then clearly this is just what the laws of chance predict. What about 60 hits? Well, the probability of this

J.B. Rhine (right) and one of his card-guessing subjects at Duke University, North Carolina, a photograph first published in Rhine's ground-breaking book New Frontiers of the Mind *(1938).*

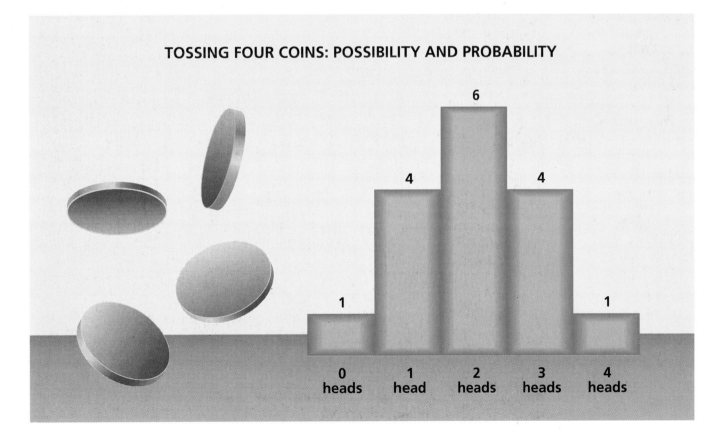

TOSSING FOUR COINS: POSSIBILITY AND PROBABILITY

0 heads	1 head	2 heads	3 heads	4 heads
1	4	6	4	1

is slightly larger than .05; we would need 61 hits to obtain a probability of .05. So 60 hits is not sufficient evidence for us to infer that anything other than chance is operating. If our subject scored 70 hits, however, the probability is around .001, a 1,000-to-1 shot (an inexact expression, but the concept of '1,000-to-1 odds' is readily grasped). We would feel pretty certain that such a result was not due to chance alone. And if our subject scored 80 hits, the 'odds against chance' lengthen to about 50,000 to 1.

The exact numbers of this example are not crucial. What is important is that, for any given number of guesses, we know exactly what the chance average score is; we can measure 'coincidence'. We also know that results increasingly far away from chance are more and more unlikely, and the lower the probability the more certain we can feel that chance, or coincidence, is *not* a plausible explanation. If we do an ESP test and find that our receiver has scored so many hits that the odds against his performance are 1 million to 1, we have an objective confidence in that finding which we cannot truly have in any reported spontaneous case of alleged ESP, no matter how subjectively interesting we might find it.

Similar principles can be applied to testing for PK. A long-used procedure is to have dice thrown by a machine while the subject in the experiment wishes for one particular face to come up. Clearly, if only chance is operating (no PK, and the dice are not biased) then one die in six, as an average, will come up with the desired face showing (since there are six possibilities).

The act of measurement allows us to compare different conditions, experiments, people, and so on. Potentially, it allows us to say that 'Mr. X has stronger ESP ability than Mr. Y, and condition A is better for ESP than condition B in our experiments'. We can also measure whether, on guesses where the subject feels especially confident that he is right, he scores significantly better than on guesses where he is not confident. Making such comparisons is vital if we hope to learn where ESP and PK are most likely to occur, how to make them operate at levels where they might be useful to us, and in many other attempts to gain understanding of psi. Spontaneous cases cannot give us formal, measured differences which allow us to make such comparisons with any real confidence.

The laws of chance apply to bodies of experiments as well as individual ones. Consider 20 experimenters, each conducting an ESP experiment. Nineteen of them get results fully consistent with the laws of chance. The other gets a score with a 1-in-20 probability, so he publishes his results — and it is assumed that this is evidence of ESP. Clearly, this is an error. In fact, selective reporting is not really a problem in parapsychology, because unsuccessful experiments are often reported (far more often than in other areas of science, we regret to say). Both authors have published unsuccessful psi experiments. The odds against chance in many parapsychology experiments are so huge that whether there are some unsuccessful experiments lying around unpublished or not is an irrelevance. We will return to this issue in the final chapter of this book.

Looking at the evidence

The statistical methods summarized above have been the basis for thousands of experiments on ESP and PK conducted over the past 60 years. The literature of parapsychology — published accounts of experiments and findings — has consequently grown to sizeable proportions. What is a rational plan for examining this vast store of claims and reports?

First, surely, we should examine some of the strongest evidence suggestive of psi and see if we can explain it in terms of known and understood abilities. If we cannot, we will increasingly have to consider that there is a high probability that psi, or at least something which is genuinely anomalous and unknown to science, does occur. We are not setting out to *prove* that psi exists. Proof is a concept which applies to formal logic and mathematics. Rather, the legal notion of *reasonable doubt* guides our enquiry. We might say: 'The evidence is strong. It therefore appears to us that it is probable, or even highly probable, that psi exists.' Or we might find the evidence not impressive at all.

If we do find the evidence for psi strong, then many interesting questions arise. Do different people differ in terms of their psi abilities? Surely we would anticipate that they should, since they differ in terms of every other ability or skill one can think of. Are there particular conditions which are favorable for psi? If so, why? How might psi work — can physics explain it? Or does psi contradict the 'laws' of physics? Finally, is psi relevant to the age-old concept of body and soul? Is there, as Rhine claimed, some 'non-physical' component in us which is responsible for psi — and which might survive death?

So many questions! First, though, we have to appraise the evidence, the best and strongest evidence within the literature. As we look at that evidence, we will explain why we consider it to be strongly suggestive of psi, or at least of some genuine, unexplained anomaly (from now on, this qualifier will be dropped to avoid pedantic repetition). Four pieces of evidence are surveyed in the next two chapters: two remarkable 'psychic' individuals, and two sets of formidable machine-PK experiments. This evidence will give us much food for thought as we begin our journey, hoping to explain as much of the unexplained as we can.

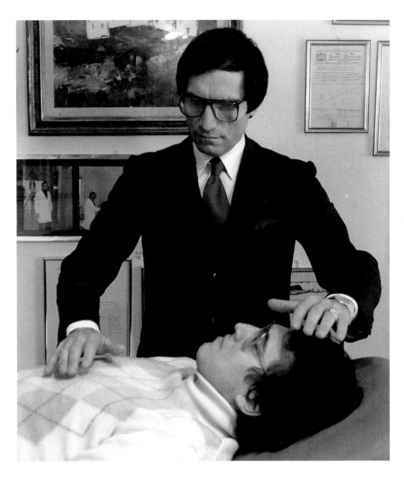

Many people report benefits from faith healing. While such reports are anecdotally interesting, they tell us very little about how psi operates. For that, we need controlled experiments whose design allows us to use statistical methods to determine the strength and direction of possible psi effects and the conditions under which psi is most likely to occur.

Psi stars

I f psi abilities exist, then there are a handful of people who could be referred to as 'Psi stars', individuals who have been able to produce apparently paranormal events, for prolonged periods of time, under conditions which allowed careful observation, and in the presence of many investigators and observers. Their exploits form part of the best evidence we have for the possible existence of psi, and may tell us something about what is possible with psi, what unknown human abilities may be capable of. We have selected two particular individuals from the literature of parapsychology, the nineteenth-century medium D.D. Home, and the Czech Pavel Stepanek, whose remarkable performances in ESP experiments during the 1960s earned him an entry in *The Guinness Book of Records* as the world's most psychic man.

The amazing D.D. Home

Daniel Dunglas Home, born in Edinburgh, Scotland in 1833, was reared by an aunt and taken to America at the tender age of nine. A somewhat neurotic and sickly child, whose mother was thought to have 'second sight', Daniel very quickly began to follow the family tradition. At the age of 13 he saw an apparition of a close friend. The 'spirit' form made three circles in the air, and Daniel told his aunt and uncle that this must mean that the boy had been dead for three days. The relatives scoffed, but the news soon came that the boy had died just three days before his spirit appeared to Daniel. Four years later Daniel's mother died, and he saw her ghostly form also. After that, he claimed to be in almost constant communication with the spirits of the dead.

Mary Cook and her husband certainly had an odd child in their care. One can imagine their distress when the spirits young Daniel conversed with started thumping and making rapping noises all over the house (a trademark of the *Poltergeist*, or 'noisy spirit', as we shall see later). Believing that the boy must have brought Satan himself into the house, the Cooks threw Daniel out onto the streets.

All this took place at a time when America was in the grip of a craze for spiritualism. Generally considered to have begun in 1848 in New England, where three sisters had announced that they were in communication with spirits of the dead, a local sensation ballooned into a national obsession. Soon thousands and then hundreds of thousands of people all over America were attending seances at which allegedly psychic mediums produced a bizarre selection of effects to convince those present that they were indeed in contact with another world inhabited by the spirits of the dead. These effects included

Daniel Dunglas Home, physical medium extraordinaire, photographed during the 1860s. The variety of effects Home produced, from levitation to fire-handling, set him apart from many thousands of contemporary mediums.

Opposite: D.D. Home levitates himself and household objects during a seance in the home of a French nobleman. In 1863 the court of Napoleon III saw Home demonstrate his powers.

Props used to fake 'apparitions', 'ectoplasm', and other effects during seances. At the height of the spiritualist craze mediums were under tremendous pressure from a credulous public and used all sorts of gadgets to produce unearthly effects.

mysterious rappings, voices and unearthly music seemingly coming from thin air, luminous apparitions, automatic writing, and even levitations. In this milieu Home, himself a fast-developing medium, did not have to look far for wealthy patrons. Within a short time he was giving seances at which the spirits of the dead regularly conveyed messages to the living.

In this there was nothing to mark him out from the 15,000 or so other mediums estimated by one contemporary commentator to be operating in the United States. It quickly became clear, however, that the variety and scale of the physical effects which occurred during Home's seances set him in a class apart. Levitation of objects, levitations of Home himself and of other people, rappings, the grip of unseen hands clearly felt by those attending the seances...all of these phenomena were frequently attested by many witnesses. It is these effects which are of interest to us. If they really did happen as reported, they are strong evidence for the existence of PK.

Rapping, levitation, body elongation, and fire-handling

What exactly did Home do and under what conditions did he do it? To begin with, it is a remarkable fact that during a long and astonishing career, spanning decades and involving seances at the courts of Napoleon III and Czar Alexander II, Home was never caught in fraud, nor was any serious, substantiated allegation made against him. This despite the fact that he unquestionably made enemies who would dearly have liked to discredit him. Also, Home preferred bright light for his seances, and he asked researchers to treat him with skepticism. He did not request payment for his seances, and was not infrequently poor during his lifetime, although he could easily have become a rich man had he wanted to. In all these respects Home was not at all like the overwhelming majority of so-called 'physical mediums'.

Spirit rappings were common at Home's seances. Home would go into a light trance, at which point bangings and thumpings would be heard by sitters in the seance room. Two particular examples show that these effects could be very dramatic, and hardly capable of production by simple fraud.

In a brilliantly-lit chamber at the Napoleonic court in January 1863, Home levitated a cloth from a table and was standing several yards from it when an enemy of his, the skeptical Prince Metternich, decided to leap under the table to discover what equipment or trickery Home was using to produce the effect. The bewildered Prince was greeted by a barrage of raps which *came from within the table itself.* During one of Home's seances in England, at which six witnesses were present, the highly distinguished physicist Sir William Crookes observed 'very strong vibrations of our chairs, then the table and floor, and at last the very walls and windows seemed to shake'. These events are clearly very difficult to explain away. To fabricate them would have required machinery, confederates, or both. The whole problem of trickery will be dealt with later, but for now we will merely note that the scale of the effects in the Crookes seance (and others) verged on the enormous.

Levitation was another effect regularly observed at Home's seances. Lord Adare, formerly a foreign correspondent for the London *Daily Telegraph*, kept a model record of many of Home's seances, written down immediately after they had happened. He documented no fewer than sixteen levitations of tables, some of them too heavy for a man to have lifted alone (even a far burlier one than the thin and unfit Home). Home also levitated other people and, sometimes, himself. Crookes computed that, at one time or another, over a hundred people witnessed Home levitating. On frequent occasions the witnesses were actually hanging onto his legs! Crookes himself observed Home levitate a chair together with a woman sitting on it.

Crookes, being a man of science, undertook controlled experiments with Home, concentrating particularly on the levitation effect. Home enjoyed music, and one of his favorite phenomena was the levitation of an accordion which would waltz around the room playing, appropriately enough, 'Home Sweet Home'. So Crookes purchased an accordion and sealed it inside a locked cage where Home could not reach it. Despite this, the instrument levitated and flew around inside the cage, playing edifying tunes as it did so.

Home's most spectacular effects were documented towards the end of his career. Throughout his life he was often met with hostility — Napoleon III paid conjurers and magicians to try and discredit him (which they failed to do) and he was expelled from Rome because he was thought to be a wizard (questions were raised in the British Parliament about his treatment). However, we are lucky in that we have two long contemporary accounts of his later activities made by men with sufficient sympathy for him to observe him watchfully and record their observations and experiments. Both Sir William Crookes and Lord Adare recorded, together with examples of levitation, several instances of two other major effects, body elongation and fire-handling.

Body elongation is a curious phenomenon which, again, was witnessed by dozens of people. On occasions, Home would stretch his body, seeming to add as much as six inches to his height, while people held onto him. Home generally asked spectators to watch carefully for any evidence of fraud. As he said to Crookes: 'Now, William, I want you to act as if I was a recognized conjuror, and was going to cheat you and play all the tricks I could.... Don't consider my feelings. I shall not be offended.' Yet, surrounded by people watching for tricks, holding all parts of his body, Home was still able to extend his form. One witness reported how he felt Home's ribs passing under his hands. There are even a few reports of Home elongating the bodies of *other people*.

As for *fire-handling*, at one seance Crookes saw Home take from the fire 'a red-hot piece nearly as big as an orange.' Home put the coal on his right hand, 'covered it with his left hand so as to almost completely enclose it, and then blew...until the lump of charcoal was nearly white-hot, and then drew my [Crooke's] attention to the lambent flame which was flickering over the coal and licking round his fingers...'. Adare, too, witnessed this and both Crookes and Adare were treated (if that is the right word) to the sight of Home lying prone before an open fire and *actually placing his head among the live coals!*

This last phenomenon is quite incredible. It cannot be compared with the practice of fire-walking, where a person's feet are only intermittently in contact with hot coals; it seems that such brief contact can be repeated for a short period of time (the walk) without harm from burns (although we are amused to note that, in one recent experiment, the only persons who could not successfully fire-walk were two skeptics, who spent some time in hospital with severely burned feet). Crookes tested the fire-handling effect as best he

One of Home's favorite effects was to levitate his accordion. When Sir William Crookes locked the instrument in a wire cage, Home still managed to levitate it. According to Crookes, it played 'a sweet and plaintive melody' as it moved about inside the cage.

could, by actively seeking out others who claimed to have this ability. He found that one black man he tested was able to hold a red-hot iron for an extremely short time, but that 'the house was pervaded for hours after with the odour of roast Negro'. There was never any smell of burning when Home handled fire, and no one else could tolerate anything like the prolonged exposure Home showed. Crookes also examined Home's hands after these feats and found them to be 'soft and delicate as a woman's'. On some occasions, Home used handkerchiefs given to him by other people to hold the coals. These handkerchiefs were not even singed. Crookes chemically analyzed one such handkerchief and found nothing out of the ordinary about it.

Explaining Home away

The first possibility we must examine is that witness reports were untrustworthy. In this respect, the Crookes and Adare papers are a rare treasure since they are contemporaneous written documents. The possibility of subtle errors of perception and memory is not going to explain away events such as levitations in bright light or people observed lying with their face in a fire.

Could some form of mass hallucination, then, explain these reports? Was Home, perhaps, some amazingly gifted hypnotist? One 'scientific' contemporary commentator in *Nature*, the distinguished journal of science, actually suggested that Home was either a mass hypnotist or a werewolf. That the latter possibility entered the pages of *Nature* showed how desperate and confused Home's critics had become!

The hypnosis/hallucination theory runs into many problems. The major one is that very few people are so susceptible to hypnosis that they will hallucinate if appropriate suggestions are made to them. Yet many people gave accounts of witnessing Home's levitations, fire-handling, and the like, not just a few. Home actually preferred conditions for sittings which certainly would not favor hallucinations. He liked to work in brightly lit rooms; he always liked bright lights. Finally, Crookes conducted experiments which showed that Home could influence the weight of objects, results which were recorded instrumentally. Instruments don't hallucinate.

Of course, some of Home's witnesses were probably untrustworthy. The nature of the times, with wild spiritualist beliefs gaining many adherents, made many folk credulous. But Adare, Crookes, Metternich, and others (such as a self-styled group of Dutch rationalists who sat with him in Amsterdam in 1858) who initially showed skepticism towards Home are not so easily dismissed.

Overall, it is agreed, even by Home's later detractors, that hallucination alone cannot explain a fairly substantial chunk of what was reported of this strange man's life. What this case must come down to, in the end, is that Home was either fraudulent or some genuinely unidentified force was operating in his presence.

Was Home a fraud?

Some of Home's effects certainly have the aura of conjurer's tricks about them. On occasion he *did* conduct seances in the dark, or ask for lights to be dimmed before a levitation or some other dramatic effect. Sometimes he levitated glasses and made then reappear in a different place after flying into the air. Nonetheless, it is a puerile exercise to do what so many critics have done and try to show that some of the most trivial effects are explainable by fraud or conjuring. We should look instead at the most dramatic and evidential effects produced by the man.

Home's seances were often conducted in public places or in the houses of interested people to which Home had no advance access. Home sometimes didn't know where a seance was to be held until immediately beforehand. Then again, before, during and after seances, Adare, Crookes, and others carefully checked for any kind of apparatus being used. If we consider the levitation of heavy tables or human bodies, it is extremely unlikely that some kind of improvised conjuring using a small piece of apparatus which could be smuggled in and out in a jacket pocket could have been used!

So far as accomplices are concerned, this possibility seems to be equally implausible. They would have had to be paid, and paid well, yet Home was not paid for seances and was often broke — at one time he was so poor that he had to give literary readings to feed himself. He would have needed a fair supply of accomplices, and the financial reward for any of them who cared to sell their story to the newspapers would have been enormous. No one ever came forward.

The fire-handling phenomena seem virtually unfakeable. The fires were real enough; observers could feel the heat from the coals burning in Home's hands.

One further episode from the extraordinary life of this man is worth discussing because it sheds light on the psychology of some critics. In 1855 Home conducted a seance at the home of the poets Robert and Elizabeth Browning. As they sat around the table with other sitters, a wreath of clematis picked by the Brownings' children levitated and settled gently onto Elizabeth's head. Robert got up to watch it move through the air.

Unfortunately, Home suggested that perhaps Robert had moved so that the wreath might fall on *his* head. Robert was already jealous of his wife's poetic talents, and after this seance Elizabeth championed Home. Robert Browning's recollections of events showed an interesting change with the passage of time. *At the time* he wrote letters to friends in which Home was mentioned, but there was no hint that he thought him a fraud. *Only in later life* did he convince himself that Home was a fraud and that he had actually caught him in the act of cheating. The motivation for this warped memory is obvious.

Robert vented his spleen in 1864 by publishing *Mr. Sludge the Medium*, a long, venomous poem about a fraudulent and vain medium. The link with Home was obvious (except to Home himself), and in some quarters the story grew that Robert Browning had exposed Home as a fraud, which is ridiculous. Browning's letters at the time show that this was not so, as do his statements to the pioneer psychical researcher F.W.H. Myers. Later, G.K. Chesterton commented that *Mr. Sludge* was 'a reality tangled with unrealities in a man's mind'. How stories grow in the telling — and not just on the credulous side.

Perhaps the greatest tragedy of Home's life was that, with the exception of Crookes,

Elizabeth and Robert Browning, the most famous poetic duo of the Victorian era. Robert's venomous attack on the fictitious medium Mr. Sludge, construed by some as an exposé of Home, may have been an indirect attack on Elizabeth, whose reputation as poet stood higher than his own. Elizabeth was a devotee of spiritualism in general and of Home in particular.

contemporary scientists were too afraid to test him. Time and again Crookes invited eminent scientists to test Home, without restrictions, yet they failed or refused to take the opportunity to do so. We must bear this in mind when considering the merit of skeptical assertions about Home. Many contemporary skeptical men of science clearly possessed all the cowardice of their convictions.

What are we to make of all this? Crookes's attitude was unequivocal: 'To reject the recorded evidence on this subject is to reject all human testimony whatsoever...'. While this may be exaggerating, we are faced with an abundance and quality of testimony which cannot be ignored. At some point we have to trust human testimony. After all, even scientific reports are the output of recording devices (of whatever kind) *as viewed by human eyes.*

Some of the effects reported in connection with Home might well have been the products of unreliable testimony, errors of memory, skilful illusions, or mass hallucination. However, a sizeable residue remains which cannot be explained away so easily. Skeptical books on Home are a sorry collection. Compared with the Adare and Crookes documents, the amount of special pleading, empty 'What if...?' speculation, unsubstantiated assertion, selective quotation, and the like is fairly damning. None of them amounts to a credible and substantial critique of Home and his powers. Nevertheless the reader intrigued by Home will find that the Bibliography on page 186 includes these skeptical works; there is no point in addressing only one side of the story.

Home is dead and gone. We have not seen his like since. But let us jump forward a hundred years to another individual whose longevity as a psi test subject is still unrivalled: Pavel Stepanek.

The Czech parapsychologist Milan Ryzl discovered the amazing powers of Pavel Stepanek almost by accident — in early experiments Stepanek proved to be a poor hynotic subject. Did Stepanek's powers prompt Ryzl to try another method of eliciting psi?

The bank clerk from Prague

Russians and other Eastern Europeans have always had a keen interest in the links between hypnosis and ESP, perhaps with good reason, since hypnosis appears to be conducive to ESP (see Chapter 6). One researcher fascinated in this area was Milan Ryzl, trained in life sciences and keenly interested in the paranormal. At the beginning of the 1960s he started experimenting with hypnosis as a tool for training ESP abilities. His test procedure was long and complex: volunteers were trained to develop mental imagery ('seeing with the mind's eye') and to relax into deeper and deeper trance states; they were then asked to use ESP to complete various tasks such as detecting objects sealed inside boxes. It was in the course of this work, which provided some promising leads, that Ryzl first encountered Pavel Stepanek.

Stepanek, a quiet and unassuming bank clerk, came along because of an interest in the psychic. Ryzl tested him to see if he would be a suitable subject for his hypnosis/ESP experiments, but Stepanek turned out to be a poor hypnotic subject and after two visits Ryzl was nearly ready to give up. A third session proved only slightly more promising, so Ryzl decided not to use Stepanek in his training experiments and instead tested him for ESP using some cards lying around from previous studies. The cards were 3 inches by 5 inches, white on one side and black on the other, and concealed within light-proof, opaque cardboard covers. Ryzl presented each cover (containing a card) to Stepanek and asked him to

For more than ten years Pavel Stepanek demonstrated extraordinary levels of ESP in tests with many different researchers. The odds against his powers being due to chance were huge, in one experiment as huge as 1,000 million million to 1.

guess which side of the card — white or black — was uppermost within the cover as it was laid flat. Even in this informal early work, Ryzl made sure that the sequence of black/white 'targets' was random. Stepanek responded by guessing correctly well above 50% of the time. After a few weeks, Ryzl and Stepanek were ready for formal research.

The first formal experiment was completed in July 1961. At this time, Stepanek worked in a state of very light hypnosis (abandoned in later research). Ryzl's assistant, working alone in a closed room, took ten index cards and placed them inside opaque covers, deciding randomly whether a card should have the black or white side uppermost within the cover. The covers, with the cards inside them, were given to Ryzl, who then held one cover after another in front of Stepanek. Stepanek, however, could not see the covers; his face was shielded by a screen. *Stepanek neither saw nor touched the covers*, but simply guessed 'White' or 'Black'. Ryzl recorded each guess. After Stepanek had completed ten guesses, Ryzl checked the guesses against the list of targets prepared by the assistant.

It has to be said that this looks like a very tedious experiment indeed. One has to admire Stepanek's stoicism for staying with variants of this procedure for so many years. But, while the experiment is simple to the point of dullness, the results Ryzl obtained were dramatic. In the first experiment Stepanek completed 200 tests with 10 guesses per test, making 2,000 guesses in all. Since the chance of being correct with each guess is 50% (there are two equal possibilities), one would have expected Stepanek to score around 1,000 correct guesses by chance alone. He actually scored just over 1,140 correct, a scoring rate just above 57%. The odds against this happening by chance are well over 10 million to 1.

Ryzl, however, wanted to try for a higher scoring rate, and devised an ingenious method of doing so. He reasoned as follows. Suppose that, when Stepanek is guessing, he only uses ESP now and then (not all his guesses are correct, so this must obviously be the case). This can be thought of as an *infrequent signal* — something gets through around every seven guesses or so (since Stepanek gets around four right every seven, the other three out of six would be a chance level of success). If the one-in-seven is a *signal*, and the other six are just *noise*, then there is a particular technique that can be used to amplify that signal: *Stepanek must guess at the same series of targets over and over again.* The signals will then begin to add up and stand out more clearly against the background noise.

This technique is termed a *majority vote* experiment. If, for one particular target, the subject says 'Black' seven times and 'White' three times, then the majority vote is taken to be Black. If he says 'White' seven times and 'Black' three, the majority vote is White. Fifty/fifty splits are discounted.

Accordingly, Ryzl had his assistant prepare a set of 100 cards, randomly ordered, each sealed inside an opaque envelope, with extra opaque packaging on the outside. This sequence of 100 targets was presented to Stepanek ten times in succession. A majority vote was recorded for 93 targets (in the case of the other seven, Stepanek said 'White' and 'Black' an equal number of times). Using the majority vote technique, Stepanek's scoring rate increased to 66 correct out of 93, or 71%. The odds against this result occurring by chance exceed 20,000 million to 1.

For the time being, let us assume for the sake of argument that Stepanek was using ESP to detect the target cards correctly. If this was the case, then the majority vote procedure suggests that ESP operates in a lawful manner. If it is some kind of 'weak signal', then the majority vote procedure *should* boost the scoring rate, which indeed it did. This is reassuring.

Stepanek's performance in independent tests

The results of Ryzl's early tests were so remarkable that Western scientists soon developed an interest in them. Gaither Pratt from the Parapsychology Laboratory at Duke University, North Carolina, visited Ryzl in Prague in 1962. A long-time colleague of J.B. Rhine, Pratt was a highly experienced and knowledgeable researcher. He observed and examined Ryzl's test procedure in some short tests, which produced a scoring rate above 50%, but only slightly so. When Pratt returned in 1963, however, Stepanek was in top form. Of 2,000 guesses in the experiment conducted with Pratt and Ryzl, Stepanek scored 1,133 successes, a hit rate of 56.65%. Once again, this was a '10 million to 1 shot'.

In between Pratt's two visits, Stepanek produced his most remarkable single feat. Ryzl considered that if a majority vote with ten guesses per target had boosted scoring to 71%, a majority vote with even more guesses might obtain a still higher scoring rate. So, Ryzl presented a series of 15 targets to Stepanek literally *hundreds* of times in succession. At the end of the experiment, Stepanek had got *every single one correct* — 100% success, with the odds against chance being exactly 32,767 million to 1.

Now for the first twist in the story. As the experiments progressed, Ryzl noticed that Stepanek began to make particular guesses quite consistently when a particular *envelope* was presented to him. Were little sensory 'cues' on the envelopes — marks, scratches, and so on — distracting him? Was focusing on the *envelopes* inhibiting his ability to guess the *cards* inside them using ESP? To exclude this possibility, Ryzl and Pratt modified the test procedure. The cards were sealed inside envelopes, as before, but now the envelopes were concealed within covers. Since Stepanek could no longer see the envelopes, it was hoped that he would not be distracted by them and would use ESP successfully on the cards.

What the researchers found was that Stepanek *continued* to make particular guesses whenever certain envelopes were presented, even though he could no longer see them. It seemed that his ESP ability had moved from the cards to the envelopes. When the order of envelopes within a series of covers was changed, Stepanek still continued to make consistent guesses relating to the envelopes. Stepanek thought he was using ESP to detect the cards, but he was actually using it to detect the envelopes, or so it appeared.

It was at this time that Pratt — who came more and more to the fore as the major researcher with Stepanek — conducted one of the two experiments which, in his words, provided 'conclusive evidence that P.S. (Stepanek) was demonstrating ESP' During this experiment, Pratt collaborated with J.G. Blom, a Dutch scientist from Amsterdam.

Blom and Pratt prepared 40 cards (green and white now, as in most of the work with Stepanek after Ryzl's early work), sealed inside 40 envelopes. They did this in such a way that neither of them alone could have known which envelope contained which target color (card). Pratt randomized the order of the envelopes, and took eight at a time, concealing each inside an outer cover. Stepanek made his guesses in Blom's presence when these card-envelope-cover packages were offered to him. The two experimenters carefully recorded guesses and targets for each session, and 1,000 guesses were made each day. This time, after four days' work and 4,000 collected guesses, Stepanek showed apparent ESP detection of the cards. He scored 2,154 correct, not a very high scoring rate, only 53.85%, but the odds against such a scoring rate occurring by chance are around 0.5 million to 1.

The white and green cards used in experiments with Stepanek were concealed in envelopes. After a while Stepanek's ability seemed to transfer itself to the envelopes rather than the cards inside them, so the envelopes were concealed inside covers. When Stepanek transferred his attention to the covers, the covers were put into jackets.

Over the next few years, without deluging the reader with endless numbers and statistics, two features of the work with Stepanek stand out very clearly. The first is that Stepanek was able to show scoring rates significantly higher than 50% in tests with many research scientists from all over the world. What had begun with Ryzl, then drawn in a first independent researcher (Pratt), then another (Blom), drew in still more. This is an important point. Stepanek was able to succeed with many different researchers, which adds to the value of the experiments. His success was *repeatable.*

The second notable feature was that Stepanek's apparent ESP ability detached itself from the cards completely, moving first to the envelopes and then to the outer covers! So the covers had to be concealed within heavy jackets.

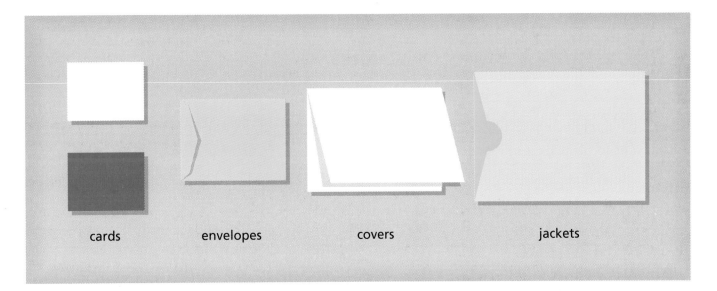

cards   envelopes   covers   jackets

Since the covers themselves were quite bulky, the jackets had to be padded with cotton and carefully weighed to make sure that they truly concealed the nature of the covers within them. This increasingly awkward, but still effective, test procedure was used when Stepanek visited the University of Virginia to work with Pratt and Dr. Ian Stevenson, and also with Dr. Jurgen Keil from Tasmania. In February 1968 Stepanek consistently called certain covers 'Green' and others 'White', and there were also particular covers for which he consistently guessed *one side* 'Green' and the other 'White'.

What appears to have happened with Stepanek, as his powers declined, is that his putative ESP became confused between cards, envelopes, covers, jackets, and the heavy-duty mailing bags (!) which comprised the target packages in later research. It must be stressed that, although the effects shifted, they stayed consistent for a number of experiments, so there is no question of the researchers just lifting out any old statistical anomaly from one study to the next. Nevertheless, despite the eventual decline, for a decade or so this modest and retiring man produced some of the most remarkable results in the history of parapsychology. What are we to make of his career?

SOME OF STEPANEK'S BEST ESP PERFORMANCES

Experiments	Odds against results being due to chance
1. Two majority-vote experiments, run by Ryzl, attempting to get a very high score rate on the cards by guessing over and over at the same targets. Results: 71 percent correct in the first study, 100 per cent correct in the second.	20,000 to 1 112 million million to 1
2. Two key experiments viewed by Pratt (who ran them) as the best from the point of view of evidence of ESP. One (November 1963) was done with J.G. Blom of Holland as colleague, and the ESP effect was shown as a high score on the cards. 2,154 correct guesses out of 4,000. The other (February 1968) was done with Ian Stevenson and Jurgen Keil as colleagues, and in a series of three sub-experiments Stepanek's ESP effect revealed itself as a very high score rate on the concealed covers.	500,000 to 1 10 million to 1
3. Stepanek was particularly successful with visiting researchers. In the 1963 study run by Dutch experimenters, he scored 1,216 correct and only 832 incorrect for his card guesses. In other experiments with visiting Japanese, Indian, and Dutch researchers (among others) he was also very successful.	1,000 million million to 1 1 million to 1

ESP or some alternative explanation?

The first point we can make, and there is no dispute about this, is that chance cannot possibly account for the results obtained in a string of experiments conducted by numerous researchers. Everyone agrees on this. Instead, we need to know if there is any reasonable alternative to ESP (or some similarly genuine, unknown force or agency) operating in the Stepanek experiments. The word 'reasonable' has to be stressed. It is, after all, theoretically possible that Stepanek and the sixteen experimenters who obtained and reported evidence of ESP with him were all engaged in a gigantic conspiracy to defraud the world in general and science in particular. On the other hand, only a paranoid lunatic would regard that as a reasonable alternative to the ESP theory.

In a very few of the early experiments, it seems just possible that Stepanek could have been using *heat cues* from the cards. The black and white sides of the cards may have reflected detectably different amounts of heat through the envelopes. However, there are no data on thermal sensitivity which we can look at to assess this possibility in the conditions of those experiments. In any event, such a possibility could not apply to those experiments in which envelopes *and* covers were used (as in the Pratt-Blom experiment), nor to those in which Stepanek did not touch or even see the envelopes. This needs to be mentioned because the 'skeptical' reviewer whose opinions we shall now examine fails to mention this.

When Pratt and others published papers in *Nature* and in the less prestigious *New Scientist* magazine about Stepanek, they encountered considerable skepticism. Much of it was summarized by the British critic C.E.M. Hansel, then Professor of Psychology at Swansea University. In 1966 Hansel published a book on ESP research which devoted 22 lines of text to Stepanek, quoted on the next page. In 1973 Pratt corrected the many errors and false inferences the Hansel text contained. When Hansel updated his book in 1980 he managed to correct some of the errors (for example, the claim that Blom was one of Ryzl's colleagues, which undermined the importance of the *independence* of the Pratt-Blom experiment), but other points remained unchanged. To take one instance, Hansel wrote in 1980 that 'In 1965, I suggested that cues due to warpage of the cards might be responsible for this result (i.e. high scoring on the cards in the earlier experiments).' In fact Pratt had controlled for precisely this possibility, carefully flexing the cards and studying the warping of unattended 'control' samples left alone to see how warped they might become due to the grain of the material, and so on. In 1973 Pratt had pointed this out, carefully noting his attention to the problem and how he had dealt with it. In his 1980 revision Hansel simply ignored these careful statements. He also repeated the inaccurate claim that Ryzl was a biochemist at the Institute of Biology in Prague; this is not a serious mistake, but the failure to correct mistakes when they have been pointed out is not a characteristic of a careful critic.

While Hansel's critique is a perfunctory affair, in 1989 the ebullient popular science journalist Martin Gardner penned what might at first sight appear to be a meatier criticism of the Stepanek experiments. By this time Pratt had died, but in 1990 Jurgen Keil provided a spirited rejoinder, illustrating how Gardner had misunderstood key elements of experimental procedures and had made much of possible trickery when it could only have applied to a small portion of the experiments (and there was no evidence that such trickery had ever taken place). Keil notes that Gardner, as a journalist, is very liberal with pejoratives like 'ridiculous', 'laughable', and 'preposterous' when the Stepanek experiments are *bona fide* scientific experiments and deserve more serious and attentive scrutiny (to be sure, we described D.D. Home's phenomena with terms such as 'amazing', but that would be agreed by anyone, whether they considered them to be PK or trickery!). On this score, Keil is surely correct. Gardner is good entertainment when one is bored (his book is listed in the Bibliography), but for a coolly scientific appraisal we must look elsewhere.

It is also worthy of note that other skeptics have expressed different opinions. The British mathematician George Medhurst wrote to Pratt saying: '...so far as I am concerned this [work with Stepanek] looks like a clear demonstration of ESP.'

There are, in fact, many possibilities for normal sensory communication being involved in *some* of Stepanek's successes — weight differences between packages, visual clues, heat reflection, and so on. But all of these possibilities were examined and controlled for as the experiments progressed over a decade, and Stepanek's high scoring still continued. Our judgement is that none of these factors could explain — even in combination — much of Stepanek's success (that critics such as Gardner must perforce resort to claims of trickery is an admission of this). The random determination of target sequences eliminated any predictability which might have enabled logical influence to be used. Nor could Stepanek have gained any information unwittingly from the experimenters, since those testing him virtually never possessed any information about the targets (these having been determined by people who were not part of the face-to-face testing). Unless deliberate fraud, implicating many researchers, was involved, we have to say that some genuine anomaly was involved, and that anomaly looks awfully like ESP.

FLAWED CRITICISM OF STEPANEK

Italics have been added to identify specific statements requiring comment.

Hansel's critique, 1966

In recent years, parapsychologists have discovered that ESP research is in progress behind the Iron Curtain. In Prague, Milan Ryzl, *a biochemist at the Institute of Biology of the Czechoslovak Academy of Science*, has claimed extraordinary clairvoyant powers for his subject, Pavel Stepanek.

Stepanek's act, for it can hardly be called more than that, is as follows:

An observer is given a *pile of envelopes and cards*. One side of each card is *black*, and the other is white. *The observer places the cards in the envelopes with either the black or the white side uppermost. The pack of envelopes is then sorted by Stepanek,* and he is able to distinguish envelopes in which the card has the black side uppermost from those in which the card has its white side up. The envelopes are specially made and consist of *two pieces of thin cardboard stapled together. Since Stepanek handles the envelopes,* it is likely that he utilizes *cues due to bending or warping of the cards.*

Stepanek has been tested by several independent investigators. When tested by Pratt and *J. G. Blom, one of Ryzl's colleagues,* he produced very impressive results, but *when the experiment was conducted by a psychologist,* John Beloff, of Edinburgh University, *he failed to display any clairvoyant ability.*
Beloff had supplied his own cards which were made of plastic.

Pratt's comments, 1973

From about 1960 Ryzl had no salaried position but worked unofficially in ESP research.

P.S. did not set the conditions for the research, so he could not have worked like a stage magician, as this sentence implies.

Most of the research involved cards in envelopes plus outer covers.
Most of the tests used white and green cards.
This description reads as if someone present in the room with P.S. placed the cards in the envelopes and immediately handed them to him to call. The testing was not the casual affair that Hansel implies, but was carefully planned and carried out by experimenters who had full control over the materials and conditions for excluding sensory clues.
One strip of cardboard was folded and the edges taped for the envelopes. For the outer covers the edges were fastened by stapling them together through heavy cardboard ribs or stapling strips.
This statement ignores conditions used to control explicitly against bent or warped cards.

Blom was from Amsterdam and he had not even met Ryzl when our research was done.
Several other investigators were psychologists (Pratt, Barendregt, Freeman, Otani, Kanthamani) who obtained highly significant results.
P.S. obtained highly significant results with Beloff present, although not with the novel materials and test proceedures used in Experiment 1.

Personality factors

One final point is surely of interest to all of us. What sort of man was, and is, Pavel Stepanek? Common sense suggests that anyone who spends a great deal of time over the space of ten years guessing 'Green' or 'White' for concealed cards is no ordinary soul. To many people this would seem a dreadful prospect, boring beyond comprehension. Yet Stepanek enjoyed it and indeed was never very successful with other types of psi experiments. Why was this?

Formal personality tests on Stepanek, and the opinions of those who worked with him and know him, point to one significant feature in his psychology. Stepanek is a rather anxious person, who adopts one particular type of defense against that anxiety: compulsive and slightly obsessional habits, the performing of rituals. Pratt wrote: 'His life is governed more than anything else by the need to avoid social complications.... He strives to keep matters so arranged that he can be ·in control at all times.... He is afraid that personal involvements that overlap with his daily routine might make his life complicated, and he has a strong desire to *keep it as simple as possible...*'. Pratt also stressed Stepanek's punctuality and his deep-seated conviction that a man's word should be his bond.

Most psychiatrists would consider this to be an obsessive-compulsive personality, reflected particularly by the need for order, control, and predictability. Simple ESP card-guessing experiments were ideal for Pavel Stepanek — precise, simple rituals, prearranged and adhered to at the stated time and place. There is something important to be learned here which we will discuss at greater length in Chapter 4, which concerns ESP and personality. Different types of people may prefer different types of test. It is not so difficult to see why a type of test which would have bored most of us to tears appealed so much to Pavel Stepanek, still *The Guinness Book of Records'* most psychic man.

Mind over machine

The techniques used to test Pavel Stepanek derived directly from the simple card-guessing experiments of Rhine and other pioneers. In the age of the computer, new techniques have been developed to simplify the laborious business of preparing and handling materials and recording results.

A German-born physicist, working 20 years ago for Boeing Research Laboratories in Seattle, was the first researcher to use this technology to test psi in a thoroughgoing and systematic way. This man, Dr. Helmut Schmidt, devised an automated psi test machine which generated random numbers, registered subjects' guesses, and recorded all data in a form that was both easy to access and easy to process. With his machines, Schmidt hoped to conduct experiments which would eliminate errors of recording, inconsistencies of method, and other pitfalls.

Schmidt's research has furnished some of the most powerful evidence for psi yet recorded, and his work has also led to others duplicating his efforts. We will examine that subsequent research later, but first we need to understand the basic principles of his machines and test procedures. Obviously, over more than 20 years, these have developed and changed, but the basic principles remain much the same.

At the heart of Schmidt's psi-testing machines is a naturally occurring random process — the radioactive decay of the isotope Strontium-90. As atoms of Sr-90 decay, they emit rapidly moving electrons at random, wholly unpredictable, time intervals. The radioactive decay is detected and registered by a Geiger counter. In turn, the Geiger counter is linked to a very high-speed electronic oscillator. That oscillator cycles constantly between a number (usually four) of different electronic states, over and over. When the Geiger counter detects the emission of an electron, a counter driven by the oscillator stops, registering the state — 1, 2, 3 or 4 — of the oscillator at the microsecond of emission. A simple visual display of numbered lamps allows one to see which state is being registered.

This set-up was used in much of Schmidt's work to test for precognition and psychokinesis. Subjects were asked to guess which of the numbered lamps would light next — a precognition experiment — or they were asked to concentrate on making one of the lamps light more than 25% of the time — a test for PK. The advantages of this kind of machine testing are clear. The test is simple and readily understood; the events to be predicted or controlled are truly random, and allow a clear measurement of subjects' successes in their psi tasks relative to chance; and the machine records results automatically, eliminating human error in recording (especially important in precognition tasks).

ESP and the Schmidt machine

Schmidt published the results of his first ESP experiments in 1969. For these tests, subjects registered their guesses by pressing one of four numbered buttons. Pressing a button triggered the machine to produce a target which duly resulted in one of the four lamps being illuminated. The guess and the target (the lit lamp) were recorded on punched paper tape. The whole process, for one guess, was completed within half a second. To guard against cheating (or inadvertent error), the machine was constructed to ignore trials in which a subject pressed two or more buttons simultaneously, although if there were more than a millionth of a second delay between the pressing of two or more buttons, the

Opposite: Machine-testing of psi suggests that PK can have a biasing effect on all sorts of systems which generate random events. Modern aircraft are equipped with sensors that monitor essentially random events — second-by-second fluctuations in temperature, pressure, acceleration, air speed, magnetic fields, and so on. Could PK cause a potentially fatal bias or 'glitch' in such systems?

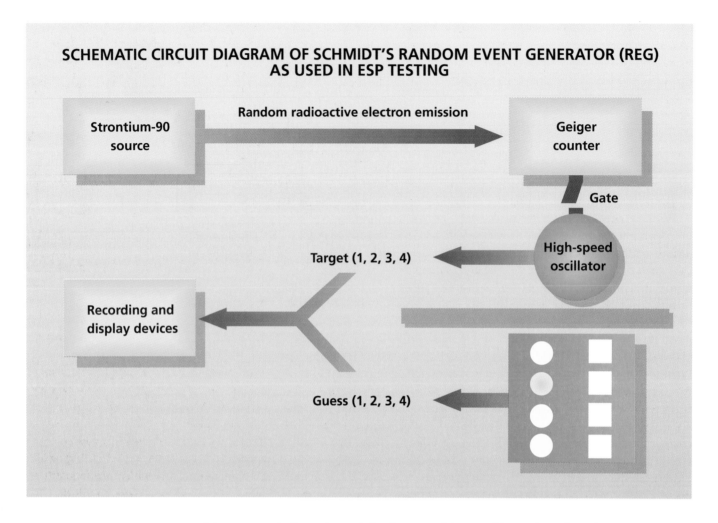

SCHEMATIC CIRCUIT DIAGRAM OF SCHMIDT'S RANDOM EVENT GENERATOR (REG) AS USED IN ESP TESTING

machine automatically registered the first signal (pressed button) as the subject's guess.

Initially Schmidt tested some 100 subjects, drawn from Spiritualist communities and churches. He did this because he considered he might have his best chance of finding individuals with psi abilities among such people. He found one seemingly gifted individual, a doctor of physics, who was able to predict the behavior of the machine to such an extent that the odds against chance for his performance were well over 100,000 to 1. Unfortunately, the man had to move away to a new job, so Schmidt was unable to test him further. However, the results persuaded Schmidt that the best approach would be to concentrate on a few gifted individuals.

Through further screening for people who appeared to have some ability, Schmidt selected three individuals for a formal experiment. All three had a strong interest in the paranormal. One was a male medium, another a teacher of 'psychic development', and the third, a truck driver, described himself as an 'amateur psychic'. Between them, they completed 63,066 guesses. The chance average score was, of course, 25%, or around 15,766 correct guesses, but the actual number of correct guesses was 16,458, nearly 700 more than chance would predict. While such a scoring rate was not very high (below 27%), because it was sustained over many thousands of guesses, the odds against it arising by chance exceeded 100 million to 1.

Schmidt began to vary his simple experiment by asking people to score high and low — asking them to use ESP to guess correctly and also to score below chance. This may seem perverse, but we'll be examining the often-reported phenomenon of 'negative ESP' or *psi-missing* later. Schmidt's medium was no longer available for testing, so this time he added the 16-year-old daughter of the truck driver as his third subject. When his subjects tried to score high they got just over 26% correct; when asked to score low, just below 24%. Again, the difference is small, but once more the odds are astronomical against this being due to chance.

Schmidt also conducted clairvoyance experiments. Here, targets were generated by the machine and stored on paper tape. The tape was then sealed inside the machine, which was then programmed to read off the tape and light lamps in the sequence corresponding to the tape. Instead of guessing future targets, his subjects had to guess targets already generated and stored — clairvoyance rather than precognition. Using his 'aim high, aim low' technique, Schmidt once again obtained results with odds against chance of around 250,000 to 1 from his expanding group of subjects (six in this study).

Helmut Schmidt operating an early random event generator. Regular checks were made to ensure that its output was truly random.

Checks and safeguards

Before looking at some of Schmidt's other experiments, it would be useful to pause and consider the question of safeguards. Obviously, the results of Schmidt's early experiments were not due to chance. Could they have been due to some bias in the machinery? Well aware of this possibility, Schmidt made many checks. Since he had the punched paper record of all the guesses his subjects had made, in the original order, he could check if there was anything peculiar about any particular sequence which might have produced a distorted result. He fed the record of the guesses into the machine and checked it against an entirely new set of targets. The comparison showed a level of hits very close to 25%, well within chance expectation. Schmidt also regularly programmed his machines to produce long sequences of targets which he analyzed for bias. In an original series of over 5 million targets generated in this 'control' condition, and also in many later checks, there was no evidence of any patterning. The machine's output was wholly random. Neither statistical peculiarity nor mechanical bias appears remotely capable of explaining Schmidt's results.

In later experiments (described in Chapter 9) Schmidt asked subjects to try to bias past REG outputs. Here a subject wearing earphones is wishing for a greater frequency of clicks in one ear than the other.

Schmidt made other checks too. In one precognition study he used his machine as a recording device, but instead of using Sr-90 as the random event source he used a standard table of random numbers published by the RAND Corporation. In a 15,000-trial experiment, he obtained results well above chance (odds of 1 million to 1). Schmidt used machines constructed by himself and also by other workers at the Boeing Research Laboratories, and found that he obtained successful results independent of the machine type. His documentation contains details of these and many other checks.

PK and the Schmidt machine

The combined results of Schmidt's ESP studies are impressive enough, but to these must be added some equally dramatic results from the PK experiments his later research increasingly focused on.

For his PK experiments Schmidt used a simplified version of his machine, with two (rather than four) output states. This is technically a *binary* (two-way) *random event generator*, or REG. This device was linked to a circle of lamps, with only one lamp being illuminated at any one moment. As the Sr-90 isotope emitted electrons, the REG converted them at

SCHMIDT'S SECOND ESP EXPERIMENT: CAN PEOPLE CONTROL THEIR ESP?

Subject	Goal	Guesses	Hits expected by chance	Hits scored	Difference	Probability by chance
O.C.	Score high	5,000	1,250	1,316	+66	1 in 50
J.B.	Score high	5,672	1,418	1,541	+123	1 in 10,000
O.C. & J.B together		10,672	2,668	2,857	+189	1 in 100,000
J.B.	Score low	4,328	1,082	956	−126	1 in 100,000
S.C.	Score low	5,000	1,250	1,164	−86	1 in 500
S.C. & J.B. together		9,328	2,332	2,120	−212	1 in 500,000

Probability of the difference between +189 and −212 arising by chance is less than 1 in 100 million.

random into negative or positive electrical pulses. When a pulse of one kind was delivered to the display, the currently lit light went out and the next one clockwise on the display lit up. Correspondingly, when the other type of pulse was delivered, the next counter-clockwise light lit up instead.

The basic principle of Schmidt's machine remained unchanged. Instead of a box with four buttons and lights, the subject sees a clock-face of eight bulbs. In his PK tests, Schmidt instructed his subjects to sit quietly and try to 'will' the machine to generate pulses so that the lamps would 'jump' in a clockwise direction more often than in a counter-clockwise direction. If no PK effect is operating, the machine ought to take a 'random walk', with the direction of movement being equal in either direction.

In his initial experiment Schmidt found what appeared to be *psi-missing*: his subjects scored below chance. Schmidt selected the most consistent of his psi-missers and conducted a total of 32,768 trials (one trial being a single jump). With chance alone operating, the light ought to jump clockwise 50% of the time, but in Schmidt's experiment it did so just over 49% of the time. Again, the effect is small, but the odds against it being due to chance exceed 1,000 to 1.

While Schmidt has continued to report successful studies over the years, we cannot summarize all of them here, but four others (one by Schmidt, three by groups including Schmidt) deserve special mention. In the first of these Schmidt used a 'simple' REG (a binary system, as in the clock-face experiment) and also a much more complex one; this generated a large number of individual random events, computed how many there were of each type, and then presented the most commonly generated target to his subjects (this is the same principle as the majority-vote experiment with Stepanek, except that here it was applied to the target, not to the guesses). The scoring rate in this experiment was well beyond chance expectation (odds exceeding 100,000 to 1), and subjects scored the same rate of success on both machines. This is an important finding for understanding how psi might work, and we will return to it in Chapter 9.

Independent confirmation

The three other experiments are of especial note. In these Schmidt 'channelled' the output of an REG to *independent researchers* (at Syracuse University and elsewhere). These other researchers had *their own independent, random systems* for deciding whether the target should be one pulse type of a binary output or the other (actually, the experiments were more complex than this, but this was the basic principle). The point here is that Schmidt could not possibly have faked the results. Of the three studies done in this manner, two showed statistically significant results, while the third showed above-chance scoring which was not statistically significant, although it was not very different from the scoring rates in the other two experiments (so it could not reasonably be classified as a complete failure). In other words Schmidt proved that he could reproduce his results with outsiders in control. The scoring rates were not very high, but then the subjects recruited by the independent researchers were almost certainly not comparable with Schmidt's carefully selected subjects.

Disarming the skeptics

By our computations, the odds against chance for Schmidt's studies taken as a body of evidence are so huge that, if we gave them, the word 'million' would fill several lines. No one has suggested that his results are compatible with chance.

Early on skeptics realized that Schmidt's work was of a high standard. The view that his experiments are soundly conducted, properly recorded, and rigorously statistically checked is not ours alone by any means. Technically-minded readers will find many of Schmidt's research reports cited in the Bibliography. Fraud is not a credible hypothesis because of the success with other researchers, and indeed because of the other work we will be considering in this chapter. In fact many skeptics have come to agree with the assessment of Ray Hyman, a skeptical commentator on parapsychology: 'By almost any standard, Schmidt's work is the most challenging ever to confront critics such as myself. His approach makes many of the earlier criticisms of parapsychological research obsolete. [I am] convinced that he was sincere, honest, and dedicated to being as scientific as possible...the most sophisticated parapsychologist that I have encountered. If there are flaws in his work, they are not the more common or obvious ones.'

This was written before Schmidt's collaborations with other researchers were published, and when the notorious American National Research Council report on parapsychology was published in December 1987 (we'll return to this in our final chapter) the first of Schmidt's successful independent collaborations was omitted without explanation, despite the fact that the design of the experiment had been published well in advance in 1982 and the results reported in 1986! This is, in its way, a breakthrough. Schmidt's evidence had reached such a high standard that the critics of the NRC could only ignore it. However, this research is not going to go away!

Robert Jahn's PK 'operators'

Since this book was originally published, a mass of reports has emanated from the Princeton Engineering Anomalies Research (PEAR) group at Princeton University. The head of the research group, Robert G. Jahn, is a scientist of unquestioned distinction, holding a prestigious post at a prestigious university. Like Schmidt, Jahn has used binary REGs and tested whether subjects can influence the outputs of these devices. And, like Schmidt, he has found that this indeed appears to be the case.

Jahn's research is formidable for any reviewer to deal with. The technical reports of the Princeton group are exhaustively documented, with data summaries which attain the size of telephone directories (fortunately, Jahn and his colleagues have written a summary book which is listed in the Bibliography). We cannot summarize all of the research here, but the key findings are readily appreciated.

Equipped with headset, data glove, and joystick, a player prepares to enter the totally computer-generated world of Virtual Reality (VR). If Jahn's finding, that some 'operators' show characteristic patterns of PK skill, is true, some VR players should be consistently more successful than others.

Jahn's basic protocol uses both *volitional* and *instructed* tests. In a volitional test the subject decides which way he wants to 'will' the display to go, above or below a chance baseline level of scoring. Theoretically, this allows for either PK or precognition to occur. In an instructional test, subjects do not have free choice: the machine itself triggers a random event to determine which way they must try to use their will to influence its output. Also, Jahn's group runs machine control checks, including tests where the subjects (whom Jahn refers to as 'operators') are physically present and either ignore the machine's output or wish for nothing in particular to happen. This gives an empirical baseline condition, and the results from this are of as much interest as those where operators are actively intending to use PK.

The initial core of the Princeton data comes from experiments with rigidly fixed conditions (50 trials per run; a fixed number of samples — 200 — used to determine each trial outcome, like Schmidt's 'complex REG'; and predetermined numbers of runs per experiment). In experiments where subjects were asked to score above chance, they did so not 50% of the time (chance level) but 61% of the time. When asked to score below chance, they did so 64% of the time. Overall, the differences in scoring rate are very small. The scoring shifts from the chance average of 50% by a fraction of 1% only. But because the number of trials and runs is very, very large, the results are immensely statistically significant.

To appreciate the details of the results, it is important to realize that Jahn's group has not actively sought out people thought to have some special 'gift', as Schmidt did in his early research. However, the Princeton group has certainly reported results from one or two exceptional individuals who have come their way. Thus, from a first experiment with their now famous 'Operator 10', Jahn found that if asked to score above chance the man did so with odds against chance of 300 to 1; when asked to score below chance, he did so with odds against chance exceeding 100,000 to 1; and the difference between the two conditions was so large that the odds against that being due to chance exceed 3 million to 1. While the size of the possible PK effect is small, Jahn's results are no less statistically startling than those of Schmidt.

A really thought-provoking finding by Jahn is that operators have what he terms characteristic 'signatures' in the results of their experiments. Some can score above chance when asked to do so, but fail if asked to score below chance. Some show the reverse pattern. Others score above chance all the time, whether asked to score above or below. Different individuals show different patterns of apparent PK skill. The reason why this cannot be dismissed merely as a random collection of disparate patterns arising from chance variance is that the operators show relative consistency from one test to the next. Jahn is, in effect, reporting test-retest reliability for his subjects. Lump them together, even once one has excluded the exceptional subjects, and the overall results still show significant correlation with intention.

What is also intriguing is the result of the baseline series, as reported in 1987. From time to time a series of truly random events will throw up an exceptional result. This is the scatter effect we referred to in our first chapter. On average, once in every 20 experiments there will be a result which has a probability of 1 in 20, or .05. Chance predicts this. What Jahn actually observed in 76 reported baseline series is that *not one* showed such a deviation. The machine output went on hugging the chance baseline in every case. This in itself is an unlikely event (probability around 1 in 50, not immensely

A subject in Jahn's Princeton laboratory tries to influence the output of a binary REG. The Princeton group's results were achieved with 'ordinary' people rather than psi stars.

small, but interesting). It is as if Jahn's operators were using PK to make the machine conform to chance during the baseline tests!

However, even eschewing such exotic possibilities, and even if we do the Princeton group a disservice by lumping all of their published research together, their work constitutes a really huge database — it comprises over 1.5 million trials. The effects are very small (a shift of only a fraction of 1% from chance expectation), but the overall odds against chance are over 20,000 to 1. In fact, this analysis does not do justice to the Princeton results because it obscures the different types of results obtained with different operators. Much larger anti-chance odds have been obtained in well-defined and controlled experiments with particular individuals who have produced databases of many tens of thousands of trials.

Boosting PK effects

At first sight a shift of less than 0.1% does not appear very impressive. However, a 1991 report by Brenda J. Dunne of the Princeton team points to a way of enhancing it. Dunne reports experiments in which pairs of operators teamed up, attempting to use PK together in co-operation to affect the output of the REG. Separated into same-sex and opposite-sex pairs, the results make interesting reading.

Robert Jahn and Brenda Dunne of the Princeton Engineering Anomalies Research Group. Behind them is the random mechanical cascade apparatus used to test for intentional PK.

The same-sex pairs obtained poor results, tending to score high when they aimed low and vice versa. Their results can be ascribed to chance. The opposite-sex pairs, however, scored impressively during their 92,000 trials. They scored high and low in accordance with their intentions, with the difference having anti-chance odds of some 2,000 to 1. The 'combined operator' effect was some four times greater than the effect of operators working alone. The effects are still small, still below 1%, but this co-operative approach suggests they might be susceptible to further increases. It is also worth noting that the highest scoring of all came from opposite-sex pairs who were, to use a charmless American term, 'bonded', suggesting that people who know each other well and have an established

relationship might be most successful at such co-operative PK work.

If we return to Schmidt's experiments for a moment, we find other possibilities for increasing the magnitude of PK effects. Schmidt conducted one experiment with 1,000 trials using a four-way REG, and here he worked with groups. Individuals were made to walk out before the whole group and step individually to the test machine, and then a single trial was generated (this experiment used many groups and took a long time!). Subjects were asked to use PK to *stop* a light appearing on the machine (which, by chance, it would do once in every four trials). Schmidt's instructions were: 'See how many safe steps you can make before stepping on the light. When this accident happens, imagine you have stepped on a bomb or you got an electric shock. Be extremely careful.'

Obviously, such vivid suggestions might be expected to make subjects apprehensive and nervous. As he expected, Schmidt obtained significant psi-missing. That is, the light came on significantly more often than 25% of the time, opposite to the intentions of the subjects (who were trying to stop it coming on). The actual hit rate was not the chance level of 25%, but a startling 30.6%. A surplus of +5.6% over the chance odds is a sizeable and highly important result. The odds against it occurring by chance are around 10,000 to 1.

Summing up the Princeton research

Jahn's experiments using the random mechanical cascade set-up seen here confirmed results obtained with REGs. As found in other kinds of PK experiment — using dice, magnetic tape, metal objects, enzymes, microbes, blood cells — PK effects seem to be 'material independent'.

We have given only the basics of Jahn's researches here. The Princeton group has also reported significant PK results with a 'random mechanical cascade', in which a mass of polystyrene balls bounce in complex random fashion through an array of nylon pegs, accumulating finally in collecting bins at the base of the apparatus. The distribution of the balls is found to be distorted as a function of the intention of operators trying to use PK to alter it. However, we will not discuss this work here since this chapter really concerns Schmidt's work, and that of the Jahn group, with REGs as strong evidence for PK. However, the Jahn group has obtained success in a range of PK settings and experiments, and although the effect size of the Jahn data is small, there are clear indications of how that yield might be increased.

We are not aware of any significant critique of Jahn's work other than the scrutiny of the NRC, and we will return to that report in Chapter 11 (at this stage we will merely observe that it is a fiercely criticized document). Indeed, critical attention to the Jahn group's research has been a fairly limp effort. Here is a sample, from Victor Stenger's book *Physics and Psychics*: 'I can only speculate, and again I must make it clear that this is not an accusation of fraud, just a critical examination of the possibilities. Electronic circuits are known to "drift". They are often sensitive to heat, shock and humidity. Perhaps the operator noticed a drift over the weeks, and took advantage of it. Perhaps she simply kicked the apparatus, turned it upside down, or blew on some of the transistors.'

Such remarks hardly qualify as 'critical examination'. The conditions of Jahn's experiments simply do not allow the kind of tampering suggested, especially since a larger body of remote experiments, generated under double-blind conditions, with the operators up to several thousand miles away from the machine while it was running, produced significant results similar to those of local experiments. The contrast of high- and low-scoring conditions eliminates the drift possibility (which is also specifically excluded by the counting circuitry of the device and confirmed by ongoing calibrations). Again, the curious reader should consult Jahn's original reports (see Bibliography). We can assure the reader that the kind of criticism quoted above makes an interesting comparison with the quality of Jahn's own documentation.

Perhaps such lackadaisical criticism is motivated by the fact that the effects in Jahn's studies are typically so small. We have already addressed that issue, but a final point might be noted: quantum physics also deals with effects which are sometimes incredibly hard to detect. Trapping neutrinos, for example, requires very expensive equipment and a great deal of waiting time. The effects in this branch of science are sometimes so fleeting as to make Jahn's effects look highly robust by comparison!

Towards a broader base of evidence

So far, then, we have looked at two putative 'Psi stars' and at the work of two research laboratories on machine PK. Our conclusion is that these sources of evidence form a strong basis for considering that human beings may possess some kind of faculty or ability which allows them to sense, and act, in ways which do not accord with the known 'laws' of physics. We cannot swallow the mass-hallucination/mega-fraud explanation of D.D. Home. We do not consider that Schmidt's work can be ascribed to as-yet-undocumented faults in his experimental technique (in over 20 years no hint of what such a fault might be has ever been suggested by critics or fellow researchers), and unless there has been a conspiracy among research scientists fraud is not a credible claim either. Such a conspiracy would have to include Schmidt and others who have worked with him, the Jahn group, and many other individuals.

In 1989 the Princeton scientist Dean Radin reported summary results from a series of 27 studies conducted with a 'Schmidt machine' and analyzed with the help of statistician Jessica Utts of the University of California at Davis. Of the 27 studies, one would have expected an average of 1.35 to have given results with chance odds of 1 in 20 (27/20); actually, eight of them did so, so that Radin's experiments were statistically successful some six times more often than chance would predict. The probability of this body of results, taken as a whole, arising by chance is around 1 in 27,000. Radin's results are hardly wildly exceptional; others have reported successful results with Schmidt-type machines too.

This is where the basis of the evidence shifts. While the effects produced by D.D. Home and Stepanek, and the results of Schmidt, impress and puzzle us, it would be wrong to think that such 'demonstrations' are necessarily the best evidence for psi. They are only part of the picture. What we really need are *groups of experiments*, reported by different researchers, that show consistent patterns of evidence. Then the accumulation of results — none of which need be overly dramatic taken in isolation — would form a persuasive overall picture. This is a 'bundle of sticks' argument. Taken individually, the sticks (individual experiments) may be easy to break. Bound together (considered as groups of related experiments), they cannot be so broken.

Now, in fact, something of such lawful repeatability has already emerged from our discussion of Home, Stepanek, and Schmidt. Many independent observers witnessed Home. Many independent scientists were able to verify the experimental results with Stepanek. Schmidt's work has been replicated in co-operation with others and by independent experimenters. It is this quality which makes the evidence impressive, not just the dramatic nature of the some of the evidence reported.

While purported 'Psi stars' such as Home and Stepanek are rarities, it would be surprising if psi abilities were confined to such exceptional people. We'll now begin the task of looking at the evidence for individual differences in ESP ability, keeping in mind that if such differences can be shown repeatably and reliably, they form evidence for the reality of ESP just as persuasive as the more glamorous, dramatic happenings associated with D.D. Home and other exceptional people.

Who is psychic?

Although people such as Home and Stepanek are exceptional, many ordinary people believe that they have some experience of psi. Thus, it is reasonable to test the possibility that psi abilities exist in unselected individuals. Indeed, the results obtained by Jahn, and to a lesser extent by Radin and Schmidt, suggest that psi abilities are not confined to a few rare and special people.

Human beings differ enormously in intelligence, memory ability, personality, accuracy of perception, and a whole gamut of skills. One would surely expect differences in psi ability also. Is there any link between psi ability and such factors as age, race, sex, intelligence, or personality? If so, why might this be? Does the explanation lie in genetic factors, upbringing, differences in lifestyle, or differences in brain activity?

Believers and disbelievers

How can we start to answer these questions? Let's begin by dividing people up according to whether they are disposed to believe or disbelieve in psi. Mediums have always claimed that the presence of skeptics at seances tends to inhibit their powers. The skeptic claims that he is a hard man to fool, and that mediums dare not play their tricks with him around! However, in controlled testing, we can find out whether attitudes to psi affect scoring in psi tests.

The experimenter whose name is synonymous with investigating the effects of belief and disbelief on psi is Gertrude Schmeidler. Her decades of research at the City University of New York are a landmark in parapsychology. In 1942 she started testing the psi

Gertrude Schmeidler was the first researcher to investigate the relationship between ESP and belief/disbelief. Her finding that belief in psi is conducive to psi has stood the test of time.

abilities of psychologists and students from Harvard University. Volunteers had to try to use ESP to guess the order of ESP cards in 25-card packs placed in a different room where no one was looking at them (a clairvoyance experiment). Before testing, Schmeidler interviewed her subjects to ascertain whether they were 'sheep' or 'goats'. The sheep were the believers, although in this context that meant only that they thought ESP was at least a *possibility*. The goats were the real hard-liners, simply refusing to believe that ESP was even possible, although they were prepared to be tested, probably to help Schmeidler with her experiment.

The first three experiments gave quite clear results. Schmeidler's 46 sheep averaged 5.31 correct guesses per pack; although this is not far above the chance average of exactly 5, the odds against it being due to chance are around 1,000 to 1. The goats, however, showed an even more intriguing result. One might have expected them to score at chance, but they did not. They scored consistently *below* chance, showing the *psi-missing* effect we referred to earlier in some of Schmidt's work.

Between 1945 and 1951 Schmeidler performed a series of 14 further experiments with sheep and goats. The results were very consistent. Sheep scored above chance, goats scored below chance. So marked was the difference between the two groups that the odds against

Opposite: In Schmeidler's terms the apostle Thomas was a 'goat'; he refused to entertain the possibility of resurrection until he had actually touched the wounds of the risen Christ.

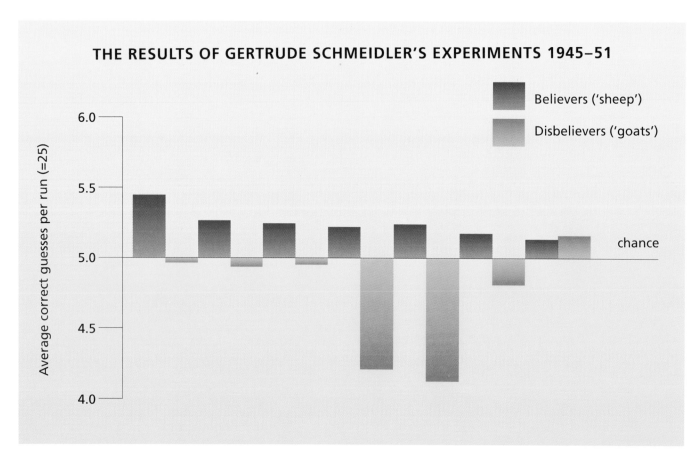

THE RESULTS OF GERTRUDE SCHMEIDLER'S EXPERIMENTS 1945–51

Believers ('sheep')

Disbelievers ('goats')

Average correct guesses per run (=25)

6.0

5.5

5.0

4.5

4.0

chance

This graph displays the results of 14 experiments done by Schmeidler. In only one experiment did 'skeptics' score slightly above chance.

chance being responsible comfortably exceeded 10 million to 1. While the reader may be getting a little fatigued with anti-chance odds by now, 10 million to 1 is very long odds!

Schmeidler's work is a major landmark on two counts. First, it showed reliable patterns of ESP from research with ordinary people — at least, from people who claimed no special gifts or abilities. It also established a link between ESP and individual psychology (the psychology of belief or disbelief). In total, Schmeidler collected some 300,000 guesses from 1,308 people. With numbers like this, her findings cannot be lightly dismissed. Her work has been subjected to rigorous scrutiny, but never seriously questioned. The validity of Schmeidler's findings must rest on the ability of other researchers to repeat her results. There is no reason in principle to consider that other experimenters, testing other unselected groups, should not be able to obtain the same results. And this is what has happened.

Results from a large body of experiments, including ones conducted in Britain, India, Czechoslovakia, Argentina, and other countries were collated and analyzed by Californian researcher John Palmer in 1971. While his analyses have been updated since, Palmer's approach to the evidence deserves special mention for its rigor, and because it has turned out to be a pointer towards key advances in parapsychology as it enters the last decade of the century.

Solidity of the 'sheep-goat' effect

Palmer reasoned that if there really is a difference between sheep and goats, then Schmeidler's huge database might be taken as a good indication of how powerful the difference between them truly is. Taking her results as an estimate of the true sheep-goat difference, Palmer predicted that 84% of all subsequent experiments would show sheep scoring higher than goats. That not every experiment would do so is expected from the notion of scatter we referred to in our opening chapter. Sometimes scatter will produce an oddball effect. When Palmer came to look at the results of experiments by researchers other than Schmeidler, he found that sheep scored higher than goats in 76% of them, compared with the 84% he predicted (in the 20 years since, the percentage has come closer to 84%; Palmer himself returned to the fray in 1977 and reached the same conclusions). If only chance is at work, of course, sheep should score higher than goats about 50% of the time. As it turns out, using an undisputed statistical analysis, the difference between 76% and 84% is not of any importance. Palmer was satisfied that Schmeidler's results were essentially correct, a reflection of a real difference between believers and disbelievers, and that her results had been confirmed by later researchers. Palmer's analysis was one of the most statistically sophisticated of its time and has never been criticized for false logic or deduction.

So the sheep-goat effect has stood the test of time. Half a century on, Schmeidler's results are still being repeated by other researchers. Methods of measuring attitude and belief have certainly moved on, from Schmeidler's early interviews to written questionnaires, and a variety of psi test procedures have been used, but the sheep-goat difference remains.

We do not wish to suggest that this effect is perfectly repeatable. Some experiments have certainly failed to observe it, and one recent (1991) study in Iceland produced a fairly dramatic reversal of the effect, with goats scoring much higher than sheep. It is also the case that some researchers have used the sheep-goat variable in experiments and failed to report their observations (the direction of the effect in those experiments is thus unknown). Further, there is a definite need for standard measurements of belief which can be used by different researchers (although the fact that the sheep-goat effect holds up despite different measures of belief suggests that the effect must be moderately robust!). Nonetheless, the clear majority of experiments have provided results which confirm Schmeidler's original observations. Indeed, if the results were more clear-cut, they would *not* be consistent with what Schmeidler reported. This seems almost counter-intuitive, but there is always chance scatter in a large body of experiments. That scatter produces some negative results and the odd freak reversal.

The real puzzle, of course, is why goats score below chance, rather than at chance. Does this suggest that they have some ESP ability and are consistently misusing it?

One possibility is that goats feel silly taking part in experiments they believe to be bunkum. After all, if you don't think ESP is even possible, you're going to feel rather silly in an experiment designed to test it! As a result, goats may be in a state of some mental conflict which may systematically distort their use of ESP-acquired information, and so they show psi-missing. If this is so, it might be revealing to see if neurotic individuals (who show chronic levels of conflict) also show below-chance ESP test scoring. Another possibility is that there may be personality differences between sheep and goats. Some research suggests strongly that sheep are more extravert, friendly, and outgoing than goats. Because so many ESP experiences in the real world seem to involve communication about and between people, someone who is friendly and gregarious may be more likely to experience ESP (especially telepathy) and thus be more likely to become a 'believer' (actually, just open to the possibility of ESP) than a social isolate. This possibility certainly seems plausible and needs further research.

Correlations between personality and ESP ability

Some cases of spontaneous ESP (deathbed apparitions, premonitions of disaster, and the like) have a high emotional content. On the other hand, the Stepanek, Schmidt, Jahn, and Schmeidler experiments were fairly low-voltage affairs emotionally. Do psychoanalysts and other alleged explorers of the emotional depths of the human mind provide any clues as to

Extroverts like to party because the excitement pleasantly boosts their level of cortical arousal, or so the theory goes. They make better ESP subjects than introverts, but whether this is because their levels of cortical arousal are generally lower than introverts' is still controversial.

possible links between personality and ESP? The literature on this theme is abundant, but the facts are pretty thin.

The trouble with the psychoanalytical approach adopted by followers of Freud and their kindred is that it is infinitely subjective, tends often to attach huge importance to entirely trivial or allegedly symbolic aspects of behavior, and lacks any kind of experimental support. Many psychoanalysts claim that their fee-paying clients have telepathic experiences involving deep-seated emotional drives and repressions. Unfortunately, the wholly unscientific nature of these interpretations (which often violate common sense) makes them valueless to the parapsychologist engaged in a search for truth. We need scientific methods for looking at personality, or we cannot hope to relate psi to personality in any reliable or repeatable manner.

Scientific personality researchers use one or more of three types of evidence to construct personality profiles: biographical material, objective measures of behavior, and questionnaires which record opinions, preferences, thoughts, and so on. Each source has certain advantages and disadvantages. The most exhaustive research into the measurement of personality has been that conducted by Hans J. Eysenck and Raymond B. Cattell in America. Their notions differ in detail, but not in essence: the two most reliable and readily measurable components of human personality are extraversion-introversion and neuroticism-stability. It is around these two components that parapsychologists have concentrated their research efforts. Once again, the early research was conducted in the United States, by Betty Humphrey at Duke University, North Carolina.

Extraverts come up trumps

Humphrey used a standard personality test of the time — now thought of as rather primitive — to divide her subjects into extraverts and introverts. She then ran them through ESP card-guessing, as Schmeidler did, and consistently the extraverts scored above chance while the introverts scored somewhat below chance. However, there are some rather arcane statistical problems with the manner in which she analyzed the results of her early experiments, so we must treat them with due caution (she lumped together the results from all extraverts and all introverts, into group comparisons, so that differences between *individuals* were not properly explored). However, a few years later in 1953, together with J. Fraser Nicol, she came up with results which can be treated with more confidence. She and Nicol administered the best personality measures available at the time to 30 subjects prior to an ESP card-guessing test, and found a clear extravert-introvert difference as before.

In the many years since this pioneering research, confirmation of the extravert-introvert difference has come from South Africa, Sweden, Britain, America, India, and elsewhere. Some experiments failed to produce a conclusive difference, as one would expect. In 1981 one of us (Sargent) examined all published studies and looked at the clear-cut differences, updating earlier surveys by Palmer in 1977 and by Eysenck ten years earlier. Clear-cut differences are experiments in which extraverts and introverts differed significantly in their scoring rates. The definition of 'significant' is the one we introduced in our first chapter; a difference is significant if there is a probability of 1 in 20, or even less, of it occurring by chance.

Now, if there is no true difference between extraverts and introverts, extraverts should outscore introverts on ESP tests as often as introverts outscore extraverts. However, what Sargent found was that out of 19 studies which showed clear-cut differences, extraverts outscored introverts in 18 cases — and the single exception really does prove the rule. From many different countries, with thousands of different people, experiments have shown this difference to be a real one.

Sargent's analysis was updated by American psychologist Daryl Bem, together with parapsychologists Charles Honorton and Diane Ferrari, in 1990. They suggested that, while some of the extraversion/ESP results may have been due to a mistake in the way extraversion measures were recorded (*after* the ESP test, so that subjects' knowledge of how they had performed on the ESP task might have influenced their questionnaire answers), in a substantial number of free-response experiments the effect remains clear-cut and highly significant. Free-response studies are described in the next chapter; they are, in essence, picture-guessing rather than simple card-guessing experiments.

Accepting the extravert-introvert difference as a real one, what might account for it?

Introverts and the 'busy brain' theory

In 1967 Eysenck offered the suggestion that extraverts might be better ESP test subjects because they have lower levels of cortical arousal (activity in the cortex of the brain) than introverts. This is a well-attested finding in personality psychology; it may exist because extraverts are better than introverts at suppressing the activity of nerve cells in the medulla (the 'hindbrain') which relay incoming sensory signals to the cortex. Eysenck suggested, from anecdotal evidence, that low levels of arousal might be favorable for ESP. If this is true, then the extravert-introvert difference in ESP reflects a difference in brain function.

To test this idea, the most obvious course of action would be to measure brain activity during ESP experiments. Simple as this might sound, different researchers have come to completely different conclusions. This is disappointing, but not surprising. Many different EEG (electroencephalograph) measurement methods have been used in different experiments, with different EEG variables, and different ESP tests.

The 'brain wave' research of the 1970s concentrated on one particular pattern of brain activity known as alpha rhythm. This is the rhythm of alert but relaxed states of consciousness. Experienced meditators, for example, can 'turn on' alpha rhythm at will. Alpha activity represents an intermediate stage of arousal between beta activity (one's normal, busy, waking state) and delta/theta activity (characteristic of sleep). Unfortunately, the evidence on extraverts and alpha rhythm is weak (this comes from conventional psychology, of course). Extraverts and introverts do tend to show different alpha patterns — extraverts tend to have higher alpha frequencies but of a lower amplitude — but the results of many experiments have yielded weak and inconsistent results.

There are now some powerful new technologies available for studying brain structure and activity. A welter of acronyms (PET for positron emission tomography, MRI for magnetic resonance imaging, and others) has grown up, denoting these new techniques. They allow researchers to see levels of activity throughout the brain, and surely offer the best approach to a direct study of brain function and psi. Unfortunately, the technology needed for using these techniques doesn't come cheap, and parapsychologists receive virtually no funding from state sources. So the research which cries out to be done here has not yet begun.

Another way of examining the cortical arousal hypothesis would be to use drugs. Amphetamine or 'speed' is a highly arousing drug; barbiturates and tranquillizers such as diazepam (Valium) have the opposite effect. So one would expect amphetamine to reduce ESP ability and diazepam to increase it. There is a little evidence that this is so, but more experiments — with more selective arousing and depressant drugs — need to be done.

Present evidence on the cortical arousal theory is inconclusive. There is simply not enough of it, from consistently designed experiments, for us to evaluate the theory. Let us hope that aspiring young parapsychologists put that right before too long.

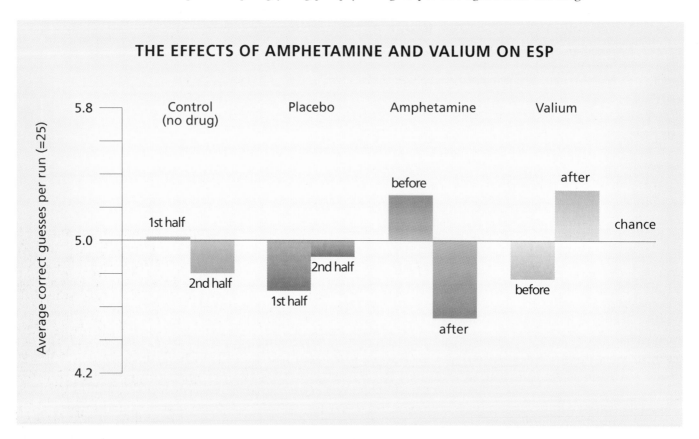

THE EFFECTS OF AMPHETAMINE AND VALIUM ON ESP

In this experiment, using traditional ESP cards in packs of 25, amphetamine depressed ESP scoring and valium increased it, but not significantly. Further research needs to be done in this area.

Effects of the social environment on ESP performance

A second theory concerning the extravert superiority in ESP tests has been offered by K. Ramakrishna Rao, an Indian-born researcher who has for many years worked at the Parapsychology Laboratory established by Rhine in North Carolina. Rao suggests that the extravert-introvert difference is basically a social one. The atmosphere in which an experiment is conducted is all-important, Rao suggests. A friendly, relatively informal, approach is vital. This is easier to achieve with extraverts because they are friendly and sociable, but more difficult with introverts because they tend to be shy and aloof. This seems plausible enough, but are there facts to support the idea?

Some ESP experiments have involved asking subjects whether they liked, and got on with, the person testing them. If the experimenter is liked, one would expect the test atmosphere to be good and the results to be fairly conclusive. In fact, this has not always been the case. But the whole notion of 'liking' the experimenter is naive. Unless the experimenter is a complete monster, most subjects will be polite and say: 'Yes, he was OK', which is too superficial a judgement. We need better measures than that. There is some evidence that experimenters who are extraverts (as measured by personality questionnaires) obtain better results in ESP experiments than introvert experimenters, but too few studies of this type have been done for the results to be clear-cut. Obviously, one would expect this if Rao's social theory is correct; no one will have more effect on the general social atmosphere than the person running the show.

Attempts have been made to have experimenters behave in different ways to their subjects. One study showed that experimenters told to act in a friendly manner obtained better results than those told to act in an unfriendly manner. This gives some support to Rao's theory, but not strong support. Such manipulation is rather false, and is hardly relevant considering the way in which the vast majority of experiments are conducted.

Yet the social theory predicts some interesting effects. For example, one might expect extravert/introvert differences to disappear with repeated testing. Initially, in an experiment, introverts may feel very unsure of themselves — part of the definition of introversion is an unsureness of oneself in new social situations. But, as they become more familiar with the strange environment of an ESP test in a laboratory, they will come to feel more relaxed and comfortable in it, and therefore perform better. On the other hand, extraverts who bounce into the place on Day 1 with a loud 'Hello' and a grin to the experimenter may become bored after a string of tests and therefore perform less well — proneness to boredom is a well-attested trait of extraverts. So, with time, we might expect the extravert-introvert difference to become less and less.

The evidence here is not clear-cut. Humphrey and Nicol found that extraverts tend to improve with time in ESP card-guessing experiments. In free-response experiments,

however, the extravert-introvert difference does seem to decline with time (these may be situations where social factors play a more powerful part). Not for the first time, we run into an irksome barrier; we need more evidence!

The extraversion story is frustrating. There is little doubt that the effect is a real one. However, we do not know why it exists. Many more experiments need to be done.

High neuroticism, low ESP?

When it comes to studies of neuroticism and ESP, the picture is more confusing, but also perhaps more exciting, than with the extraversion studies. The first element of confusion is that the personality factor Eysenck refers to as 'neuroticism' is referred to by Cattell as 'anxiety', so that the description within psychology differs slightly. There are also debates over sub-components or sub-factors of neuroticism (tension level, guilt proneness, and others). The second awkward element, hinted at when we discussed Pavel Stepanek, is that the relationship between ESP and personality tends to vary with the environment in which experiments are conducted.

John Palmer's fine review of all the published experiments on neuroticism and anxiety is 15 years old now, but the broad conclusions he arrived at still appear to hold true. Palmer found that in every experiment where a clear-cut (statistically significant) difference appeared between high- and low-neurotic individuals, the latter showed superior ESP performance. The effect appears to be genuine, but we have to take note of an important moderating influence: whether people are tested individually or in groups.

Palmer reached the conclusion that the neuroticism/ESP effect appears to exist in a

Anxiety in a test situation tends to hamper performance, particularly if one is the anxious/neurotic type. In individual ESP tests high-neurotics perform less well than low-neurotics, at least initially. As the test situation becomes more familiar, they tend to do better.

In this test low-neurotics scored significantly above and high-neurotics significantly below chance when tested individually. When tested as a group, the low-neurotics scored more or less at chance, while the high-neurotics scored well above it. Clearly, group situations enable high-neurotics to shed some of their anxiety.

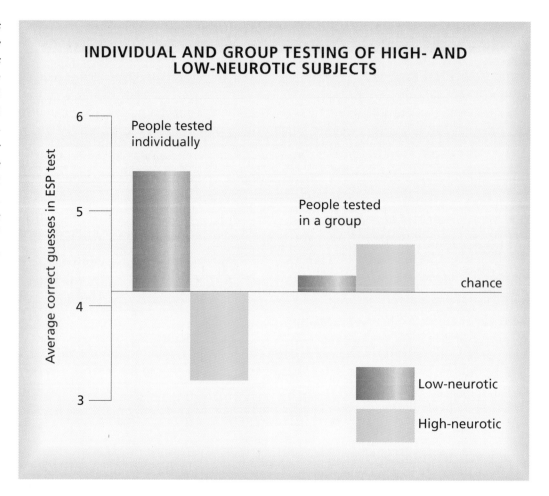

clear-cut way only if experiments are conducted with individual testing (people being tested one at a time). If groups of people are tested, the effect vanishes.

Palmer's conclusion was supported by a study reported in 1982 by Sargent and Trevor Harley. Subjects were given a short personality test followed by an ESP test in which they were asked to imagine a die falling down a chute and coming to rest with one face showing — which one? Twenty-five guesses constituted a test run for each subject. The chance scoring level here was 4.17 correct (⅙ x 25). A total of 186 people were tested, 36 individually and 150 in two groups. When tested individually, high-neurotic individuals averaged just over 3 correct guesses, low-neurotic people just over 5. When tested in groups, the difference vanished, with high-neurotic individuals actually scoring somewhat higher than the low-neurotic individuals. Let us hope that more experiments will support the results of surveys of old evidence and confirm them in this way.

Palmer's theory for this effect runs as follows. Neurotic people feel anxious about being tested individually, if they agree to be tested at all. Even if a researcher is friendly and reassuring, they still have 'ESP *test*' at the back of their minds, even if the experimenter is at pains to point out that we don't know enough about psi for us to *test* it in the same way as an examination tests knowledge, and that the experiment is an exploration rather than a test. They become anxious, and a degree of 'noise' builds up in their nervous system, interfering with ESP. Low-neurotic individuals do not have such an attitude, or if they do, they are not so bothered by anxiety. In groups, however, the neurotic can lose himself in the crowd. He is not being singled out for attention, so he does not become anxious, so his ESP scoring is not impaired.

What is the 'noise' we refer to here? It is not the high level of brain-cortex activity

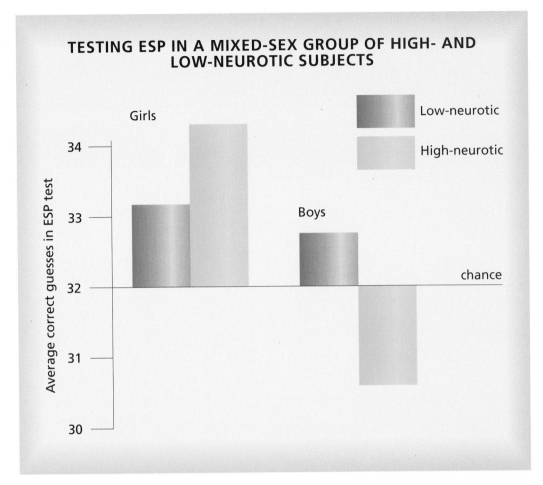

TESTING ESP IN A MIXED-SEX GROUP OF HIGH- AND LOW-NEUROTIC SUBJECTS

In this experiment girls greatly outnumbered boys. The boys, consciously or unconsciously threatened by a situation in which they were in the minority, performed less well than the girls. The high-neuroticism/below chance scoring effect was only apparent in the minority group (boys).

characteristic of introverts. Introversion and neuroticism are quite separate elements of personality. Rather, as Eysenck, Cattell, and others agree, a typical trait of neurotic people is a very active and reactive (responsive) autonomic nervous system, or ANS. The ANS is that part of the nervous system which controls automatic, involuntary activity of many kinds — the production of hormones, relaxation and contraction of the gut and other 'involuntary' muscles, heart rate, breathing, sweating, surges of (nor)epinephrine (adrenalin and noradrenalin) and other stress responses. Thus, high-neurotic people tend to sweat more heavily, to overreact to startling or surprising stimuli, and to show signs of stress more readily. These 'activation' factors may be 'noise' to the ESP signal just as over-arousal within the brain is. This theory draws considerable support from experiments which have used relaxation exercises, meditation, and other 'quietening' techniques to enhance ESP performance (the following chapters review a great deal of evidence on this score).

Finally, Palmer's arguments about groups may need further refinement. Some classroom experiments by Sargent suggest that the neuroticism difference still exists in a group for those members who are in a clearly defined minority within the group. For example, a minority of boys among girls will show a neuroticism difference, as in individual testing. Being in an obvious subgroup may *not* allow a high-neurotic person to lose himself in a crowd. Future researchers will have to consider very carefully what considerations have to be met for a test to be defined as a group test. For the moment, it appears that the social environment can influence ESP every bit as much as personality can.

Belief, extraversion, and neuroticism clearly relate to performance in ESP experiments. There are far too many experiments, with results which are too consistent, for this body of personality-related evidence to be dismissed. In their way these experiments form evidence for psi at least comparable with the more glamorous and dramatic phenomena associated with D.D. Home. Why? Because they concern ordinary people and because the experiments can be repeated. All we have left of Home is historical evidence.

The skeptical psychologist Ray Hyman has written in *Contemporary Psychology*: 'Such summaries of the hard-core laboratory data convince me that "something" is there...the critics, if they are to be fair, must find ways to account for the virtually hundreds of experimental studies that are summarized herein before they summarily dismiss parapsychology as a pseudoscience.' Years have passed since that comment, and we will return to such verdicts in the final chapter of this book. For now, let us look at other psychological factors which might correlate with ESP.

ESP ability related to age and culture

Whether there are age-related differences in ESP is an important question. Given that our society places very different demands — chiefly in the form of rewards for ordered, logical behavior — on adults as opposed to children, one might expect some differences between them in ESP ability. Then again, twentieth-century industrial societies have very little in common with the hunting, hunter-gatherer, pastoralist, and early farming communities of our history. Has this social evolution, which has tended to dismiss allegedly primitive, magical, animist beliefs, affected how psi functions? Can we explore that possibility by studying those 'primitive' cultures that still survive today? Is ESP is evolving in or out?

Since ESP is potentially useful, it could be argued that evolution might favor it. On the other hand, it is usually weak and sometimes unreliable (judging by the evidence we have considered to date). Humans are highly visual creatures, not half as gifted in other sensory departments as many other animals. Perhaps ESP is going the same way as our sense of smell, and evolving out.

Playtime in the laboratory

In this experiment by Susan Blackmore children were given cuddly owls and thinking caps to help them concentrate on sending and receiving images of pictures on cards. Would adults do better in ESP tests if they had similar props?

Taking age first, the relationship is not simple. Certainly no researcher has ever reported a near linear relationship, positive or negative, between ESP and the whole age range. However, many researchers have reported consistently strong results with young children as ESP subjects.

The classroom experiments of Margaret Anderson, a very creative ESP researcher, are recognized as a classic series of studies in parapsychology. Although she used simple tests for ESP, she dressed some of them up as a science fiction game in which good (above-chance) ESP test scores helped to launch a 'space rocket' and keep it on course during its mission. Such a presentation would have appealed greatly to children, especially during the 1950s when space travel was still a great novelty. Anderson's many experiments with

children obtained consistently high, well above-chance scores.

Direct comparisons of children and adults were made by Dr. Ernesto Spinelli of Surrey University, working with large groups of subjects of all age ranges. His findings were that children aged between three and eight scored well above chance on a telepathy test, with the youngest obtaining very high scores indeed (more than double the 20% chance average in some studies). However, because only some of these experiments used randomly selected targets, a direct comparison can only confidently be made with his 19–21 age group (all whom were university students — it would be helpful to have had a more representative group of adults than this).

Nonetheless, Spinelli's results are impressive, and we could adduce further evidence of high-scoring experiments involving children and even babies. What we lack is a direct comparison with varied groups of adults, so we cannot speculate with too much confidence about child-adult differences. However, Spinelli found a decline in scoring even in his child groups; the youngest scored best, the oldest the lowest, and those of intermediate age were in between. On the basis of this, he not unreasonably offered a theory of why children might possess superior ESP.

Spinelli's suggestion is that the development of formal, logical, analytical thought and reasoning in the growing child is inhibitory to ESP. Asking a three-year-old: 'Can you guess which symbol John next door is looking at?' will probably elicit a cheerful 'Of course I can!' Adults, and older children, think they know better. Spinelli has also reported that ESP scoring declines dramatically if subjects

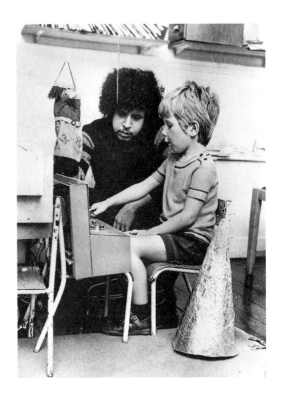

Ernesto Spinelli and one of his child telepathy subjects.

are given tricky mental tasks to perform while doing ESP tests. If a person is bound up in logical, analytical thinking, ESP inhibition occurs.

There are alternative explanations here. Belief (the sheep-goat effect) could be part of the story (children are not natural skeptics). So could personality and spontaneity (people tend to become more introverted as they grow older). The way in which Spinelli administered his tests to children was brilliant. He used a pair of glove puppets to act out the test and explain the procedure and what the children had to do. He also gave the children 'thinking caps' to help them read each others' thoughts! One has to wonder whether, if the enthusiasm and spontaneity and sense of fun the children felt could be produced in adults, adults might not score well too.

Schools put higher value on formal reasoning than on imagination. Does this progressively suppress psi ability?

However, the mental interference effect reported by Spinelli suggests a definite possibility of intelligent, analytical thought being inhibitory to psi. As abstract reasoning skills develop, psi may decline. For adults to 'tap in' to psi abilities, they may have to suspend those skills. The next two chapters describe ways of doing just that.

A voodoo ceremony in Port-au-Prince, Haiti. Belief in good and evil spirits, in the power of spirits to govern the daylight world, is almost total in Haiti. Spirits may even bring corpses to life (zombies) for their own purposes. In such a society, simple laboratory tests of ESP are meaningless.

Below: Mowanjum aborigines in dance costume. Although comfortable with certain aspects of what Western researchers call ESP, psychokinesis is regarded as a special power, safe only in the hands of 'clever' men. Interestingly, the original meaning of the word 'clever' was 'adroit with the hand'.

Psi and the 'primitive' mind

Anecdotal reports suggest that some pre-industrial, tribal societies accept psi, most often in the form of beliefs about spirits and magic, as part of everyday experience. Unfortunately, there is little in the way of good research in this area. The most extensive, from the 1950s, was conducted by Ronald and Lyndon Rose among Australian aborigines, Maoris, and Samoans. The Roses carried out ESP card-guessing tests and PK tests with clearly divergent results. The ESP tests got high scores (except from the Samoans), but the PK tests were uniformly unsuccessful. These findings may well relate to cultural beliefs about psi — the sheep-goat effect in another form. The aborigines, for example, were adamant that only the 'clever men' of the tribe could possibly influence the dice used to test for PK; ordinary tribesmen were adamant that they could not do so. And they didn't.

A little PK testing was done with the 'clever men', unsuccessfully, but very few were tested and their attitudes to the task were unclear. Realistically, good tests would need to be shaped to the culture of the community being tested. One would hardly approach a voodoo *houngan* (priest) with a pack of ESP cards and ask him: 'Can you guess these symbols please?' It would be meaningless. Yet if one adapted the nature of tests to the circumstances and familiarities of different cultures, it would be difficult to draw comparisons. Overall, we can only say that so-called 'primitive' societies may well be fertile ground for further research, but at this stage we can draw no firm conclusions from the available evidence.

Intelligence, sanity, and madness

Returning to Spinelli's work, his suggestion that analytical intelligence inhibits ESP seems plausible. Intuition and analytical intelligence are often antithetical. Research on formal measures of IQ (and also cases of major mental illness, where rational thought may be considered to have broken down) might shed further light on this general area.

The relationship between psi and adult IQ is easily summarized: none exists, or at least none is suggested by present evidence. However, it is often difficult to separate intelligence from other factors. One ESP experiment conducted by Robert Brier with American Mensa members showed clear and strong psi-missing (below-chance scoring). The Mensa members had high IQs, but were also very skeptical about psi, so the results could well be due to the sheep-goat effect rather than to high IQ.

Intelligence is not a single skill. There is evidence that it is hierarchical, and composed of different related skills. There are also sex differences. Men are better on tests of mathematical reasoning and some spatial IQ tests (especially those involving perceiving hidden shapes, or rotations of objects in space), while women seem to show higher verbal fluency, item-matching, and mathematical calculation (as opposed to reasoning). These are only generalizations, of course, but an increasing body of evidence suggests there may be structural brain differences which underpin these sex differences. There have been attempts with ESP tests, using words versus pictures with subjects of both sexes, to pin down related differences, the theory being that differential IQ-related skills might show up in different levels of scoring by men and women on different types of targets. The results of these experiments can be said to have been consistently inconsistent. In fact, this is rather reassuring; it would be surprising if the simplistic test differences employed in these ESP tests had shown any male-female differences, since they were based on an understanding of sex differences in IQ skills that was much less sophisticated than it is today.

Many people suffering from psychotic (schizophrenic, and more rarely manic) illness believe that they have telepathic powers, and/or that they are being persecuted telepathically (quite common in paranoid schizophrenia). Far-fetched as it might sound, some psychiatrists have suggested that psi might actually be a trigger for psychosis; a person who is too 'open' to disturbing telepathic 'messages' may be pushed over the edge into madness.

Trying to test ESP in schizophrenics is fraught with problems. The first problem is ethical. Can we ethically conduct such tests with deeply unhappy and confused people? Might we not expose them to mental trauma if they do

This painting by a psychiatric patient expresses an intense, anguished inner world. Hallucinations and delusions have ESP-like components. Could malign telepathy or PK produce the profoundly disturbed mental states that we label paranoia, mania, psychosis, and so on?

show ESP, opening their minds and brains to stimuli they might perceive as threatening? There are also major practical problems relating to diet, drugs, (mis)diagnosis of illness, subtype of schizophrenia, and so on. Trying to control for such factors is a nightmare, as anyone conversant with journals of psychiatry will be well aware. Trying to get around these problems requires a lot of time and money, careful screening of patients, great expertise, clinical skill, and the goodwill of psychiatrists and nurses involved in caring for the mentally ill. It is hardly surprising that none of the work done by parapsychologists with schizophrenics meets acceptable standards. Most of it is outdated now (the diagnostic definition of schizophrenia has been radically altered in the interim), but for the record it was not conclusive. Sometimes very significant ESP test scores were obtained with psychotic subjects, sometimes not.

Overall these studies, and others with other categories of mentally disturbed individuals, cannot be interpreted as meaning that mental disturbance equates with marked ESP ability. If anything, the opposite is the case. Research using measures of social adjustment and maturity tend to show small positive correlations with ESP talent, although the findings are not striking.

The myth of female superiority

Virtually every survey ever conducted shows a strong sex difference in relation to psi experiences. Women tend to have more ESP experiences than men or, to be accurate, they *say* they do. In telepathy experiences, men are in the majority as 'senders' and women as 'receivers'. This looks suspiciously like a reflection of well-worn gender stereotypes, with passive-intuitive females receiving messages while active-dynamic males send them. Changes in how surveys are conducted make it difficult to see if this pattern shows any sign of weakening over the decades in which feminism has influenced gender stereotypes.

There is virtually no evidence to suggest that, in ESP experiments, there is any stable or consistent pattern of difference between the sexes. In both the dream studies and in at least part of the ganzfeld studies reviewed in the next chapter males performed rather better than females as receivers, but the difference was not great. Most experimental investigations have actually focused on sex differences with children, again without clear-cut results. It

A great deal of mythology — the feminine principle as lunar, hidden, somehow linked with an invisible, darker world — underpins the common assumption that women are more psychic than men. In the laboratory this apparent sex difference disappears.

has been suggested that women are more worried by laboratory tests than men, and are therefore inhibited from displaying their superior abilities. If this were the case, then one might expect female subjects to show rather more of that extra ability when working with female experimenters, but that has not been observed. Also, from Anderson and Spinelli's work, it seems clear that almost all the children involved in ESP experiments entered fully into the spirit of the thing; the girls did not seem to be more inhibited than the boys.

So, while we cannot rule

out a sex difference between women and men, there is no evidence for it. This is an important finding, for it suggests that a long-held assumption based on surveys of experience does not reflect any real difference in experience. It simply attest to the fact that women are more willing to acknowledge and discuss their experiences than men, although men will open up if their experience is compatible with a socially sanctioned image of active masculinity.

The story so far

What we have found is that three factors appear to correlate fairly reliably with ESP ability: belief in the possibility of psi, extraversion, and low levels of neuroticism/anxiety. The first of these is really a commonsense finding. It has parallels with the 'placebo effect' in medical research, in which groups, of sick individuals given a sugar-coated, utterly inactive pill almost always improve as compared with groups not given any treatment at all. Belief is a powerful thing. Mediums who complain that skeptics inhibit occurrences at seances may not be just making excuses; the psi effects of 'goats' appear to be negative, and would inhibit any genuine psi on the part of the medium.

The other factors, extraversion and low levels of neuroticism, may exert their effects through a common mechanism, that of decreasing 'noise in the system'. Whether this is noise in the cortex of the brain or noise in the autonomic nervous system of the body and brain, it seems that a reduction of noise may be conducive to psi.

We have also found that some psychological factors do *not* seem to relate to ESP. In some cases, the negative evidence is plentiful. This is especially true for sex differences. In other cases, there is not enough research to be sure, but it doesn't look as if there is any relationship. If everything we studied seemed to relate to ESP ability, we would begin to wonder whether our experiments were sound!

Returning finally to our 'noise' notion, there is now a large body of research that has focused on attempting to increase the strength of ESP 'signals' by cutting down internal noise. This research is based on clear theory and on surveys of ESP performance, and it employs elegant and appealing test techniques. It provides much further evidence for us to contemplate.

ESP, dreams, and the Twilight Zone

We have examined whether there are personality traits which might be favorable for psi, but clearly the use of any human skill, ability, or sense depends on the environment in which it is exercised. Much exciting work has been done to create environments, physical and mental, which might favor the occurrence of psi.

This research really began in the 1960s, when a younger generation of parapsychologists, many trained by Rhine, began to feel that his methods for testing ESP were sterile and his philosophy somewhat naive. Rhine's own pioneering work had taken place in the 1930s, when the dominant school of thought in psychology was *behaviorism*. In essence, behaviorists assert that psychologists can only study events and behavior which take place, measurably, in the external world. Internal events and processes get very short shrift. Thus, a behaviorist might attempt to show that a particular type of electrical activity in the brain is associated with some mental state, but argue that one cannot study the mental state itself, which is too subjective a territory to measure.

Immersed in this dominant ideology, Rhine wanted to beat the behaviorists at their own game by using experimental techniques which could have been lifted straight from any behaviorist's manual of 'how to do psychology'. Thirty years on, however, a new spirit was abroad in America. Increasing use of hallucinogenic drugs (including LSD and mescaline) and interest in cross-cultural psychology drew the attention of many psychologists to the inner mental life and its study. Behaviorists ignored people's introspections about their inner mental lives, but the new generation of psychologists felt that ignoring such matters could breed only ignorance.

Parapsychologists began to look afresh at reports of psi from many different sources and periods in history. Anthropological research showed that many allegedly 'primitive' people claimed that naturally occurring hallucinogens (including varieties of the fabled 'magic mushroom') produced or enhanced psychic experiences. Ancient Sanskrit texts on the practice of yoga and meditation seemed to suggest that psi experiences, including ESP and more dramatic phenomena such as levitation, occurred in the course of certain meditation exercises. In the more recent past, the reported demonstrations of hypnotists showed that normal human behavior could be transformed in strange and unexplained ways. All of these sources, and many more, suggested many potentially fruitful new approaches to studying psi through altered mental states, changing normal consciousness through drugs, hypnosis, or meditation.

The dream-watchers

One particularly promising line of enquiry seemed to lie in the field of dreams. From ancient times, dreams have been believed to have occasional supernatural significance. Historical accounts of prophetic dreams, such as Pharaoh's dream of future famine, interpreted by Joseph and narrated in the Old Testament, are common. Moreover, a very high proportion (some 50%) of reported experiences of spontaneous ESP occur when 'receivers' are asleep.

Landmark research in dream-ESP testing was conducted in America by Dr. Montague Ullman, later joined by Dr. Stanley Krippner and his associates. As a practising

Opposite: 'To sleep, perchance to dream...'. Dreams seem to access levels of information that the conscious mind cannot or will not process. During dreaming sleep the eyes flicker beneath the eyelids, and breathing and pulse rate become irregular.

Dreaming Head, a painting by John Armstrong. Research has shown that dream recall is very vivid if one is woken during a dream. Even five minutes afterwards recall is hazy; after ten minutes it is almost non-existent.

psychoanalyst, Ullman had become intrigued by apparently precognitive dreams reported by his patients. This group's experiments, conducted over several years, were funded by the Irish-born medium Eileen Garrett through the Parapsychology Foundation, which she set up to promote scientific research into parapsychology (and which remains an active, and important, promotor of scientific research in this field). Between 1962 and his retirement in 1978, Ullman's dream research was based in the Dream Laboratory of the Maimonides Medical Center in Brooklyn, New York.

Ullman's research was greatly assisted by the discovery of psychologist Nathaniel Kleitman that it was possible to detect periods of dreaming during sleep through external signs. Kleitman found that, during sleep, human beings show bursts of strong, rapid fluctuations of activity in eye muscles. If a person is wakened from a period of Rapid Eye Movement (REM) sleep, he is much more likely to report a dream than if awakened at other times (NREM — non-REM sleep). REM detectors, linked with an EEG machine to record electrical activity in the brain, can reliably be used to pinpoint episodes of dreaming sleep as they occur. Kleitman's results, soon repeated by other researchers, provided an objective measure of dream activity which could be incorporated into dream ESP study.

The best way to show how the Maimonides dream-ESP experiments worked is to examine a study Ullman conducted in 1964. His single subject was a psychologist, Dr. William Erwin. Twelve test nights were planned but, due to illness on Erwin's part, only seven were completed.

The experiment took the form of a telepathy test. While Erwin, wired to up to an REM/EEG apparatus, was asleep in one room, a sender in another room tried to use telepathy to send the content of a target picture (not just a simple ESP card symbol) to Erwin. The picture was chosen from a large collection of art prints, using a table of random numbers. The sender viewed the target picture during the night, and that target picture only. During the night, the experimenter with Erwin would send an electronic signal to the sender when Erwin was dreaming (in REM sleep), so the sender could then make a special effort to communicate the content of the picture to him and influence his dream content. At the end of each burst of REM sleep (there are typically a handful of REM bursts during a night's sleep, each lasting anything from a few minutes to an hour or even more), Erwin was woken and asked to report his dreams. The content of his report was written down by the experimenter with him. During the night, the sender had no direct contact with Erwin or the other experimenter. In the morning, he left without seeing the other participants. Erwin was asked by his experimenter to report any extra associations to his dreams (extra details, anything in the dream which reminded him of associated memories and images, and so on).

How could it be established whether Erwin was detecting target information accurately or whether he was using ESP to do so? An experiment like this does not use simple, clear-cut guesses. Unlike ESP card-testing experiments, which are *forced choice* experiments in which subjects are allowed to make only one of a narrow range of guesses, a dream experiment is a *free response* experiment; the dreamer can report anything.

Judging the issue

After seven nights of experimenting Ullman had used seven different target pictures and collected seven nights' worth of reported dreams from Erwin. The pictures and the dream reports were then despatched to three independent judges who were asked to carry out a simple task: to look at each of the dream reports, and then to arrange the seven pictures in order, from one to seven, giving first place to the picture which seemed most like the dream and seventh place to the picture least like the dream.

Now, the judgements of people checking through dream reports and pictures are clearly going to be subjective. Not all of them will see things the same way. Despite this problem, it is still possible to use the method outlined above to check for ESP. If a judge compares dreams with pictures and *consistently* puts the target picture first against its corresponding dream report, then chance cannot account for this. By chance alone, one would find a mix of results — occasionally the target will be placed first, but equally-often

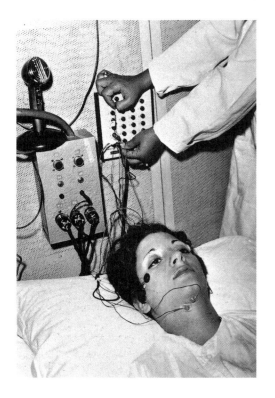

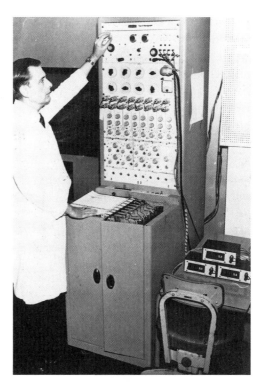

Far left: A dream ESP volunteer being wired up to an EEG and a polygraph in the Maimonides Dream Laboratory. The EEG records electrical activity in the cortex of the brain, and the polygraph records changes in blood pressure, respiration, and pulse rate.

Left: Dr. Stanley Krippner conducts a dream telepathy experiment at Maimonides.

it will be placed last or anywhere in between. In the Erwin study, with seven dreams and seven pictures, we would expect by chance alone that only one of the seven pictures would be placed first against the correct dream (because there are seven trials, with a 1-in-7 chance of being correct each time). We would also expect that the average *rank* (placement between one and seven) given to the right picture would be the middle number, 4.

The judges must, of course, be *blind*. In this context, that means they must not know, or be told, which targets correspond to which dreams. This seems obvious, but the pitfalls can be subtle. For example, if Erwin had been shown the targets *after* he had made his reports, he might have inadvertently made comments about earlier targets in later dream reports ('It seemed like the thing I saw last night when I got the Van Gogh...'). If the judges knew the order of the targets, this could inadvertently give them clues about the match-up of targets and dreams. Some free-response studies have fallen into such traps in experimental design. Fortunately, the Erwin study did not. So how did the judges score Erwin's dream reports when their different judgements were averaged out? On only one occasion was the average rank 4.0. On six occasions, it was lower (better than chance), suggesting that the right pictures were being scored high against the matching dreams. From his statistical analysis, Ullman concluded that ESP had been demonstrated in this study, but because the experiment had not run for the formal, pre-determined length of time (which left him vulnerable to the accusation that he had stopped experimenting when the results looked good), he decided to repeat it.

Getting more involved

For the second Erwin study, which completed its pre-designated length of eight test nights, a strong innovation was made in the experimental method. The sender didn't just *look* at target pictures. Ullman and Krippner developed what they termed 'multisensory materials' to supplement the pictures. The sender, Feldstein, must have been embarrassed by this at times even though he had suggested the idea. On the second night of the experiment, the picture to be 'sent' was a Japanese painting of a man with a parasol trying to escape from the rain, so Feldstein had to wander around in the Maimonides shower room holding a toy umbrella!

From the second Erwin experiment, the results were remarkable. Of the eight nights of the experiment, six gave direct hits — on six occasions the judges ranked the correct target picture first against the dream report. The other two pictures were ranked second and third, respectively, against their targets. Chance alone would have given one hit, or 12.5% correct. Erwin scored 75% correct. The odds against chance for this result, from a very small-scale experiment, are well over 1,000 to 1.

The Maimonides team went from success to success with this type of experiment. One particular example of their work is of particular note, because of the nature of the experiment and the tremendous success it enjoyed. The idea for it emerged as a result of intriguing examples of apparent spontaneous precognition which manifested themselves during the normal course of laboratory experiments.

For example, in 1969, a telepathic dream session was conducted with Alan Vaughan (co-author with Ullman and Krippner of the book *Dream Telepathy*) as the dreamer. In the post-dream interviews, Vaughan commented: 'Chuck Honorton was there in my dream and he was marking a transcript and he was using the letter F.... He said: "Oh, F is for failure"...then I looked at the television set there and this television set actually seemed to be part of the experiment as well...as I looked at it, the whole thing began to move and come to life, and there was a man holding a knife...and behind him was a monkey lying on the floor.... I wonder if there might sometime be an experimental thing like this...'.

That was on 9 April, 1969. On 17 July, Vaughan wrote to Ullman suggesting that this dream might have been a precognition of a session yet to come.

On 12 January, 1970, the Canadian TV personality Norman Perry arrived at Maimonides to act as a subject in the research. Vaughan was there as a 'back up' just in case Perry found it difficult to sleep in the unfamiliar laboratory conditions, which included having electrodes attached to his scalp (we can confirm from experience that this certainly doesn't help one to doze off). The selection of the target, from the random number table, produced a picture showing a monkey holding an orange. To add impact to this image the sender took an orange and *ripped it apart*.

Perry dreamed not of a monkey, but of a large white nondescript animal. However, he placed the monkey picture first when given six different pictures to choose from, because *the monkey in the picture was white*.

Meantime *Vaughan dreamed of someone ripping up a loaf of bread*. When he looked at the pictures after the dreams, he put the monkey at the bottom of the pile, a complete miss. *Honorton was the experimenter. F for failure.*

Vaughan watched Perry make his choice as he was being *filmed for television* ('this television set seemed to be part of the experiment as well...') and watched Perry place the monkey picture first, *flat on the floor* ('...a monkey lying on the floor...'). The second choice by Perry, which he placed next to the monkey, was a picture of *a man holding an axe* ('...and there was a man holding a knife...').

Now, all of this could be no more than coincidence, although the sheer number of correspondences is disconcerting. It is interesting to note that, in a formal experiment designed to use an ESP-conducive state of mind, spontaneous ESP can pop up around the edges of the experiment! Given that the inspiration to conduct dream-ESP studies came in part from study of such spontaneous cases, there is an amusing element to this. Of course, the Vaughan/Perry saga cannot be scientifically evaluated, but one can see why the Maimonides team were keenly interested in precognition. Two of their most remarkable experiments gave them the opportunity to study it with a most unusual individual.

Precognitive dreaming

During 1969, and again the following year, a young Englishman named Malcolm Bessent arrived at Maimonides. With a history of ostensibly precognitive and other psi experiences, Bessent became one of the stars of the Maimonides research program. This is how the experiments with Bessent were conducted.

Malcolm Bessent's ability to dream accurately about the next day's events was uncanny. The Maimonides team did not even choose his dream targets until the morning after his dreams.

In each of the two experiments there were eight experimental nights. This was determined before the experiments began, of course. On each night, Bessent slept with the REM/EEG monitors attached as usual and, on being awakened from REM sleep, was asked to report his dreams. In the morning, he added any final thoughts, images, and associations. So far, this follows the pattern of the previous Maimonides studies. But with Bessent, there was no sender and no target picture!

After the night's events, an experimenter who knew nothing of Bessent's dreams used a complex random scheme to select a target word from a standard psychological text, *The Content Analysis of Dreams* (which has absolutely nothing to do with cheap potboilers offering spurious interpretations of what dreams 'truly' mean). The experimenter matched the word with a target picture, and from that picture the experimenter devised a dramatized experience for Bessent. One notable example will serve to show how this worked in practice.

On one occasion, the word 'corridor' was selected as the target word; this determined the choice of the target picture, Van Gogh's *Hospital Corridor at St. Rémy*. This picture was chosen because it was the first in the collection to have the word 'corridor' in its title, a quite objective selection. A bizarre charade was inflicted on Bessent. Shortly after

SOME OF MALCOLM BESSENT'S PREDICTIONS

The predictions listed below were made in December 1969.

Bessent's prediction	What actually happened
'A Greek oil tanker, black in color, will be involved in a disaster having international significance within 4–6 month's time. (Onassis connected — perhaps the danger is symbolic, but I feel that the ship may represent him personally)'	Two months later the Onassis-owned tanker the *Arrow* was wrecked off the coast of Nova Scotia. The resulting pollution did indeed become an 'international incident'.
'General de Gaulle will die within one year'	Eleven months later de Gaulle died — but he was an old man!
'Prime Minister Wilson in change of government next summer (1970)'	The Heath government took office in the summer of 1970 in Britain and confounded political pundits and opinion polls, which had put Labour well ahead. But Bessent's prediction is not exact. He did not state that Wilson would be defeated, although, to be fair, this is the usual sense of 'change of government'.
'Nixon will not serve another term as President'	Wrong. Nixon was overwhelmingly re-elected in 1972. And yet right, for Nixon did not complete his term of office, being forced out of it over the Watergate scandal.
'Senator Muskie will be the next President'	Wrong!

dreaming, waking up, and reporting his dream, he was hauled off along a dark corridor, given an innocuous pill to take for his 'condition', addressed as 'Mr. Van Gogh', and shown paintings by mental hospital patients. Bessent's dreams *the night before this experience* reflected uncannily what actually happened to him the next morning (see opposite page).

In order to assess whether precognition was occurring, Bessent's dream report for each night was sent to three independent judges together with the target word and seven other randomly selected 'dummy' words (on the 'St. Rémy' night, the other seven words were 'parka hood', 'desk', 'kitchen', 'teaspoon', 'body back', 'leaves', and 'elbow', all culled from *The Content Analysis of Dreams*, which explains their rather strange nature in some instances). The judges, who as usual were not told which word was the correct target, rated 'corridor' as the best fit to the content of Bessent's dream from the eight possible choices.

Actually, the judging procedure here seems to us to be almost designed to *lose* information. One might have expected the most striking results if the judges had been given the correct target picture, together with seven dummy pictures, rather than the correct target word and seven dummy words. Even so, Bessent's results were phenomenal.

During 16 nights, chance would predict two hits (correct target word matched to dream), since the judges had eight alternatives to choose from. Bessent scored 10 direct hits, five times the chance rate of success, with very large anti-chance odds.

PRECOGNITIVE DREAMING: A TEST SESSION WITH MALCOLM BESSENT

Bessent's dream report

'Impressions of green and purple...small areas of blue and white. There was a large concrete building. A lot of concrete, for some reason. But it was architecturally designed and shaped...and there was a patient from upstairs escaping...it might have been a woman...she had a white coat on, like a doctor's coat. Kind of a feeling...of hostility toward me by people in a group I was in daily contact with.... My impression was that they were...doctors and medical people.... The concrete wall was all in natural colour.... It's like a carved wall...I felt that...a patient had escaped...and got as far as...the archway. I was dreaming...about breakfast...the cups were all white...drinking... eating...the cups and things were rattling...'.

Events the next morning
Target word (random choice): Corridor
Target picture (first picture in pool with word 'corridor' in title): *Hospital Corridor at St. Rémy* (1889) by Van Gogh

Bessent's post-waking experience
Rosza's 'Spellbound' played on phonograph. Recorder laughing hysterically.... Bessent welcomed as Mr. Van Gogh.... Paintings by mental patients shown on slide projector. Bessent given a pill and a glass of water. Bessent 'disinfected' with acetone daubed on a cotton swab. Bessent led through a darkened corridor of the lab to reach the office.

The Bessent experiments are also notable because they completely excluded any possibility of what is known as 'sensory leakage'. In ESP experiments it is obviously essential that receivers must not be able to gain any information about targets by normal sensory means. One might wonder whether, with senders taking showers in the laboratory and so on, one could be totally confident about this. In fact, from reading the Ullman-Krippner technical specifications and having visited Maimonides, we are confident that sensory leakage was not a possibility. But the crucial point here is that the Bessent experiments eliminate this *in principle:* no one can have sensory knowledge of a target which doesn't even exist when they report their dreams!

More dream studies
The full body of studies from Maimonides, reviewed in *Dream Telepathy* (see Bibliography) and presented in numerous scientific papers, clearly showed far more successes than chance would predict. In the most dramatic series, such as those with Erwin and Bessent,

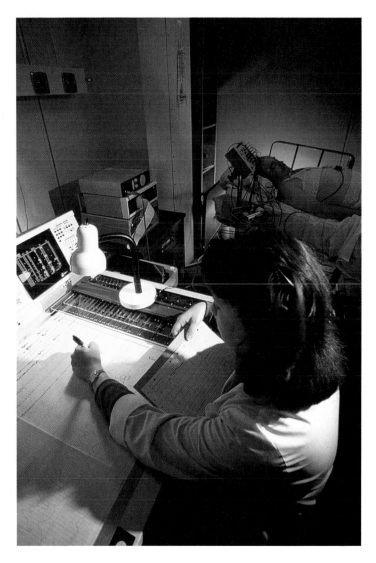

A researcher monitors EEG data from a sleeping volunteer. Although dream ESP research has yielded promising results, the time, expense, and dedication involved have steered 'altered states' ESP research in other directions.

the scoring rates were phenomenal. The major problem has been repeating these experiments elsewhere, and the major problem with that has been lack of money. Equipping a dream laboratory with secure sound-proofing for telepathy experiments, and paying experimenters to work long nights in teams, is a very expensive business. Since the Maimonides research, no one in parapsychology has been in a position to mount a research program anything like it. Our best hope is that a sleep/dream researcher in conventional psychology will develop an interest in dream psi and revitalize this area of research.

Much simpler dream studies have been done, in which dreamers simply record their dreams when they wake in the morning (or sometimes during the night, with alarm clocks waking them up). These lack REM/EEG monitoring, and there is no doubt that much information is lost (people report far more in the way of dreaming when woken from REM sleep than they can recall in the morning). Obviously, with such information loss, any ESP-derived information a dream might contain will be harder to detect.

Nonetheless, several researchers have reported success in ESP dream studies with this much simpler procedure. The psychologist Robert Van de Castle, himself a high-scoring ESP-dreamer at Maimonides, used this method with members of an American summer camp and obtained positive results. A five-experimenter team at Cambridge reported significantly above-chance results from a study in which each of eight dreamers contributed six dreams, being given sealed and tamper-proof packages to take home and put under their pillows. The correspondences between the dreams and the sealed pictures were assessed by two judges (Sargent and Matthews) who were given a duplicate of the correct target and three dummies. The average scorings were significantly better than chance, and each individual judge's scorings were also better than chance — but the judges seemed to be attentive to different elements of the dreams! This is how they ranked the targets:

Judge	Target Picture Rank			
	First	**Second**	**Third**	**Fourth**
Sargent	17	15	10	5
Matthews	20	9	10	9

(Sargent's total is only 47 because of a faint possibility of sensory leakage in one of the 48 trials). This suggests that in free-response experiments we need to study the judges. Matthews spotted direct hits very strongly. Sargent may have been more sensitive to 'partial information' coming through which allowed him to rank the correct picture among the first two choices but did not enable him to see direct hits as well as Matthews did. Despite this, both sets of judgements correlate very highly, so the judging cannot be considered to have been overly subjective.

One of the subjects from this study, Trevor Harley of Warwick University, reported a further significant dream ESP study with himself as a subject in 1989, but here he obtained psi-missing (scoring well below chance). Interestingly, this scoring pattern became stronger and stronger throughout the night, with very powerful psi-missing on dreams recorded later in the night.

At the 1992 convention of the Parapsychological Association, researchers Kanthamani and Broughton from North Carolina reported a dream experiment with 20 subjects in which they obtained strongly above-chance scoring (odds against chance of over 400 to 1). Their experiment is of note not least because two earlier ones by them had not produced such strong results. It may need time, and experience, to learn how to work with dreams and ESP.

Summarizing all the reports which have been published, we estimate that some 45% show scores that diverge significantly from the chance level. That is, they show evidence of possible ESP about nine times more often than chance would predict. The skeptic might say: 'Yes, but that's because there are many unpublished chance results around! If we knew about them, the results would not appear anywhere near so strong.' One could make many replies to that, but three points are worth making. First, negative studies *do* get reported (like the first two North Carolina studies). Second, dream studies are expensive and time-consuming and it is simply not possible to conduct whole batches of them and just publish the ones which appear to be successful. Third, the vast majority of significant results show psi-hitting (the Harley result being an exception); if only chance were at work, we would expect psi-hitting and psi-missing in equal measure.

Dream ESP studies are showing something of a renaissance at the present time, but towards the end of the Maimonides program it became clear that the expensive and time-consuming nature of such research was something of a handicap. It would clearly be advantageous if, somehow, an ESP-conducive state as favorable as that of dream sleep could be developed which would be faster and cheaper to conduct experiments with. Such a procedure was soon to be found.

Ancient and not-so-ancient texts

One researcher involved with the Maimonides team, who subsequently worked at Princeton and Edinburgh, was the late Charles (Chuck) Honorton. Although other researchers used the technique he pioneered in parapsychology, the ganzfeld technique (to be described shortly), Honorton is rightly given credit for primacy with this, having conducted a formidable number of studies with it.

Honorton's approach was informed by his own surveys of historical accounts of psi experiences, ranging from the yoga sutras of Patanjali, written 3,500 years ago in India, to the detailed surveys of J. B. Rhine's wife Louisa and the nineteenth-century publications of the British Society for Psychical Research (SPR). He also examined the memoirs and writings of mediums and psychics. In Patanjali's texts, for example, ESP and PK effects are spoken of as taking place at the deepest levels of meditation, *samadhi. Samadhi*

In most cultures and religions asceticism is seen as a path to higher spirituality. This holy man in Puttaparthi, South India, has lived alone in the same cave for more than 15 years. He spends most of his time meditating.

Charles Honorton, pioneer of the ganzfeld technique of 'quietening' the mind.

is the final stage of a process of disengaging the mind from the distractions of the senses, and concentrating it until it achieves absolute stillness. The work of the SPR showed that a high proportion of psi experiences occur not just when people are dreaming, but when they are daydreaming, lost in reverie, dozing, on the verge of sleep, or in some other highly relaxed state. In the writings of psychics, too, Honorton observed a common refrain: the best conditions for psychic experience are those in which the individual is relaxed and making a firm but gentle effort to empty the mind of extraneous thoughts. Honorton identified two common elements, a 'quietening' of the normal sensory mechanisms and an inward-looking mental orientation, as favorable to reported ESP. But why should this be so?

Honorton offered the model of ESP as being something akin to a 'weak sense'. If this is the nature of ESP, it might well be drowned out by the strong activity of our conventional senses. Consider the vast amounts of information that enter our eyes whenever we open them; if ESP signals are weak, that mass of input is actually noise. Our brain is too busy processing ordinary sensory input to attend to or register ESP signals. However, in altered states of consciousness — dreaming, hypnosis, meditation, and so on — the operation of our normal senses is sharply reduced. This might be the reason why such altered states are favorable to ESP.

Sensory deprivation and ESP

Honorton initially experimented with complete sensory deprivation as a means of screening out all extraneous 'noise'. It is well known that people insulated from their environment for a period of time begin to show signs of disorientation which include changes in body awareness, visual hallucinations, and other signs of a clearly altered state of consciousness. Eliminating normal sensory inputs might well be expected to boost ESP success.

Honorton's study involved 30 individuals. Each one wore a blindfold and ear-mufflers, and was confined to a cradle suspended so that it could be freely moved in any direction.

Complete sensory deprivation is an extreme way of inducing altered mental states. Imagine yourself floating in water which is neither warmer nor cooler than your skin, seeing only darkness, hearing only silence.... The ganzfeld method of reducing sensory input is far gentler.

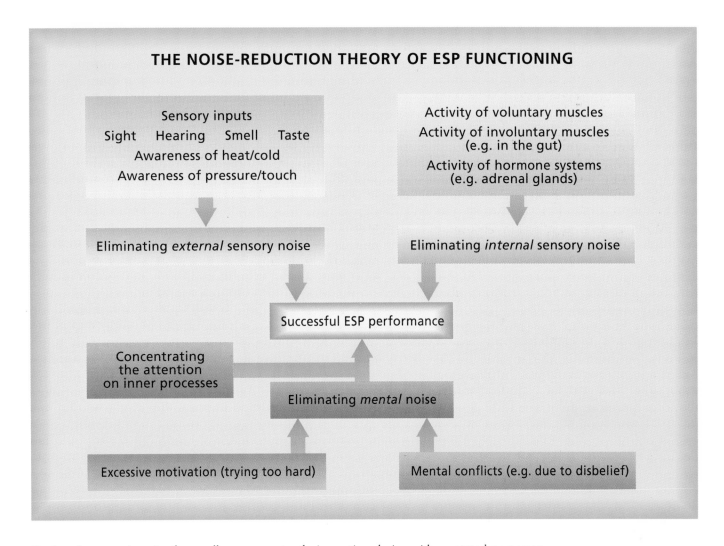

THE NOISE-REDUCTION THEORY OF ESP FUNCTIONING

During the experiments, the cradle was constantly in motion, being either rotated or swung backwards and forwards. Each subject had to report the ideas, thoughts, and mental imagery he experienced. During the session, a distantly-located sender looked at a randomly selected target picture. After the session (which lasted 30 minutes), when the receiver had recovered from his time in the cradle, he was shown four pictures, one of which was the target, and asked to select the picture which most closely matched what he had experienced. This is very similar to dream-study measures of ESP, of course.

Honorton had two specific predictions he wished to test, both made in advance of obtaining results. First, he expected positive, above-chance scoring in the ESP experiment. This prediction was not confirmed; he obtained above-chance scoring, but not to a degree which was outside the limits of chance. His second prediction was that the best ESP scores would come from those subjects who experienced the most radical changes in consciousness during the experiment. This prediction was confirmed, significantly.

Honorton's experiment suggests, then, that ESP *is* associated with disorientated mental states induced by insulating people from their environment. However, the effects of sensory deprivation are really rather extreme for it to be used as a standard experimental method. The experience is by no means a pleasant one for everyone; indeed, the reader may have felt somewhat uncomfortable just reading our description of it. Even the prospect of sensory deprivation is anxiety-arousing for many people, and anxiety appears to inhibit ESP.

In an attempt to produce a milder, less threatening experimental procedure, Honorton adapted a procedure known as 'ganzfeld isolation' (German *Ganzfeld* = 'whole field') from

*In the picture below,
the subject tries
to decide which
of four pictures
most closely matches
her ganzfeld
impressions.*

psychology. This method of creating the noise-reduction/inward-attention mix is subtly different from and much more pleasant than sensory deprivation. Instead of trying to eliminate all sensory inputs, the ganzfeld (GZ) approach maintains those inputs at a constant level. If the same sensory signals are fed into the brain over and over, continuously, the brain eventually stops attending to them. To put it simply, brains are programmed to respond to change; if nothing changes, attention moves elsewhere, to internal mental events. This process is technically known as *habituation*.

Honorton's ganzfeld experiments

In a ganzfeld experiment the receiver is encouraged to relax in a restful, controlled, non-threatening environment. He or she lies on a mattress or in a reclining chair. A constant level of noise, white noise (sound spread equally across all audible frequencies) or rhythmic sea-shore sounds, is relayed to the ears through headphones. The person's eyes are covered with halved ping-pong (table tennis) balls, sealed around the edges with cotton wool, over which a dim light source (usually red or orange) is directed. The material of which the balls are made has just the right degree of translucence to spread the light evenly. The relaxation is designed to eliminate internal noise (from muscular activity, anxiety, etc.). The white noise drowns out the intermittent sounds of the outside world (for experimenters with the resources, a soundproofed room is often used). The diffusion of light through the ping-pong balls creates a warm, hazy glow which soon becomes uniform, without pattern or feature, eliminating the changes our eyes normally register every millisecond of our waking lives. The reason for using ping-pong balls is that they are cheap and simple to use. In at least one experiment using goggles, people's eyes watered and they became very uncomfortable; the cotton wool around the edges of the ping-pong balls (which are not a perfect fit) eliminates that problem.

What happens to people in this strange environment? The experience is pleasant — very relaxing, comfortable, and warm (use of 'cold' blue light has been found to be less pleasant than the warm glow of red-orange). The noise may be experienced as the gentle fall of rain, or the sea, or even distant thunder. As time passes, and the attention of the brain shifts to internal events, the effects of GZ isolation grow stronger.

*The ganzfeld
environment is
comfortable and
unthreatening.
Here and above,
Carl Sargent
is the experimenter.*

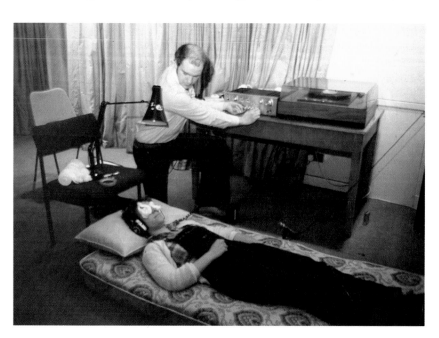

Now for the ESP part of the exercise. At a distant location, a sender views a randomly selected target picture. At the end of the session, the receiver (or in other experiments, independent judges) is given the transcript of what he or she reported during the GZ session (usually 30–35 minutes). This transcript is then compared with a copy of the target picture (ideally the original used by the sender should *not* be used, because subtle sensory clues such as fingerprints might be present on it) and a number of dummy pictures — (usually three). The receiver is then asked to decide which of the four pictures most closely matches what he or she experienced and reported in the transcript. With four pictures to choose from, a chance level of correct first choices would be 25%.

Honorton's first study yielded 13 correct first choices in 30 trials, 43% correct. The odds against chance for this result are not great, only around 60 to 1, but the experiment was small-scale and the 18% increase over chance is a sizeable effect, not comparable with Erwin or Bessent, but still hefty. One drawback with this experiment was that the receivers were not given duplicates of the target pictures used by the sender, so there was a very tiny possibility that they could have used marks on the target pictures, rather than ESP, to make correct choices.

However, the above-chance results of other studies by Honorton, using different types of targets (videotape sequences and duplicate targets) cannot be explained in this manner. Over many experiments spanning nearly 20 years, Honorton and his colleagues ran nearly 1,000 GZ sessions with a direct hit rate of around 35%, compared with the 25% expected by chance. This 10% surplus cannot possibly be ascribed to chance, and since no one claims that it can, we'll forbear to quote the odds.

One of the two best chunks from this heroic exercise uses a special method of measuring ESP effects. In the book *The Content Analysis of Dreams* (published in 1967) the authors give ten different categories for recording dreams according to the presence or absence of certain elements. Honorton borrowed this scoring system for use in his GZ work.

Taking all the possible combinations and permutations of these ten categories, there are 1,024 possibilities in total. Honorton built up a pool of 1,024 target pictures covering every possible combination (from a blank white slide with no categories present to the ten-categories-present combination). Every picture can be coded as a ten-digit binary number, from 0000000000 (blank slide) to 1111111111 (every category present). The receiver is tested in the usual manner, but his or her GZ perceptions are encoded as a ten-digit number. If he or she reports seeing people and colors but nothing else, the binary code for that report would be 1000100000. This can then be compared with the binary code of the target. If chance alone is operating, there should be 50% correct matches, an average of five correct out of ten, for each trial. Honorton consistently reported hit rates of higher than 50% correct in the experiments in which he used this scoring technique.

OBJECTIVELY SCORING A PICTURE-GUESSING ESP EXPERIMENT

Ten content categories

	Present (1)	Absent (0)
01	color	no color, black-and-white
02	activity	no activity, static quality
03	mythical characters	no mythical characters
04	animals	no animals
05	humans	no humans
06	artifacts/implements	no artifacts/implements
07	food	no food
08	body parts	no mention of body parts
09	architecture	no architecture
10	nature	no nature features

The second major chunk of Honorton's research we will reserve for our final chapter. This work involved eight experimenters, hundreds of trials, years of work, and a fully automated test system, and can fairly be described as a breakthrough in parapsychology. We do not use that term lightly. For now, however, let us look at how other experimenters have fared with the ganzfeld.

Repeating ganzfeld results

William Braud of the Mind Science Foundation in Texas (although at this time he was still at the University of Houston) was the first experimenter to report independent confirmation of the Honorton GZ experiments. Braud introduced two innovations. First, he used both a GZ group and a no-GZ group (no ping-pong balls and white noise), to see if it made a real difference to picture-choosing scores. The second innovation was a change in the statistical analysis. Braud considered that previous free-response experiments had shown that, sometimes, people might gain a scrap of information about a target which was not quite enough to identify it unequivocally as a first choice. (As a brief note for the statistically-minded, if in a four-choice task a subject gains one 'bit' of information, this should be enough to allow him to place the correct target first or second, but not enough for him to place it unequivocally first unless that single bit is unique to the target; with rich, complex targets that is rarely the case).

Using a six-picture judging procedure rather than Honorton's four-choice method, Braud scored a 'binary hit' if the receiver placed the target picture first, second, or third (which is 50% likely by chance). In every one of Braud's ten GZ trials the result was a 'binary hit'. The control, no-GZ group, just talking off the top of their heads, scored at the chance level. This suggests a specific improvement of ESP ability through GZ isolation.

Braud himself in other studies, Rex Stanford in New York (especially in one dramatic study with Mary Schmitt), Sargent in Cambridge, and many other experimenters have obtained significant, well above-chance scoring in GZ ESP experiments. In order to take a closer look at why these experiments have been successful, let us go back to the 'noise reduction' model of ESP proposed by Honorton and examine it in more depth. This will give the reader a feel for the excitement of this research.

Implications of the 'noise reduction' theory

Honorton's noise-reduction model predicts that GZ should enhance ESP, but it predicts more than that. Here is the train of thought that leads to those further predictions.

- GZ works because sensory noise is eliminated (theory).
- Sensory noise is eliminated because the brain ceases to attend to unchanging fields of sensation; habituation occurs (observed and documented in conventional non-ESP, psychological research).
- This habituation does not occur immediately. It develops with time. The longer spent in GZ, the more pronounced it gets. Physiological and introspective evidence both show that habituation takes some 15–20 minutes, for most people, to reach a baseline depth (again, results from conventional non-ESP, psychological experiments).
- Therefore the strength of the ESP effect should increase with time as habituation strengthens.

This final deduction generates two specific predictions which can be tested. The first is that very short durations of GZ exposure should *not* enhance ESP. The second prediction is that what receivers perceive later on in a GZ session should match the target better than what they perceive in the earlier parts of the session (when they are not habituated).

Unfortunately, we know of only one experiment which has systematically compared two different durations of GZ (15 versus 30 minutes), randomly allocating receivers to one or other condition. Frustratingly, the scores were at chance level for both conditions, so it

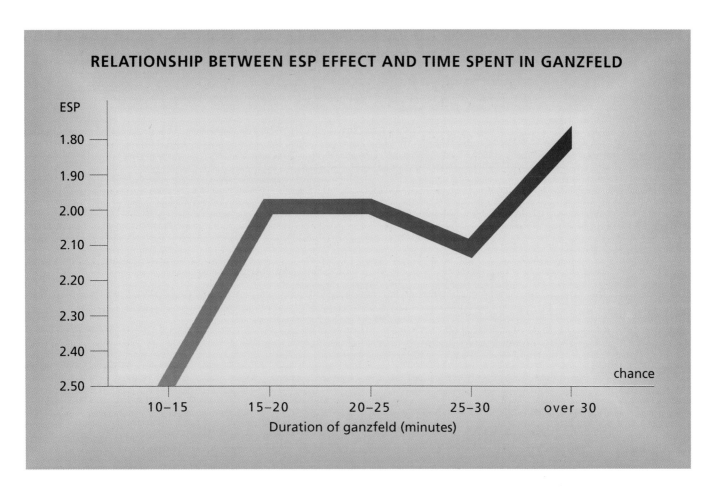

RELATIONSHIP BETWEEN ESP EFFECT AND TIME SPENT IN GANZFELD

is impossible to draw any conclusions from this. More experiments of this type are badly needed. Published experiments which used 15 minutes or less for test sessions (some experimenters used periods as short as seven minutes) tend to confirm that too short a time for GZ exposure produces chance results, but there were many differences between the experimenters concerned, between test procedures, and so on. Really, checking this is a priority for GZ research.

The second prediction, however, receives rather better support. The Cambridge group explored this by using a system of 'atomistic' judging. Each receiver was asked, after the test session, to give a score to each of the four pictures for every single image or impression he received during his time in the ganzfeld. The total scores for each picture were then added up for the first and second half of the session. Then the number of points given to the target picture were compared with the number of points given to the other (dummy) pictures for each half of the 30- or 35-minute test session. Indeed, one could chop up the GZ session into shorter sections of time and look at how the signal for the target is coming through compared with the noise (points awarded to pictures other than the target). The results of this analysis strongly supported the noise-reduction model. With increasing time in the ganzfeld, the better the signal seems to become.

The Cambridge studies also controlled for at least one confounding factor. In the first of three experiments in which this effect was checked, the primary experimenter (Sargent) was excited at having made the first test of what he considered to be an important aspect of theory. He was involved in every session of the experiment. In two later experiments a colleague suggested analyzing separately the results of sessions in which Sargent did, and did not, take part. Perhaps experimenter expectancy was important, or perhaps subjects with Sargent as experimenter were reporting their experiences later in test sessions with

ESP effects increase towards 1.00 (1 out of 4 pictures, i.e. perfect scoring) as time spent in ganzfeld increases.

A DRAMATIC GANZFELD PICTURE-GUESSING EXPERIMENT

Experiment 12, Session 16
10 December, 1979
Target picture: *The Ancient of Days* by William Blake

Receiver report: *'Picture of the night sky with a planet or some unnatural golden oval. Glowing object, fire coming off it. Clumsily-drawn picture of a woman in white nightdress...ragged hair, torch in one hand. The hands and feet are too large.... Close-up picture of Sun, can see the red flames on the surface. Sun looks black...Blake's picture of God with the dividers, creating the world.'*

In one of Carl Sargent's ganzfeld experiments the subject actually named the target picture, Blake's Ancient of Days. *Direct 'hits' in such experiments are not rare.*

more care and attention. In the later experiments, the time-progression effect was hugely statistically significant so long as Sargent was not involved. If he was, it wasn't present. Why this is so, we have no idea. The most important factor here, however, was not the experimenter effect but the confirmed prediction from the working model.

Honorton's very first study tested a further prediction, namely the *state-shift hypothesis*. Put simply, this says that the more altered a state of consciousness a person enters, the more powerful the ESP effect should become. This prediction, too, has received extensive support from experiments, including experiments conducted by researchers (notably John Palmer) who have not been able to obtain results which are significantly above or below chance overall. We will return to this topic in the next chapter — strong as the evidence we've reviewed here is, it is by no means all of the tale.

Powerful results, powerful experiences

The results of both dream and ganzfeld ESP experiments have been powerful. They are powerful because the scoring rates in them are well above chance — not the fraction of 1% obtained in some of the electronic PK studies, but way above chance. Further, the subjects in ganzfeld experiments have almost all been ordinary individuals, not people like Malcolm Bessent with some putative psychic 'gift', but students, housewives, white- and blue-collar workers, just regular folk. Moreover, the repeatability of ganzfeld studies is highly encouraging; 45% of a total of some 70 studies show statistically significant scoring rates (as opposed to the 5% rate chance would predict). What is more, many of the apparent 'failures' to obtain success are not the failures they appear to be. We will return to this point in our final chapter.

The ESP effects that have emerged from dream and ganzfeld work have also been impressive in kind. For readers who have come through the machine-PK experiments and the ESP card-guessing experiments and found little that matches up with their experience, these free-response studies are much more interesting. Statistics are a dry way of capturing the powerful correspondences that appear between targets and receivers' impressions; the judging is often conservative, and we need better techniques to measure the information which seems to emerge in these experiments. The hits are often very dramatic indeed. In future experiments, it is to be hoped that parapsychologists will develop assessment procedures more sensitive to the dramatic, apparently telepathic flow of information which may be occurring here.

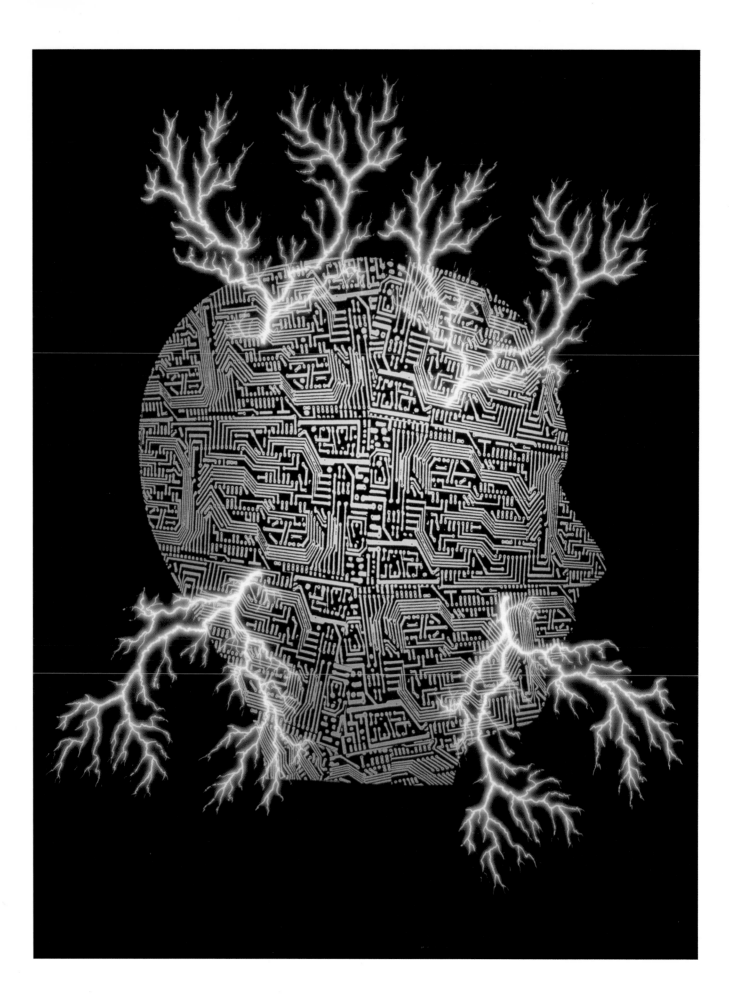

Hypnosis and other altered states

In some scientific quarters, parapsychology is deemed a disreputable business — it evokes images of fraudulent mediums, spiritualism, and other things scientists often find objectionable. Now that hypnosis is regularly involved in the treatment of smoking, obesity, phobias, other disorders, and even in dentistry, it is worth recalling just how disreputable hypnosis was in its initial form, as 'mesmerism'. Franz Anton Mesmer — who graduated in medicine in Vienna in 1764 — believed that the planets affected human beings through an influence similar to magnetism. After some attempts to treat various patients with magnets, he decided that what was most important was a force emanating from the nervous system and relayable through the hands of the physician or mesmerist. He called this force 'animal magnetism'.

The demand for Mesmer's idiosyncratic treatment grew, and in Paris he treated hundreds of people for almost every ailment conceivable. Mesmer, dressed as a magician, prowled around in the background to an accompaniment of soft music while his patients were treated with the *baquet*, a wooden tub full of water and iron filings which supposedly stored the all-curing magnetism originating from Mesmer himself. The medical establishment was not impressed and declared that the cures Mesmer reported, which were often accompanied by convulsive fits from his patients, were due to 'imagination'.

Nonetheless, Mesmer's followers carried on his work, in a more scientific and less vaudevillian manner. In England, John Elliotson and James Braid used hypnosis to anesthetize patients during operations. They would probably have been held in great esteem, but for a miserable historical accident. At almost the same time chloroform came on the scene and rendered hypnotic treatment unnecessary as an anesthetic. The medical establishment drove Elliotson from his teaching post and, on hearing that Braid had successfully amputated limbs using hypnotic anesthesia, informed him that his patients were simply *pretending* not to feel any pain as he sawed off their arms or legs.

In Europe, however, Mesmer's formidable pupil de Puységur — who disliked the convulsions and lurid sensationalism which accompanied Mesmer's treatments — found that the 'somnambulic' (sleep walking) or trance state induced by the mesmerist seemed to be an important therapeutic instrument. In this state, he considered, the magnetic influence could act on the nervous system of the patient. Hence, making sure that patients were in this state became the major consideration. Gradually, what we know today as hypnotic induction — the soft-voiced, repeatedly-given instructions to relax, to sleep, to drift away — evolved.

Opposite: The waking brain is normally too busy — too purposeful in its computations, too aware of the external environment — to tune into ESP signals. Some 'state shift' is necessary to boost ESP effects.

Anton Mesmer was one part doctor and two parts showman, yet mesmerism was the first modern therapy to formally harness the power of the mind.

Mesmer's famous baquet or tub. The original caption to this engraving says: 'He [Mesmer] uses a large tub to which are fixed pieces of cord which the patients tie around their limbs, or iron books which they apply to that part of the body in which they suffer.... The magnetizers (numbering at least 100 gentlemen of the Court to whom Monsieur Mesmer has confided his secret) place their hands upon the ailing parts to rub them, thereby aiding the influence of the cords and books...'.

ESP effects during hypnosis

Although the magnetic theory of hypnosis is no longer believed, one spinoff from it is important to us. Continental hypnotists made many claims about a so-called 'community of sensation' between the hypnotist and his subject. The 'magnetic force' flowing between them seemed to produce paranormal effects, most notably telepathy; the hypnotized person seemed to be able to read the mind of the hypnotist, even carrying out suggestions before the hypnotist had actually spoken any instructions. Mesmer himself gave demonstrations of hypnosis at a distance, in which a hypnotized person would react to his thoughts even though he was some distance away from him and out of the range of ordinary sensory communication (or so Mesmer asserted). Hypnotized people were also reported as being able to sense distant events when so instructed by the hypnotist.

Before examining the evidence for such claims, we have to ask: Why should we expect hypnosis to be conducive to ESP? Can we explain it in terms of noise-reduction and 'inner awareness', factors which seemed to be able to produce good results in dream and ganzfeld ESP studies?

Hypnosis presents one major problem; as yet, it has not been absolutely pinned down by objective recording, although some recent brain scanning experiments have suggested that the brain activity of hypnotized people differs significantly from that of people instructed to act *as if* they were hypnotized. Early results suggest that the hypnotized brain is very like a sleeping brain. However, the notion of a hypnotic trance state still needs much further exploration before we can state with confidence that it is a special, altered state of mental and brain functioning. Some psychologists assert that many of the phenomena associated with hypnotic 'trance' can easily be reproduced by people simply told to act as if hypnotized, although it is difficult to believe that a person acting as if hypnotized would not feel the pain of the surgeon's knife or the dentist's drill.

John Elliotson pioneered hypnotic anesthesia in the 1830s, but was pilloried by the orthodox medical establishment.

Fortunately, there are some features typical of hypnotized persons which are not unique to hypnosis but which tell us something about hypnosis in relation to the noise-reduction theory. Hypnotic induction techniques certainly produce a state of relaxation; the very nature of the words of the hypnotist ('You are now feeling sleepy...') encourages relaxation. Further, a hypnotist's instructions almost always involve suggestions to listen and attend only to the hypnotist, to ignore anything else going on around; this is a focusing of attention on a single external factor (the voice of the hypnotist) and a blocking-out of other factors. At the very least, attention to outside events is narrowed as compared with normal sensory function. So the combination of relaxation and elimination of distraction by external events appears to hold true for hypnosis. Thus we would expect hypnosis to be favorable for ESP.

Surveying the evidence

Charles Honorton produced a survey of all published ESP experiments using ESP card testing, and Rex Stanford further evaluated the same results. Included in these surveys are 24 comparisons of ESP card-guessing ability (or performance in very similar forced-choice tests) with hypnotized and unhypnotized subjects. This is the kind of comparison we lacked in the dream and ganzfeld experiments (save for the work of William Braud), a direct comparison of scoring with, and without, the ESP-enhancing procedure.

Of these 24 studies, 14 found significant evidence of extra-chance ESP scoring in the hypnosis condition. That is nearly twelve times more often than chance would predict. In the waking state (no hypnosis), however, only one of these studies yielded such a result (the odd exception is just what chance would predict). Again, of the 24 studies, 12 showed a significantly better scoring rate with hypnosis than without it. Remember that our definition of 'significantly better' is a difference so large that chance says we should observe it only once in every 20 similar experiments (5% of the time). The observed figure of 50% is way higher than 5%, and *none* of the studies showed a significant superiority of scoring *without* hypnosis. The results of this body of research, collected by many experimenters, are clear-cut: hypnosis is an ESP-favorable state.

There is also some evidence that, with the aid of hypnosis, people can discriminate between guesses on which they are right and those on which they are wrong. This is known as *confidence calling*; before scores are known, subjects state whether there are particular guesses which they are confident are correct. Results from a few hypnosis studies which have examined this suggest that hypnotized people may be better at making such judgements than non-hypnotized people. The importance of this is that if ESP can be trained or developed, hypnotic discrimination might be an important part of training. However, there is not enough evidence available for us to be confident about this. The evidence that does exist looks hopeful, but we need further confirmation.

Honorton also rounded up ten experiments which used a 'hypnotic dream' procedure and picture-guessing ESP tests. The ESP test was quite similar to that used in ganzfeld studies, but hypnotized receivers were told to take a nap and have a short daydream in which they would be able to detect something about the pictures being viewed by the sender. Of these ten experiments, seven gave significant evidence of ESP. In his own experiments of this type, Honorton also showed that people who scored highest on measures of 'suggestibility', and who reported being most strongly affected during the hypnotic state, produced the most exceptional scores in ESP tests. Moreover, the very best scores came from those who reported that their attention was directed inwards, rather than externally. This, of course, is exactly what one would predict from the noise-reduction theory (if the results had turned out the other way round, the theory would have been in trouble). Thus, the results of card-guessing and picture-guessing experiments under hypnosis are quite consistent with each other.

Soviet hypnosis/ESP experiments

Finally, on this topic, we come to the work of the Russian scientist L.L. Vasiliev. Although Russian parapsychology is still, even after the momentous events of the last few years, more or less a closed book to Western scientists, we do know that Soviet researchers have always had an active interest in both hypnosis and ESP. As early as 1926 the Experimental Commission on Hypnotism and Psychophysics was formed to examine the problems of hypnosis and psi with the approval of the Soviet authorities (without it, it would never have been appointed). In 1928 Vasiliev visited parapsychology centers in France and Germany, and in 1932 the Soviet Institute for Brain Research received an assignment to commence 'an experimental study of telepathy' — and Vasiliev headed the effort.

Vasiliev's most interesting studies, for which he claimed highly successful results, involved attempts to hypnotize subjects at a distance. In these experiments, people who had been established as highly susceptible to hypnosis were put into a hypnotic trance, or in some cases awakened from the trance state, by instructions from a hypnotist at distances of up to 1,060 miles. The times at which hypnotic suggestions were made were randomly chosen. Sometimes, a control experiment — using unhypnotized subjects — was employed. Regrettably, however, there were some important flaws in these experiments.

For example, although the times between the hypnotic suggestions and their apparent effects on subjects were said to be have been measured with stopwatches, some 40% of the times actually given are reported only to the nearest minute (rather poor accuracy). Also, in those experiments in which hypnotic induction of sleep was attempted, all the subjects — hypnotized or not — eventually fell asleep anyway. Vasiliev's results showed that some subjects simply fell asleep more quickly than others. For such a result to be offered as evidence of psi, we would need more accurate recordings than are reported. Also, Vasiliev's subjects should have been put into either the hypnosis or the no-hypnosis category randomly, or tested an equal number of times in both. This is essential for the following reason: what if all those people who tended to nod off easily anyway were put into the hypnosis group, while those who naturally stayed awake for longer were put in the no-hypnosis group? If that happened, the hypnotized people would show a faster onset of sleep, but that would have nothing to do with the effects of hypnotic suggestion at a distance.

We simply cannot know whether this artifact plagued Vasiliev's work, but it is clear that his experiments were not sufficiently well described or conducted for us to accept their results. Unfortunately, there have been no attempts to repeat Vasiliev's work. Since his death in 1966 none of his pupils seem to have mounted any major research efforts to confirm his results.

Russian parapsychology continues to have the support of the government and other agencies, as the accounts of a few Russian defectors and émigrés to the West confirm. It has proved extremely difficult, however, to get well-authenticated and well-documented accounts of that research. Vital pieces of information about how experiments have been conducted and evaluated are not present in the papers which have been offered. This is hardly unique to parapsychology in Russia. The same deficits affect publications in many other sciences too.

On a lighter note, the 1978 World Chess Championships in the Philippines threw interesting light on Russian interest in the paranormal. Champion (by default, since Bobby Fischer would not defend his title in 1975) Anatoly Karpov of the then USSR and Russian exile Victor Korchnoi were competing for the title. During the contest Korchnoi claimed that a member of Karpov's retinue seated in the auditorium, the mysterious Dr. Zoukhar, was hypnotizing him at a distance.

Sargent and British International Master chess-player Bill Hartston talked with Korchnoi and Michael Stean (his second in the match) about this, and Hartston also discussed the matter with Boris Spassky, another Russian exile defeated by Fischer in 1972 and by Korchnoi en route to the 1978 finals. From these discussions it appeared that Russian chess masters are instructed in ESP and hypnosis as a matter of routine. Whether this is, in reality, only a part of psychologically hyping-up and motivating chess-players, we have no idea. We do not think it likely that Russian Grand Masters will make themselves available for psi experiments!

Back to firm data, then. The results from experiments using hypnosis show a clear effect on scoring in ESP tests. Honorton's judgement, after reviewing every published paper on the topic, was: 'I believe the conclusion is now *inescapable* that hypnotic induction procedures enhance (ESP).' At the very least, one must concede that this body of experiments adds further to the accumulating mass of consistent evidence relating to ESP and altered states of mental functioning.

The great Karpov-Korchnoi psych-out? Victor Korchnoi felt sure that the Soviet camp had brought in telepathy experts to affect his concentration during his match with Anatoly Karpov. Paranoid fantasy or scientific possibility?

Relaxation — the key to ESP?

Relaxation of the body is a key element in the noise-reduction story. A relaxed body has little activity in its voluntary muscles, and this low level of activity can be easily, and reliably, measured using the EMG (electromyograph). In view of the central importance of relaxation, and the relative ease of measuring it, it is perhaps surprising that systematic research on relaxation and psi is only a relatively recent development in parapsychology. In the case of dream ESP research, parapsychology had to await Kleitman's discovery of REM sleep and dreaming activity, but the Maimonides studies were conducted not long after Kleitman's breakthrough findings. However, Jacobson's classic work *Progressive Relaxation* had been in print for nearly 35 years before William and Lendell Braud put it to use in parapsychology. Would the measurable physiological effects of relaxation be matched by any variation — improvement or otherwise — of performance in ESP tests?

In 1969 the Brauds began experiments using a modified version of the Jacobson deep-relaxation technique. Their first subject, a 26-year-old university teacher, was instructed to relax his body by alternately tensing and relaxing his muscles, and then encouraged to relax his mind (as it were) by first concentrating on pleasant imagery (peaceful countryside scenes) and then, so far as possible, to let his mind become blank and passive. Meanwhile, in another room more than 20 yards away, a sender randomly selected a target picture from a pool of 150 postcard-sized images. The sender attempted to transmit elements — shapes, colors, even tastes and smells — present in or conveyed by the picture. Work proceeded at the rate of one session and one target per day. At the end of each session the teacher was asked to write down impressions received during the relaxed state. After six sessions the six written reports and the six targets were given to an independent blind judge who was asked to match each report to the picture it fitted best. The judge matched the reports and the targets *perfectly*. The most conservative statistical interpretation tells us that the odds against this happening by chance exceed 700 to 1.

Clearly, however, results from a single individual cannot tell us about how ESP may function in people generally. So the Brauds progressed to testing 22 people, singly and in groups, in a series of seven short preliminary experiments. The test method remained the same, except that this time a binary hit evaluation (the same evaluation the Brauds used as an innovation in their ganzfeld experiments) was employed, to give a chance success rate of 50% hits. They actually observed 86% hits, and also obtained some very clear-cut correspondences between targets and the reports of their relaxed receivers. In one test session, for example, a receiver saw a glass of Coca-Cola and commented on how clear the image was. The target picture was a Coca-Cola advertisement.

The Brauds also conducted some of their telepathy studies with senders and receivers separated by distances of up to 1,400 miles, and still obtained successful results. All in all, using the most conservative statistical analysis of their results from an initial two-year period of research, the Brauds computed anti-chance odds exceeding 1,000 to 1 for their results.

In later experiments the Brauds contrasted ESP test results from deeply relaxed subjects with those from people who had undergone muscle-*tensing* exercises. The difference between relaxation and tension was measured with an EMG (to confirm that the exercises had had the desired effects on muscle tone), and the results showed that relaxed subjects scored significantly higher than tense subjects. The Brauds' results have been replicated by Rex Stanford (then at the University of Virginia) and other investigators. Later research, while confirming the Brauds' pioneer work, has not generally been able to produce such dramatic results, however. Why is this?

One reason may certainly be that other researchers have not measured relaxation as thoroughly as the Brauds. Another may be that there is no general standard for the degree of relaxation achieved by subjects given relaxation instructions. Some researchers are probably better at inducing relaxation in people than others. Without precise, and

PROGRESSIVE RELAXATION

Excerpt from a tape prepared by W. and L. Braud based on the Jacobson deep relaxation technique

'Begin by tensing the muscles in your legs, hold that tension as the count goes from 10 to 1 to zero. Feel how uncomfortable that tension is. Tense the muscles now...10, 9, 8...3, 2, 1. Relax now. Relax those muscles completely, exhale, feel the relief of relaxing. Relax all your muscles and feel how good it is. Now, tense your stomach muscles fully, really tense, hard, tight...10, 9, 8... 3, 2, 1, 0. Relax, relax those muscles, feel the relief of that, let your body sink into a state of deep relaxation now, relax....

Now we begin mental relaxation. Hold your head quite straight and lift your eyes upwards to strain them...don't blink...your eyelids become heavy, tired, heavy and tired... take a deep breath in, exhale slowly, feel how your eyes become more tired as each second passes, really tired and heavy...now close your eyes. Again feel the relief of relaxing, relax your eye muscles, relax. Relax all the tension, release all the pressures. It feels good to be so relaxed. Noises and sounds around will not distract you now, but just help you become more relaxed

Now relax your mind, no mental efforts.... Visualize something natural and pleasant, a favorite landscape or scene you love, see it in your mind's eye, without any effort, the image just comes to mind. See yourself relaxing in this place, relax. With each breath imagine yourself becoming more completely relaxed....

Now relax completely, completely, relax completely, relax. Rid your mind of any mundane worries and tensions. They don't matter now. Just relax. Think of a circle of blankness keeping out any stray thoughts. Now your mind is clear, stilled...'.

comparable, measures of relaxation from a number of other researchers, we cannot make a direct comparison of different experiments and experimenters.

A second point is important too. The Brauds' research has generally been accepted by other parapsychologists. Because the results of relaxation appear to be so strong, most researchers — no matter what experiments they conduct — now incorporate elements of relaxation procedures into their strategy for preparing people for ESP tests. Formal relaxation/no-relaxation comparisons run into the problem that in 'no-relaxation' groups people may not actually have the progressive relaxation procedure administered to them but will almost certainly be greeted with a test environment which has elements of relaxation in it anyway. This makes formal (EMG) measures of relaxation of key importance. Lacking these, further progress on the relaxation front is somewhat stymied.

However, the results of the Braud experiments, and the replications we have, add credibility to the 'noise-reduction' story, and there is still more evidence to consider.

Meditation and ESP

Historically, the practitioners of various techniques of meditation have made considerable claims for enhanced powers of the mind during meditation. From earliest times, for example, Indian yogis have claimed that they can control bodily processes, such as breathing and heartbeat, by acts of will alone. Claims about psi have also been made, although psi events are generally regarded as side-issues or distractions, certainly not as the goal of the meditator. It has been the style of mystics and prophets of many cultures to announce their 'truths' only (or mostly) in altered states of consciousness. These revelatory states are conventionally attained through the practice of some repetitive ritual act — the exercises, physical and spiritual, of yogis and mystics (chanting, dancing, fasting, breath control, and so on). Do the altered states of consciousness induced by such practices favor psi?

An Indian fakir lies on a bed of nails. If the nerve endings in his skin trigger pain signals, his mind does not admit them to consciousness. His skin does not bruise, break, or bleed.

To begin with, let us step briefly outside parapsychology and consider what has been reported with at least some meditators so far as control of bodily processes is concerned. This is necessary, not least because some readers may have seen the infamous pictures of Transcendental Meditation (TM) *siddhi* program students allegedly levitating cross-legged and been thoroughly amused by them! Despite such florid claims, there is a serious body of research which suggests that at least some meditators can achieve remarkable control over their bodies.

One researcher studying Indian yogi Swami Rama reported that the yogi was able to stop his heartbeat for so long that a member of the medical team examining him almost had a coronary from worry! TM practitioners also claim to be able to generate coherence in brain-wave (EEG) spectra during meditation, coupled with low heart and respiration rate. Voluntary control of such factors has now been well documented, and can be learned through biofeedback techniques. It has even been reported that, with such techniques, humans are capable of controlling the firing rate of a single cell in the spinal column (reported as long ago as 1969 in the premier journal *Science*).

ESP experiments in which meditation and non-meditation conditions have been compared have not yielded consistent results. Also, while meditators often produce what appear to be strong ESP results, the nature of these is not predictable and the meditator's control over them is poor. Here are a few examples, to show what we mean by this.

John Palmer reported a ganzfeld ESP experiment with 20 TM practitioners as receivers, and found that the scoring rate was well above chance as assessed by two pairs of independent judges rating the comparisons of pictures and impressions. The TM practitioners, however, rated the correspondences well below chance. What could be seen by four outsiders as better-than-chance scoring was not seen as positive ESP by the meditators. This is decidedly odd.

In a PK experiment with a TM instructor, Charles Honorton reported that, whether the man tried to aim high (above chance) or low (below chance) in the test, he scored high all the time. After meditating, his scores diverged, and he scored below or above chance as he wished. Just to confuse the issue, when his EEG showed him to be in a deep state of meditation he scored very nearly significantly below chance. There may well be evidence for PK in this pattern of results, but the lack of consistency and control are again surprising.

K. Ramakrishna Rao, working in India, found high scoring in an ESP test *after* meditation — but almost equally strong psi-missing in an ESP test given *before* meditation! Meditation did not appear to enhance the strength of ESP, only to change the direction of the scores from above to below chance.

The results of these and other studies with meditators and meditation have not produced findings which we consider to be consistent. This is infuriating, because meditation has produced enough evidence of psi effects for it to be considered an avenue worth exploring further.

Can ESP be learned?

The fact that altered states appear to enable ESP signals to be distinguished from incidental noise prompts the question: Can people learn to recognize and detect such signals and therefore become better at using ESP? There are some hints, from work on confidence calls and in other directions, that this might be so.

Some research conducted with forced-choice ESP tests, in normal states of consciousness, has suggested that the possibility for learning may exist. Charles Tart, of the University of California at LA, created something of a furore with the publication of a book in 1976 describing his attempts to train ESP with machines which provided feedback (immediate information about whether a guess was correct or not). According to learning theory in psychology, feedback facilitates learning. If ESP is akin to a form of skill, which is a rather questionable assumption, it should be trainable using feedback techniques. Tart's conclusion from his research, which used careful screening of individuals who appeared to have some definite ability to succeed in ESP tests initially (as he pointed out, one cannot train an ability which isn't there to begin with), was that ESP is trainable.

Tart's work, it must be said, stands in contrast to most of what parapsychology has learned over the decades. Far from showing learning, many 'star' subjects seem to lose some of their ability over a period of time. Tart suggests, quite reasonably, that factors such as boredom and extraneous interference (remember how Stepanek's ESP appeared to displace from card to envelope to cover) might have a lot to do with this, rather than any intrinsic decline in abilities.

Tart's experiment has been fiercely criticized on technical grounds. Reviewing all the pros and cons of many years of lively debate about it would simply take up too much space, but we have some sympathy with Tart's view that if his critics had spent one-tenth of their critical energies on trying to repeat his experiments, much more would have been learned by now.

Surprisingly enough, very few experiments with altered states of consciousness have

Above: Buddhist monks chanting. In such communities meditation is a daily discipline from boyhood. Since the goal of Buddhism is union with the One, demonstrations of ESP would be seen as unimportant.

Right: In this painting from a Buddhist shrine in Bhutan fiery demons fail to distract a hermit from his meditations. Ancient texts emphasize that any ESP or PK effects during meditation are distractions.

actually looked for learning effects. On reflection, this is perhaps not surprising. Altered-state, free-response experiments are time-consuming (a single ganzfeld session can take over two hours, while a dream session obviously requires an entire night). To check for learning, one also needs a reasonable number of subjects (at least a dozen or so) and a reasonable number of sessions for each subject (again, at least a dozen). Even with such small numbers, the sheer time and expense of conducting a learning experiment would be very considerable. Parapsychologists simply do not have the money to be able to conduct such ambitious projects.

The few altered-state studies which have explored this area, the best of which have been conducted by Professor Robert Morris and Dr. Deborah Delanoy at the University of Edinburgh, have not produced clear-cut learning effects. We have to draw the conclusion that this is a case unproved either way. All too often, scientists say 'more research is needed' (which usually means 'give me another research grant'), but it is surely true here.

Alternative views on altered states

The study of altered states of consciousness has provided parapsychologists with important insights into the operation of psi effects. However, the best of the evidence, Honorton's masterly *auto-ganzfeld* experiments, will not be presented until the final chapter of this book, so there is more to come. Strong psi effects, not just 1% or less above the chance odds, can be elicited and have been regularly reported. The experimental techniques developed are increasingly refined, although they are still time-consuming.

From an esthetic point of view, dream and ganzfeld conditions simulate the real-life conditions in which spontaneous psi seems to occur — in moments of relaxation, reverie, detachment from the world. Clearly, altered-state experiments appeal to something in us which says that ESP experiments should be *relevant* in ways that card-guessing experiments are not. Historically, card-guessing studies have been important and done yeoman service, but it is clear that the techniques which have replaced them yield stronger effects.

The claim that parapsychology is a science with many purported facts and no theories wilts under the evidence of relaxation and ganzfeld studies. A clear theoretical working model underlies these techniques, and that model can generate testable predictions for new kinds of experiments. Put most simply, the greatest strength of the noise-reduction model is that *it works*.

This is not to say that there isn't a great deal still to be learned. The concept of 'noise' is still all-embracing and needs further refinement. Some of that refinement has already been undertaken by Rex Stanford, as we shall see in Chapter 8.

John Palmer, who has worked extensively with ganzfeld studies, has proposed a more complex model of the relationship between ESP and 'noise' than Honorton. He accepts that altered states of consciousness (ASCs), whether induced by ganzfeld, hypnosis, or other means, tend to produce ESP scores which are far away from chance. What the ASC does is to increase the *magnitude* of the ESP effect, boosting the strength of the signal. What determines the *direction* of the effect (above or below chance) is different. This distinction is not explicitly present in Honorton's working model, which seems clearly to suggest that the ASC tends to produce a high *positive* (above-chance) score (unless the person in the ASC is deliberately trying to score below chance, presumably).

Palmer's model has two weaknesses. The outstanding one is that virtually all the significant ESP results obtained in ASC experiments have been above chance, as Honorton's model predicts. This does not conflict with Palmer's model, but Palmer's model would not have predicted this whereas Honorton's model does. The second problem is that Palmer's model does not state exactly what the factors influencing the direction of scoring are. Personality may be one of them, since extraverts consistently score higher than introverts in altered-state tests of ESP. Palmer's model suggests that social factors, the atmosphere in which an experiment is conducted, are decisive here, but this needs some more precise detailing. Honorton's model does not make specific predictions about such factors. If these factors are of major importance, we need better ways to measure them — but this is as much a problem for orthodox psychology as it is for parapsychology.

Nonetheless, there is one way in which the models can be compared and contrasted which does appear to support Palmer's model. Honorton's model suggests clearly that there should be a positive relationship between ESP scoring in, say, a ganzfeld experiment, and a person's report of how successful the ganzfeld was at inducing an ASC in him. People who experience a radical shift in their normal state of consciousness should score best in ESP tests. The relationship between ESP scores and what we can term 'state shift' should be positive. For Palmer, this is not so. Palmer's model predicts that it will be so if, and only if, the overall ESP score in the experiment as a whole is positive. If, overall, the ESP score is negative (the experiment shows psi-missing), then the relationship of ESP success and state shift should also be negative. Why should this be?

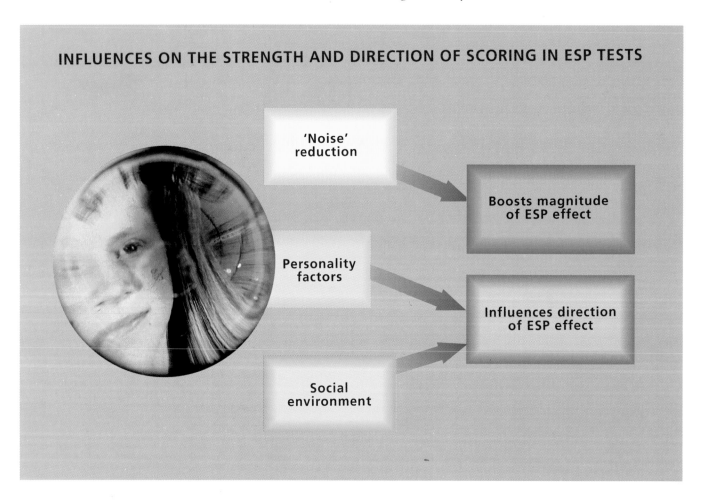

INFLUENCES ON THE STRENGTH AND DIRECTION OF SCORING IN ESP TESTS

'Noise' reduction

Personality factors

Social environment

Boosts magnitude of ESP effect

Influences direction of ESP effect

Palmer argues that this is to be expected because the people who are most strongly affected by an ASC will be the most sensitive to the social atmosphere around them, which will reflect itself in strongly above-chance scoring if the atmosphere is right and strongly below-chance scoring if the atmosphere is uncomfortable, formal, unpleasant, or tense.

Thus, for Honorton, individuals who are strongly affected by an ASC should score *very high* (above chance), but for Palmer they should score *very strongly* (above or below chance, the direction being determined by other factors).

All the studies we have collated show uniform support for Palmer's model. When the overall score is above chance, scores correlate positively with state shift. When the overall score is below chance (which is rare), scores correlate negatively with state shift. In both cases, individuals most strongly affected by state shift score furthest away from chance and show the strongest evidence of ESP.

This suggests to us that the strength and direction of ESP effects are influenced by altered states of consciousness, personality (and other variables within individuals, such as belief), and also by the environment of the experiment. The last-mentioned factor is one which needs a lot more investigation before we can say what is truly important about it. Mercifully, the generally high level of scoring in ASC experiments and the near-perfect uniformity of above-chance scores in them suggest that the social atmosphere of experiments may not be an absolutely key factor. Important, yes. Of major importance, probably not. Unless parapsychologists really are hopelessly inept at making people feel comfortable in their experiments, they should be able to obtain reasonably consistent results.

While the overall picture has its complexities (why should we expect stark simplicity?), the broad outlines have been sketched in. The three-factor model (noise-reduction/ personality/social environment) is an intuitively appealing one, and is both logical and commonsensical. That does not mean to say that reported ESP effects are not, on occasion, very clear and direct. People *are* capable of 'seeing' Blake's *Ancient of Days*, Coca-Cola advertisements, and other complex images almost as if they had been placed before their eyes.

Obviously, there is more to say about ESP and the formidable body of research we have been through in the last three chapters. For now, however, we wish to move on, and examine the corresponding active component of psi: PK, or psychokinesis. If telepathy experiments have produced startling results on occasion, the most recent 'bio-PK' research is of fundamental importance to our view of ourselves and of the physical world.

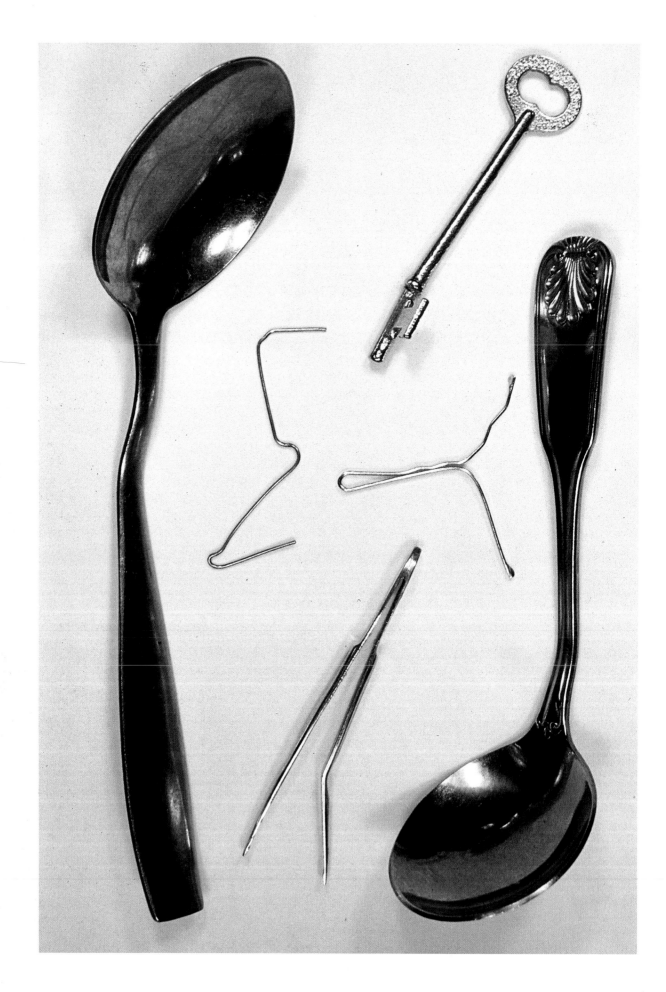

Mind and matter

I n the last three chapters we have dealt mainly with research into paranormal perception — telepathy, clairvoyance, and precognition. The weight of this evidence is such as to persuade many people that ESP is either a proven fact (a false inference, since science does not deal with proof) or a likely possibility. However, when it comes to PK (psychokinesis, literally 'movement by the mind'), opinion surveys show that most people do not consider it likely that the human mind alone can directly cause or influence events in the external world.

We have already quoted some powerful evidence for the reality of PK effects: the career of D.D. Home, and the machine-PK experiments of Helmut Schmidt and those who have conducted similar research, such as Robert Jahn and the Princeton team. We need now to examine in more detail other research that has been conducted into PK effects. We have chosen several distinctively different areas of evidence for examination.

The first of these is the poltergeist, the noisy spirit, and the second is the highly controversial area of metal-bending. Third, we look at 'PK games', computer-based work which develops the Schmidt-Jahn research. Finally, we examine 'bio-PK' research, which seeks to examine whether human will can influence organic systems (blood, skin, heart rate, etc.) directly. We will give much consideration to the latter, because it is clearly of practical importance. The 'bio-PK' research occupies a fair-sized chunk of what will be a lengthy chapter. We hope it will be a feast of information for the reader!

Opposite: The effects of PK on metal objects are not always as obvious as this. Anomalous changes also occur in the atomic structure of the metal.

Stones fly through the air in a Paris street during the building of a road between Sorbonne and Panthéon in 1846. Police and soldiers were set to guard the target of the bombardment, a coalminer's house, but the missiles continued for several weeks.

The noisy spirit

Although *Poltergeist* is German for 'noisy spirit', Germans themselves now prefer the word *Spuk*. Whatever we call them, poltergeists are associated with a range of seemingly inexplicable physical occurrences over a period of time. These occurrences take the form of strange noises, movement of objects, and so on. Sometimes, although not always, the manifestations can be fairly violent in nature. Parapsychologists have often used the charmless acronym RSPK (Recurrent Spontaneous PK) to denote a poltergeist. While we will not be using the term here, one of its virtues is that it acknowledges that poltergeist effects are, indeed, recurrent. In the large majority of cases they last for at least a few weeks; a few continue for months or even years. This makes it possible for researchers to study them, if they arrive on the scene early enough. This has a distinct advantage over the study of spontaneous ESP, where all a researcher can usually do is to collect evidence and testimony after the event.

Poltergeists are very old indeed. Reports of cases can be found in sixth-century Italian manuscripts. Later investigators were often at pains to document cases as fully as possible, so we have reports which cannot be dismissed out of hand. In one sixteenth-century tome of demonology, the author notes of poltergeists: 'I shall pass over examples, since the thing is exceedingly well-known...'. Thus, when we come to look at attempts to track the poltergeist with the

sophisticated apparatus available to us today, we have to bear in mind that the noisy spirit has been with us a long time.

Two modern poltergeists

Ask any knowledgeable parapsychologist which single poltergeist case he would offer a rational critic as perhaps the strongest and best-researched in the field, and he will probably refer you to the Rosenheim poltergeist. During 1967 and 1968, in the small (then West) German town of Rosenheim, exceedingly strange things began to happen in the office of a reputable and prominent lawyer.

Among the early manifestations were persistent and mysterious telephone calls, and the random detonation of mains fuses. The lawyer grew extremely angry about these events, suspecting sabotage or perhaps some disturbance in the power supply to the building. The local post office and power station maintenance staff were called in to research the problem. They brought in monitoring equipment to check what was going on. They brought in automatic counters, and finally in desperation an emergency power generator. The baffled engineers found that the monitoring equipment registered large and inexplicable power transients, disturbances in the power supply, and the post office equipment registered impossibly high frequencies for the number of outgoing calls to the local Speaking Clock service.

Matters were now completely out of control and specialist help was called in. Professor Hans Bender, a parapsychologist from the University of Freiburg, started a full investigation with the assistance of two physicists from the Max Planck Institute for Plasmaphysics in Munich. The physicists brought in their own monitoring equipment, and Bender himself installed cameras and recorders.

The first thing Bender found was that the strange events only seemed to occur when one particular person was in the building, a 19-year-old girl called Annemarie Sch. (her full name was not divulged, to protect her from unwanted publicity). When she walked along a corridor, lamps hanging from the ceiling would begin to swing with increasing force, a phenomenon which would persist for some time after she had gone. Bender was lucky enough to capture this on film, and checked scrupulously for any trickery, hidden wires or the like, which might have produced the effect.

Meanwhile the two physicists had been puzzling over the results from their equipment, which was monitoring the electrical effects in the building. They found the same strange electrical surges as the power station workers and post office engineers had done. Systematically, they eliminated possible causes such as fluctuations in the mains power supply, or interference from apparatus such as the X-ray equipment owned and used by a dentist who occupied part of the same building as the lawyer's offices. Their conclusions were, in essence, quite simple: something extremely strange was going on. They had checked exhaustively for normal mechanisms underlying the anomalies their equipment had detected and recorded, and they could not find any.

When Bender realized that Annemarie was the apparent poltergeist *focus* (the person around whom the effects seemed to center), he watched her very closely. By the end of the case (when Annemarie left to take another job), Bender calculated that some 40 witnesses — all thoroughly interrogated — testified to seeing a variety of inexplicable events. These included the swinging lamps Bender had filmed, swinging wall pictures (which Bender also captured on film), and many others. The witnesses were certainly interrogated, for the lawyer at one stage brought legal charges against 'a person or persons unknown' for maliciously causing the effects!

To refute the findings reported in detail for this case we have to assume that many people (including technicians, physicists, engineers, psychologists, initially skeptical journalists, many people specifically trained as observers) were deluded simpletons. In point of fact, critics of the Rosenheim case do not suggest that the effects could have occurred normally. There is too much recorded evidence on film and recorded by measuring instruments to suggest that witnesses were simply mistaken or hallucinating, and the effects clearly could not be accounted for by known physical mechanisms. The only alternative possibility to PK was that of fraud. In this respect it is worth noting that the culprit(s) was (were) facing public exposure, humiliation, and remorseless legal persecution at the hands of an irate lawyer, and if found guilty would have been sent to prison. Certainly, the lawyer was not popular with his staff, but there would have been much easier, less traceable, and equally effective ways of harassing and victimizing him.

Many people, including journalists and police, actively hunted for signs of fraud for weeks. They did not find any evidence of it. One Dutch journalist claimed that Annemarie was observed in some fraudulent activity by a policeman, but this claim was made without cited evidence or any detail as to what she was observed doing Since the journalist in question died some years ago and the alleged policeman has not publicized his claims (if he ever made them), we can hardly regard this third-hand allegation as being of importance. It is also the case that many of the effects recorded on instruments and film would have needed equipment and/or accomplices to fake, and no supported claims were ever made about either.

Papers fly through the air in the offices of Air Heating in Leeds, Yorkshire. The disturbances, which allegedly centered around a 16-year-old typist, occured in 1970 and lasted for six months.

When Annemarie left the office, the poltergeist effects followed her to her new place of work for a time (showing that the effect is person-centered rather than place-centered), and then died away.

Evidence as strong as that found in the Rosenheim case is rather rare. This should not come as a surprise. Bender's intensive research effort involved a great deal of time and money. In general, as we have already noted, research funding for parapsychology is minimal, and most researchers lack the sophisticated equipment needed to investigate poltergeist manifestations in the proper way. The cost of installing synchronized video cameras in a variety of locations in a building in which a poltergeist is thought to be active would be extremely high, and the costs of continuous recording (and checking through the tapes) would be prohibitive if the case went on for weeks. The main reason why there are not more Rosenheims is that there are too few researchers with the necessary resources, not that the evidence for poltergeists is weak.

Still, there are other cases that are worth studying because of the detail of the reports and the acuteness of the observation. In 1967, for example, Gaither Pratt (the reader will remember him in connection with Pavel Stepanek) and William Roll, then Director of Research at the Psychical Research Foundation of North Carolina, were able to observe poltergeist effects associated with a 19-year-old boy, Julio.

Julio worked as a shipping clerk in Miami, a job which involved, among other things, working in a warehouse. When he was in the warehouse, objects would fly off shelves, and Roll noted that there were certain objects which seemed to do this much more frequently than others. He experimented by putting certain objects which moved frequently in places from where levitations appeared to occur frequently, and keeping them under constant observation. Roll and Pratt were able to log ten incidents in which target objects, as they termed them, moved when they had the area in their scrutiny both immediately before and immediately after the event. In seven of the ten instances, one or other of the researchers was observing Julio. However, neither researcher actually saw an object in motion. While the keenness of perception of these observers is not in question, this frustrating inability to catch phenomena *in flagrante delicto* is all too common. Bender's filmed swinging lamps are very much the exception.

JULIO AND THE POLTERGEIST

Roll's observation of an incident in the Miami warehouse where Julio worked:

'At 11:27 a.m., a Zombie glass from the target area b on Tier 2 broke in the middle of Aisle 2. This glass had...been 12 inches from the edge of the shelf and there was a spoondrip tray, a water globe, and some notebooks in front of it. During this event there were three people in the warehouse aside from myself, Miss Roldan, who was at her desk, Mr. Hagmeyer, who was in the south-west corner of the room, and Julio. At the time of the event, Julio was sitting on his haunches at the north end of Aisle 3, placing a plastic alligator on the bottom shelf of Aisle 3. I was between five and six feet from him and facing him when this event happened. He had no visible contact with Tier 2. The position of the glass was four feet from his back. It moved away from him. None of the objects in front of the glass were disturbed. It therefore must have risen at least two inches to clear these.'

(Extract from *Journal of the American Society for Psychical Research*, 1971, paper by Roll and Pratt, Vol. 65, 446–447)

Loneliness, unhappiness, and fraud

This, then, is the type of evidence which must be considered carefully in trying to evaluate poltergeist phenomena. There is such a wealth of such evidence, from observers and experimenters all over the globe, in different cultures and at different times, that it cannot be dismissed out of hand. Still, there are clearly going to be problems which make us cautious, and which show how difficult it is to research poltergeist effects. We do not want to give the impression that Julio or Rosenheim cases are thick on the ground. Far from it.

Probably 95% of 'poltergeist' cases reported to researchers are not worth a second visit. Reports of strange goings-on may come from lonely, isolated people who really only want someone to talk to, or from unhappy families who would like a new council house. Sometimes a precise cause of apparently inexplicable events can be found. For example, one investigator studied the claim of an old lady that the spirit of her deceased husband could switch her bedside lamp on or off at request. Indeed, the investigator saw the light switch on and off without direct human touch, just as the woman described, and mostly when she asked for this to happen. Checking the flex, plug, and socket showed nothing that would explain this bewildering event. Dismantling the lamp revealed the cause: a thermal switch had accidentally been incorporated into the circuit near the bulb, causing the lamp to wink on and off. The woman had presumably learned to time her requests in accord with the natural time cycle of the lamp switching on and off.

The other major problem is that of fraud. William Roll, in analyzing an (admittedly small) sample of reported poltergeist cases, showed that for cases reported before 1949, fraud was detected in less than 10% of them. For (only 34) cases reported between 1949 and the early 1970s, the figure had increased to 32%. Now, one-third is a high frequency of fraud. The increase may be due to closer and better observation, or due to copycat cases inspired by lurid films and TV programs depicting poltergeist events. The true figure may be even higher. After all, if a researcher detects fraud early on in a case he probably won't continue his research and may not bother to publish his findings, and sometimes (with an amateur researcher and a clever fraud) fraud may go undetected. An estimate of 30–50% fraud in poltergeist cases since World War II would probably not be far off the mark.

Fraud, though, is a harsh word in this context. Most poltergeists focus around adolescents or children, and young children hardly possess the same moral sense as adults. While most exposures of fraud concern children, it is usually the family background, rather than malice, which prompts the deception.

One alleged poltergeist case which, in the course of three visits by one of us, produced no observable PK effects — but one instance of fraud — illustrates the problems well. The family home had no father, and the children — who lived in a depressingly dull suburb — liked the visits of interested strangers. After a first visit by the author, when nothing untoward had happened in his presence, one of the girls grabbed him by the arm as he was leaving and said: 'You will come back again, won't you?' Towards the end of a second visit, when again nothing out of the ordinary had been observed, the author was lucky enough to see, out of the corner of his eye, the eight-year-old boy of the household throw a kitchen brush in the air and then pretend that the poltergeist had been active.

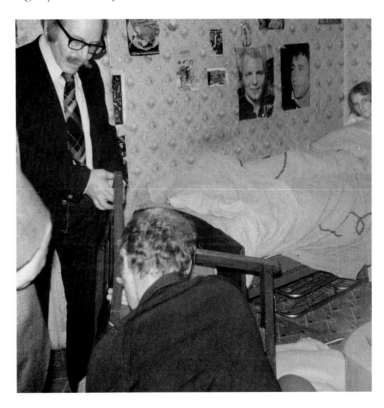

This kind of problem permits the armchair skeptic to sniff disdainfully and say 'I told you so'. It also means that researchers who want to study poltergeists had better learn to develop peripheral vision! However, to cry 'Fraud!' in the case of the family mentioned above is missing the point. The boy didn't see what he did as wickedness, and he had a good motive for doing what he did (he was seeking attention, and trying to please the adult whom he knew was looking for poltergeist phenomena). The psychology of the poltergeist and the psychology of the 'fraudulent' child have a dominating common element: the cry for attention.

We will return to the psychology of poltergeist phenomena later, but clearly the skeptic has good reason for demanding particularly stringent controls against fraud in the case of poltergeist research. However, we can now turn to a skeptical argument against the PK basis of poltergeists which has been comprehensively debunked.

Geophysical theories bite the dust

Sometimes parapsychologists are able to refute skeptical arguments with a pleasing completeness. It is actually relatively rare to find a skeptical counter-argument which is actually testable! Many skeptical comments on experimental work are vague, somewhat defamatory, or no more than assertions in the absence of any corroborating facts or logical derivations. Guy Lambert, the propounder of the 'geophysical theory' of poltergeists, cannot be criticized for any of these failings.

Lambert proposed that underground water channels, such as streams and sewers, may create poltergeist effects if they run beneath or close to the foundations of buildings. Specifically, when a head of water builds up in such channels, the building(s) may be subjected to spasmodic upward thrusts of physical force (known as 'water hammers'). In turn, these water hammers may produce seemingly inexplicable movements of objects as

Investigators examine furniture in the bedroom of an alleged poltergeist focus. The presence of interested outsiders can provide a tempting opportunity for a child to invent dramatic effects.

well as creaks and groans in the fabric of the building which might be taken for poltergeist rappings. If Lambert's theory is correct, we might expect to find a higher incidence of effects following abnormally high tides, downpours, or flooding (a testable prediction). Later, Lambert suggested that small local seismic disturbances, too weak to register on ordinary seismographs, might also contribute to poltergeist activity.

Such theories are by no means new. Concern about underground water effects date back at least 200 years. Lambert's contribution was to collect evidence in a systematic way which allowed him to test these theories. He found no difficulty in showing that some cases of poltergeist activity could be directly accounted for by subterranean events. There were, however, some questionable steps in his logic. He showed, for example, that poltergeist effects appear to cluster around coastal and tidal areas, where tidal effects are strongest. Unfortunately, as critics pointed out, these are exactly the regions which usually have the highest density of population. Historically, rivers and coastal waters have been vital for cheap transport, and settlements grew up around them (think of Rotterdam, Hamburg, London, New York, and so on). So of course there are more poltergeists in these areas. There are more people in these areas.

The first all-out attack on Lambert's theory was mounted by Dr. Alan Gauld, a psychologist at the University of Nottingham, and Tony Cornell, a Cambridge graduate with many years' experience of poltergeist research. First, they attacked Lambert on theoretical grounds. Gauld and Cornell were ready to accept that a small minority of very minor poltergeist effects, such as small-scale rapping noises and groans, could be the result of water hammers or subsidence. However, as they pointed out, geophysical theory could not account for the peculiar trajectories of moving objects often associated with poltergeists, or the most dramatic phenomena (such as movements of very heavy objects), or the seeming purposiveness of the poltergeist. The theory would also be hard-put to explain cases where effects occur in a building only when a specific person is present within it. Finally, Gauld and Cornell argued, most houses are incapable of withstanding subterranean forces of sufficient strength to actually move objects about inside them; they would simply fall down.

In 1961 Gauld and Cornell were lucky enough to get their hands (and equipment) on a number of structurally sound terraced houses which were scheduled for demolition. After extensive discussions with the municipal authorities, they were given permission to do what they liked with the houses. Equipment was brought in to produce physical forces of the kind Lambert stated were responsible for poltergeist effects — except that the forces which Cornell and Gauld produced were far greater in intensity than the ones which Lambert claimed could explain poltergeist effects.

Even when producing vibrations in a house which were so strong that they could be felt two houses away by placing a hand on a wall, no movement of objects even remotely resembling poltergeist effects was observed at any time. Both horizontal and vertical vibratory effects were generated, and at the end of the experiments they were so strong that Cornell commented: 'You could actually hear the houses singing with the vibrations.' Despite this, nothing like a poltergeist object-movement was observed. Eventually, with the real risk of the houses actually collapsing or the equipment disintegrating, the researchers concluded that Lambert's theory had been given a decent burial, and that if they pressed on with their experiment they might well be buried too.

Psychological profile of focus individuals

Alan Gauld has employed a statistical tool known as *cluster analysis* (which classifies cases into groups as a function of their similarity or dissimilarity on key features) to make a distinction between hauntings and poltergeists. This is an old distinction, of course, but Gauld was able to specify the distinction from a large body of reports and clarify it. Hauntings are place-centered — phenomena seem to focus on a place rather than a person, hence the traditional 'haunted house'. Rappings, noises, the sensation of being touched by some invisible agent, apparitions, and longevity (reports by different people over a long period of years) appear to typify hauntings. By contrast, poltergeists involve more dramatic movements of objects, are of shorter duration, include fewer rappings, and less apparent communication by any alleged spirit. However, while this distinction seems clear enough, Gauld cautions that both categories of event contain widely varying cases. Keeping this caution in mind, what can we say of the psychology of the poltergeist?

We have already touched on some of the psychological factors — desire for attention or dissatisfaction with current circumstances — which seem particularly relevant to claims of poltergeist activity. There are also some fairly clear-cut links with age and sex.

So far as the gender of focus individuals goes, females are in a large majority — Gauld and Cornell estimated a majority of 73% and William Roll 61%. However, as Roll has pointed out, in cases reported prior to this century around 80% of focus individuals were female; in this century there has been equality of the sexes. This may be due to cultural changes, for a recent Brazilian survey showed a very high (90%) proportion of females, although the sample was small. Since many recent cases have been researched in Europe or America (because that is where most of the researchers are who report cases in detail), one wonders how important Western cultural change may be here.

Age is also an important factor — the huge majority of focus people are children or adolescents. Again, there may be cultural factors at work. While 'Third World' cases continue to show this picture, in Europe and America the average age of focus people seems to have increased from 16 to 20, according to Roll. An increasing number of elderly people (age 70 or above) seem to be foci for poltergeist phenomena.

Nonetheless, the concentration of poltergeists around adolescents seems to support a frequently-voiced theory about poltergeists, namely that they are in some way linked to puberty, and therefore to sexual tensions and conflicts, a notion assiduously exploited in movies such as *The Exorcist* and *Carrie*. But is this notion justified in the light of increasing equality of the sexes with respect to poltergeist activity? In Europe and America the average age of focus people has gone up, while the average age at which puberty occurs has gone down. Further, in many early reports (and today) poltergeist activity ceased spontaneously after a few visits from a doctor or priest (or, today, from a researcher). Unless we assume professional malpractice, it is hard to see how such visits could have resolved frustrated sexuality. They might, however, have done something for the self-esteem of a confused and neglected youngster.

Mental illness is another popular explanation for the link between poltergeists and children. Many focus children, examined by psychiatrists or psychoanalysts, have duly been diagnosed as suffering from hysteria, depression, over-aggression, under-aggression, neurosis, and so on. A major problem with such diagnoses is that the person making them is likely to know why the child has been referred for an examination, and is thus all too ready to find an ailment which seems to offer an explanation. Even if that person doesn't know the reason for the referral (most unlikely) and diagnoses the child as neurotic, the child may have become neurotic precisely because she is being persecuted by a poltergeist! Unless reliable personality tests

A scene from Steven Spielberg's film Poltergeist. *No real-life poltergeist has ever produced such stunning special effects.*

of the child happen to have been done *before* poltergeist activity occurrs, how is one to know? Obviously such records are rarely available. In their absence, it is almost impossible to be sure of any picture of personality factors in poltergeist children.

'ESTHER COX, YOU ARE MINE TO KILL', AN ILLUSTRATIVE POLTERGEIST CASE

Just over 100 years ago 18-year-old Esther Cox was the centre of a poltergeist case in Amherst, Canada. A plain and (allegedly) psychoneurotic girl, Esther lived at home in conditions of poverty, sharing a bed with her (attractive) sister Jane. When Jane's beau attempted to rape Esther, an outbreak of poltergeist effects ensued.

The Cox family had to cope with disturbances in the sisters' bedroom: boxes were levitated and flew around, and the bedclothes were flung from the bed, to an accompaniment of loud banging noises. A doctor was called to attend to the feverish Esther, and was confronted with the sight of writing appearing on the wall before his eyes: *'Esther Cox, you are mine to kill.'* Later, as he stood in the doorway, plaster broke off another part of the wall and landed at his feet, having travelled *around a corner* to land there. The doctor also noted sounds which were so loud that they seemed like a pounding of the roof-shingles with a sledgehammer.

Esther started going into trances, and a minister who offered his services was greeted by a bucket of water becoming agitated and appearing to boil in Esther's presence. Fire-raising now entered the range of reported poltergeist effects and the Cox house was nearly razed to the ground.

A visiting magician, Walter Hubbell, visited the house several times and observed seven chairs falling over when he entered one room, and later suffered a number of abortive poltergeist assaults (knives were thrown at him). Hubbell's book about the case was a best-seller. Although the book is not fully reliable, the testimonies of the family, the doctor, and the ministers are difficult to ignore completely. The case illustrates many 'classic' poltergeist effects.

There is persuasive circumstantial evidence for taking seriously the theory that poltergeists are linked not with sexual tensions or mental illness, but rather with a desire for attention. In a survey of focus people aged 18 or under, William Roll noted that no fewer than 62% were living away from home when the outbreak began. Of the others, one in six had only one parent living, or present, in the home when the outbreak began. The latter figure may not be of much importance — there are many one-parent families in European-American society these days, although there were fewer for the years included in Roll's survey — but the fact that 62% were not living at home does seem rather startling. An unstable/absent family background lends some support to the 'desire for attention' theory (although we should be careful about assuming that one-parent families are somehow less stable than two-parent ones). Some additional support for the theory may be provided by the sudden increase, since 1950, of poltergeist cases focusing on old people. The attitude of Western societies to old people is notoriously less caring than in previous times. It is interesting that we cannot find evidence of a similar trend in non-Western societies, although this may be due to lack of research.

The problem here is that many neglected children do *not* become the focus of poltergeist activity. While we would hazard a guess that attention-seeking is necessary for a poltergeist outbreak, it clearly is not sufficient. We will probably have to wait many years before the extra triggering factors are understood.

So, what can we learn from poltergeists? Nothing neat and coherent, unfortunately, although there are some clear pointers. If this is PK, it is PK at its most anarchic and disordered. We are dealing with uncontrolled environments — in rare instances we may be able to observe and record phenomena, but we cannot control or predict them. Nevertheless, we have a core of well-attested cases which have been investigated thoroughly and for which normal explanations seem to have been exhausted. Even so, the PK effects here are too wild, uncontrolled, and violent for us to be able to learn anything systematic about PK. Before we turn to research which shows us a more positive, creative set of apparent PK effects, we have to deal with another area of PK research which has attracted much attention.

Metal-bending: showbiz or PK?

On 23 November, 1973, the BBC screened a TV program featuring Uri Geller, a young Israeli plucked from the obscurity of second-rate amateur conjuring shows by a maverick American scientist/inventor, Andrija Puharich. Watched by a large studio audience (including John Taylor, Professor of Mathematics at King's College, University of London, who was invited along to be the 'scientific hatchet man', as he put it), Geller bent keys and cutlery in an apparently inexplicable manner and, equally inexplicably, restarted watches which were said to be broken. Viewers wrote in to the BBC stating that, when Geller was on TV, cutlery had been bent in their own homes, long-stopped grandfather clocks had burst into fits of chiming, and objects moved around seemingly of their own accord. Media men rushed in to sign Geller up to participate in (travesties of) experiments on PK with the general public. Further metal-bending TV exploits were soon seen. The Geller Craze was born.

Twenty years on, a vast smoke-screen of irrelevant and obscuring anecdotes surrounds Geller and his career. These include accusations and counter-accusations, rumor, innuendo, 'confessions'

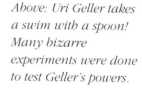

Above: Uri Geller takes a swim with a spoon! Many bizarre experiments were done to test Geller's powers.

Swiss metal-bender Silvio Meyer at work under the watchful eye of Professor John Hasted.

by ex-members of the Geller entourage (who were well paid for their statements incriminating Geller in definitely non-paranormal metal-bending), assertions by Puharich that Geller's powers are controlled by super-intelligent beings lurking in UFOs (which Geller distanced himself from), statements by magicians who claim they can duplicate Geller's feats, statements by magicians who claim that some of them could *not* be duplicated by conjuring, and much more besides. It seems clear now that Geller has been observed and recorded enhancing any PK ability he may possess by sleight-of-hand, but matters have grown extremely bitter and highly distasteful. For many years Geller has been the butt of some extremely intemperate attacks by Randall Zwinge, a conjurer with the stage name of the Amazing Randi. How this matter has ended up is summarized by George Hansen, a general commentator on the parapsychology scene. We simply quote him verbatim below, excluding the specific academic references he gives as source documents (newspaper reports, journal articles, etc.).

'In an interview for *Twilight Zone Magazine* and at a meeting of the New York Area Skeptics, Randi claimed that Eldon Byrd, a friend of Uri Geller, was a child molester and in prison. The New York Skeptics later admitted this was untrue, but Byrd sued, naming CSICOP [a skeptical group — authors' note]. Randi also claimed that Geller had launched a blackmail campaign against him, and Geller also filed a number of suits against Randi and CSICOP. This led to Randi's resignation from the Committee (i.e. CSICOP) to avoid its being named in subsequent suits. Several newsletters published an appeal from Randi that said "I'm in trouble, folks. I need help."'

Apart from discouraging anyone from giving money to an undeserving cause, we do not wish to add anything to this summary of a miserable state of affairs. What is in distinctly short supply in Geller's case is evidence from controlled studies and scientific experiments. The evidence offered by researchers closely associated with Geller is not of certain interpretation. We leave this circus world behind, and look at some more impressive evidence. This comes from Professor John Hasted of Birkbeck College, London, from Drs. Crussard and Bouvaist in France, and from studies done in Japan.

Putting a strip of metal inside a sealed glass tube precludes direct contact between the metal and the bender.

Behind the media myth

To begin with, we will examine some reported metal-bending effects which, on face value, seem to offer evidence for PK. Later, we will examine some very subtle reported effects which appear to make the claim of possible fraud or major error appear unlikely alternatives to PK.

Sealed tube bending Crussard and Bouvaist have recorded bending of metal strips in sealed glass tubes with the French metal-bender Jean-Paul Girard. Hasted and other researchers have examined the experimental method used and concluded that fraud was wholly excluded by it.

PK action at several locations simultaneously Hasted, working with (generally juvenile) metal-benders, has attempted to detect PK forces by using strain gauges mounted in metal strips. These are designed to produce electrical signals (monitored by chart recorders) if there is any bending of the metal strip. On frequent occasions, using several such gauges set up considerable distances (many yards) apart, Hasted has recorded synchronous signals from two, three, or even more of them. The measuring systems are not so sensitive that some weak seismic effect, vibrations, or equivalent would produce the recordings (as one of us has verified), nor could electrical anomalies create the effects unless there were some major problem which would be detected in other ways as well. Without some form of mechanical contrivance being used (and such a contrivance really could not be missed by the observers involved), the effect could not be created fraudulently.

PK action beyond the limit of human physical strength Hasted and the French researchers have both obtained bending of metal rods which would require a force in excess of physical strength. Crussard videotaped one session in which Girard can be seen gently stroking a metal rod, yet the deformation produced in the rod was found to require three times the known limit of human strength.

'Impossible' PK effects Hasted has reported two simple tests for 'impossible' PK. One test employed a brittle alloy bar which cannot be bent to a particular angle of deformation in less than a certain known time. If any excessive force is applied, it simply breaks. A well-attested physical constant governs the maximum deformation possible over time, which can only be produced by applying a small load continuously to effect a process known as 'creep' (a slow business, as the term suggests). Hasted has reported bending of such alloys in well under the minimum time thought to be possible with creep.

Hasted has also reported the 'impossible' effect of 'plastic deformation'. In some cases the bent area of a metal object is 'as soft as chewing gum', to quote Hasted. Such an effect could only plausibly be created in the metal by the application of corrosive chemicals (such as mercuric salts), but these would discolor metal (they are also very poisonous). Such corrosion would also have produced weight loss in the metal, but Hasted's measurements showed no weight loss.

Such evidence cannot be dismissed lightly. We are not in Gellerland here. The French researchers, for example, used the following standard procedures in their formal tests.

* All dimensions of samples (metal rods, bars, and other objects) were measured before and after bending.
* The micro-hardness of the metal was measured at several points both before and after bending.
* Residual strain profiles (a measure of crystalline structure) were examined both before and after bending.
* Electron micrograph analyses of the fine structure of ultra-thin foil specimens were generally made.
* Analyses of chemical composition at various places along the strip or rod were made.
* Samples used were individually hallmarked to prevent any substitutions being made.

This is a fairly formidable battery of tests, but some additional very subtle effects have been reported which appear to render fraud impossible in principle. A few of them can be mentioned here.

* The French team and Hasted, and sometimes the Japanese researchers, have reported local hardening of areas of metal specimens, even in cases where no bending took place (and where the test session was thought to be a failure for that reason). In one of these cases of 'anomalous hardening', the properties of the metal strip were stated by Hasted to be like those of 'a strip exposed to crushing by a weight of five tons'. However

— and this is intriguing — the pattern of strain and local dislocations in the metal was not what one would have expected from the application of such a powerful external force. It appears that what was going on was some internal stress in the metal.

  • Crussard and Bouvaist have reported an astonishing case in which a metal strip, bombarded before the experiment with radioactive Caesium atoms, was found to have a different distribution of Caesium within it after bending. It was as if the very atoms of Caesium had translocated within the strip.

  • Some research with Girard has produced changes in aluminum strips which are typical of high temperature (over 600°C) reactions; such changes can only be detected by careful metallurgical analysis.

This 'scrunch' of paperclips in the laboratory of Professor Hasted at Birkbeck College, London, was the result of a PK experiment with children.

What are we to make of all this? The authors are not metallurgists and so cannot appraise the more subtle effects mentioned above. However, the anomalous effects reported with strain gauges at several locations and with brittle alloys appear to be unequivocal. Some researchers have queried the possibility of equipment error (almost always without seeing the actual recording system), but we are not aware of any substantive critique of this research. For the moment the ball remains in the critics' court.

Metal-bending research is now rather unfashionable because of the malicious and vituperative criticism it has attracted over the years. There is nothing in this that is unexpected to anyone acquainted with scientific progress. Challenges to orthodoxy are often greeted with hostility, but in the case of metal-bending the unpleasantness of that hostility has been remarkable. Unsurprisingly, few researchers have chosen to explore PK in a world tainted by association with showbiz, rumor-mongering, *ad hominem* attacks, and even courtroom battles. We have to look elsewhere for the large body of accumulating evidence which may provide us with more understanding of PK phenomena.

From tumbling dice to virtual reality

In the course of his pioneering ESP research J.B. Rhine met a gambler who played craps and similar dice games. The man told Rhine that he, and other gamblers, occasionally felt capable of influencing the dice by an effort of will. Rather than dismissing the possibility as a gambler's fantasy, Rhine decided that the claim at least merited investigation. With his colleagues, he spent nine years testing for PK effects with thrown dice before he felt confident enough to publish the results. He was fighting enough battles to get ESP research accepted without rushing into print on the PK front as well.

The essence of Rhine's experiments was very simple. One or more dice were thrown while the subject was asked to concentrate on making them fall so that a particular face would be uppermost. With a true die, the odds of this happening are one in six, of course. As research progressed Rhine took precautions against various possible sources of error.

Dice bias A problem with standard commercial dice is that they are not true. That means that certain faces (the high numbers) tend to come up more frequently than others (low numbers). This is because the high-number faces are lighter (they have more of their surface scooped out to create the dots or pips on the die face) and the lighter faces are more likely to land uppermost when the die is thrown. Rhine got around this by using high- and low-aim PK testing (aiming to get many sixes, and then few sixes), by having subjects aim for different faces an equal number of times, and by having them aim to get a total of 7 when two dice were thrown (which only happens with one low and one high face — 1+6, 2+5, or 3+4).

Sleight of hand In later experiments Rhine used a machine to throw the dice rather than the conventional cup.

Recording errors The faces on the thrown dice were photographed, or the person recording the faces did not know which faces the subject was trying to score high on.

Rhine's survey of his early work showed that many of the initial 20 experiments yielded significantly above-chance scoring, but it was the presence of a second phenomenon which appears to have prompted him to publish the results. A subsequent analysis of score sheets by Rhine and Betty Humphrey showed a characteristic pattern of high scores early in test sessions, declining steadily through the quarters of each test session. The odds against chance for this QD (quartile decline) effect exceeded 100 million to 1. This was not the effect Rhine was necessarily looking for, but its consistency and very high anti-chance odds made him consider that it was strong evidence for a PK effect operating.

Nonetheless, many early dice experiments contained significant errors in method. A hostile review of them published by Edward Girden in 1962, and the same 'cultural' changes that produced a move away from ESP card testing, brought about a decline in PK dice tests. As it happens, the entire body of research evidence shows strong consistency (as we shall see in our final chapter), but virtually no one conducts such experiments these days. With the availability of machine-testing and computers which can eliminate such factors as bias and recording errors, dice-testing is cumbersome and time-consuming.

Many types of test have blossomed from dice research and later REG (Schmidt machine) tests (we will survey something of what has been learned about PK from them later). However, one particular line of PK research seems to us to be capable of considerable development, and the initial results have been promising.

PK and computer games

Several researchers have experimented with PK-based computer games. Some of these are very simple, little more than computerized dice-throwing using video displays of die faces for feedback. Some are based on arcade-type games such as 'Psi Invaders', a spin-off from the once-popular Space Invaders game where the player is asked to use PK to influence an REG whose output affects his chances of survival against hordes of aliens. Others have used strategy-type games, such as a stock market simulation where different players have 'accounts' and make 'contracts' on a notional commodities futures market to buy and sell over different periods of time, with an REG determining rising and falling stock prices.

Although it is not possible to review these studies as a whole, because of differences in experimental procedures and quite different goals for different experiments, consistent results have definitely been forthcoming from numerous experimenters. For example, Richard Broughton and his colleagues at the Foundation for Research on the Nature of Man (established by Rhine) have obtained a fairly reliable correlation between PK game success and anxiety levels in competitive games (but not in uncompetitive games, an intriguing and appealing finding).

Why might such game procedures be expected to be favorable for PK effects? Broughton makes a neat parallel. He notes that he has little interest in crossword puzzles, although if someone offered him a prize for completing one he would have some motivation to do it. His wife, however, enjoys such puzzles for their own sake. His motivation would only be *extrinsic* — only some external source of motivation would make him try to succeed at crosswords. His wife's motivation is *intrinsic* — she enjoys the puzzles as a challenge in themselves. Broughton suggests that psi in game-playing experiments is not strengthened by extrinsic motivation (such as offering money prizes for high scores); to succeed, subjects must have intrinsic motivation. They succeed not because of lures, but because of some internal desire or wish.

We are not convinced that this is so. Broughton's argument does not take into account the fact that certain environments create strong desires and wishes through incentive motivation of much subtler kinds than bribery. Human beings are extremely curious and many psychological experiments show that the simple prospect of learning how well one has done in some test or other (of reflexes, strategy, personality, IQ, a specific skill, almost anything in fact) is a powerful motivator. If the test is presented in an appealing and attention-grabbing way, curiosity becomes a powerful motivator. External factors very definitely affect how internal motivations are strengthened and expressed.

There are obvious ways in which this line of testing might be carried forward. First, existing computer games offer much more exciting possibilities than parapsychologists have yet made use of. Very relevant here are 'fantasy role-playing' computer games, such as those based on the world best-selling *Dungeons and Dragons* game produced by TSR Inc. (the games are developed by SSI and US Gold). In these games youngsters play the roles of computer-generated heroes of fantasy — warriors, wizards, witches, and rogues. Confronted with deadly puzzles, riddles, and traps, and mighty enemies and monsters, the computer generates pseudo-random numbers to resolve tests of skill, strategy, and problem-solving posed for the player(s). If an REG input were used instead of the pseudo-random numbers, one would have a very powerful test procedure indeed. The games are addictive and are constructed to help youngsters develop problem-solving skills of many kinds. The powerful intrinsic motivation is that of solving riddles and puzzles. Because of the variety of challenges posed to the player (thinking, riddle-solving, combat, etc.), PK tests of different types could be embedded into the game program. And because the game commands intense concentration, the player would soon forget that he was being 'tested' at all. Further, these games take place in 'worlds' (not unlike Tolkein's famous Middle Earth) in which

Screen display from Eye of the Beholder, *a computer role-play game from US Gold. If the numbers generated to put players to various tests of skill and strategy were truly random, such programs would become powerful and very appealing tests of PK ability.*

magic exists and is real, and monsters such as dragons stalk the land. Why should PK effects not exist too? If belief is an important factor, these games certainly aid suspension of disbelief. Given that people are more skeptical about PK than about ESP, this may be an important factor.

Parapsychologists could use such well-designed and appealing games for PK testing right now, provided a sympathetic games company could be found to give permission to modify and use their product. New computer technology potentially offers yet another possibility to parapsychologists, that of using *virtual reality*, or VR, to test PK. This possibility is more distant than PK testing with fantasy role-playing games, but we predict that the first tests will be conducted with it within five years. Assembling a body of results from several different researchers will take longer of course. Unfortunately, the current cost of VR equipment puts it well beyond the reach of most parapsychologists at the moment.

In VR the computer generates environments which make use of all the senses. Instead of looking at a display on a VDU screen, a person in VR is actually *within* the display, as it were. Tactile feedback given through tiny vibrational devices (usually in the form of a 'data glove' worn on the hand) allows the person to have the physical sensation of picking up objects and touching things within the visual field he sees around him. Headphone inputs allow sounds to be created to match the sight and feel of the environment. We can say from experience that VR is a very heady, and uniquely powerful, achievement of computer technology. Before long, one is completely caught up within the VR world, even though the appearance of the visual world within it is still pretty crude (a simple technical problem which advancing computing power will solve within a few years).

The VR environment is one in which suspension of disbelief is more total and commanding than in any other. If belief is important for the manifestation of PK effects, then VR is the way to go. Imagine being in the middle of a VR poltergeist outbreak, in which REG events secretly control the phenomena and you have to play the role of a researcher trying to monitor, control, or somehow dampen the effects. Almost any task, or test of skill, within VR could have a significant input from an REG and be affected by PK. The possibilities are limitless here. We anticipate startling results from research with this technology.

The psychology of PK

Before we examine our final major research area, that of bio-PK, let us review the whole field of PK research so far (with dice, REG machines, and PK games) and summarize what we know about the effects of belief, personality, social environment, and so on. Unfortunately, with PK, we do not have the wealth of evidence that we have with ESP. While there are 150 experiments concerning belief, extraversion, and anxiety in the ESP literature, there are far fewer for PK. This means, inevitably, that our conclusions about PK are more tentative.

A scene from the virtual reality role-play game Virtual Murder *(BBC). VR is an even more powerful way of sustaining disbelief than ordinary computer games.*

Belief and PK The evidence here is thin and rather inconsistent. Some studies have reported that 'PK sheep' score higher than 'PK goats' in experiments, but the nature of measurement of the belief factor is not directly comparable with that in Schmeidler's ESP experiments. At least two studies have shown superior scoring by people who indicated that they accepted the possibility of ESP. There may be a technical problem with some of the measurements, with a 'floor effect' (too many people indicating disbelief for them to be in any way a homogeneous group), but we are not too confident of that explanation. It is actually rather surprising, given the predictive power of the sheep-goat factor with ESP, that it has not been adopted as a standard measurement in PK testing.

The role of belief has been most widely researched using an entirely different approach. Following the suggestions of Kenneth Batcheldor in Britain and others, researchers have tried to create a strong atmosphere of belief in PK test sessions. Instead of measuring belief as an individual difference between people, they attempt to manipulate the factor by suspending disbelief and creating a positive, anticipatory atmosphere in which PK effects are expected to occur.

This has been done in more than one way. One approach is the 'PK party', where a group attempts metal-bending with a strong air of mutual encouragement and support, yelling 'Hey! it's going!' as a teaspoon begins to wilt. Unfortunately, this work has not progressed beyond the informal stage and there is nothing much that can be said about it from a scientific standpoint.

More interesting are the direct developments of Batcheldor's original working group. It is claimed that PK effects have been produced by creating an imaginary ghost! Members of a seance group in Toronto actually designed the character of 'Philip', his background and history, and then allowed 'Philip' to take responsibility (as it were) for the table-tilting, levitations, and other effects that were observed by the group and in some instances instrumentally recorded. Interestingly, the Toronto group began their work in parallel to Batcheldor, not knowing of his own closely related research.

This seemingly bizarre approach turns on the idea that, by having 'Philip' available as a source for the effects, disbelief can be more easily suspended. Also no single person is faced with the possibility that he or she generated the PK effect (an attempt to overcome

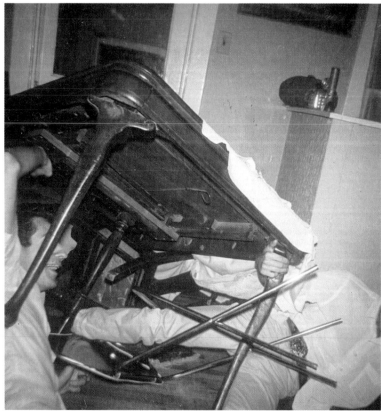

To be admissible as real evidence for PK, levitation effects need to be recorded by at least two cameras simultaneously. Here a small fold-away table apparently hangs in mid-air and a heavier table crashes down onto two observers.

what is termed *ownership resistance* — people are not comfortable with the notion that they can create PK effects). People involved in poltergeist cases, for example, are at best ambivalent about being the source of the phenomena. 'Philip' was a conjured poltergeist, if you like, but one without a focus person.

In such experiments it is absolutely crucial that recordings are made of the PK events, recordings independent of recording error, bias, and so on. It appears that the Toronto group made some kind of instrumental record, although we cannot be categorical about this. Our reservations about research of the Toronto type arise for different reasons.

Although these kinds of studies may be dramatic, they probably cannot tell us very much. They are too uncontrolled for us to be able to isolate the factor or factors responsible for generating any PK effects that might be observed. Also, with this kind of work, it is extremely difficult to compare different groups, which in turn makes it difficult to come up with a reliable formula for recreating the effects observed. Such effects may be as much due to the mix of people present (common sense suggests that any group which takes a lot of time and trouble to create an imaginary ghost may not be representative of the general population) as to the group's degree of belief, or it may be that the two factors (personality and belief) work synergistically to create the effects. Further seances of this type might be an intriguing sideline, but they are not going to provide us with much in the way of understanding. Once again, at the risk of repeating ourselves, more research and more evidence is needed in this area.

Personality and PK Research which has used recognized, acceptable measures of personality and PK tests is very thin on the ground. An Argentinian study by Mischo and Weiss suggests that sociability is linked with success in PK tasks, and sociability is a key component of extraversion. Broughton's studies, as we noted, linked pre-test anxiety with poor performance in PK tasks, and one of us has also found some evidence for a negative PK/neuroticism link. The evidence we have is modestly consistent and seems to be similar in kind to that found in ESP research. However, many studies have failed to find any PK/personality link, so we must concede that, if there *is* a link, it is a fairly weak one.

Altered states and PK Rhine himself found that hypnosis had no effect on PK scoring, and to our knowledge no one has done further research in this area. We know of only three experiments on PK and sleep, and none found significant results. We are not aware of any ganzfeld/PK experiments either, but some research from Schmidt, Braud, and others suggests that meditation may have an enhancing effect on PK, but not in a reliable or controllable way. The relationship here may be complex.

Schmidt and Marilyn Schlitz found that differently-presented PK tasks appeared to generate different patterns of success from meditators and non-meditators. Different tests suit different people. No consistent picture emerged here. There is a very real need for more research conducted along directly similar lines by different researchers. Standard laboratory practice uses elements of relaxation procedures in many PK tests, and this area cries out for more controlled comparisons of the kind carried out by Braud, comparing relaxation and tension, with ESP testing. We do have one experiment with PK testing and relaxation, but its interpretation is far from simple.

Charles Honorton reported that relaxation produced below-chance PK scores, while tension produced above-chance scores. When tested himself as a subject, Honorton produced exactly the same results — only they were more clear-cut than those of the subjects he had worked with. This raises the possibility that Honorton himself created the original effects through 'experimenter PK'. Hence the need for more independent studies, particularly since Braud himself found significantly better PK scores from people in a relaxed state than from people engaged in mathematical and logical tasks (though the nature of 'task interference' is probably extremely complex).

A related line of enquiry, which appeared promising for a time, was 'release of effort research' conducted by Rex Stanford and others. Subjects were asked to try very hard to bias a Schmidt machine using PK, and then — at the end of test sessions, as they relaxed — the researchers secretly had the machine continue running for a time, without any feedback being given. In these 'linger trials', the PK effect was much stronger than in the effortful trial session. This may have been due to relaxation, or to the fact that people didn't realize they were being tested for PK after the effort run! Later experiments have shown inconsistent results with such 'silent PK' runs, although here too the results are difficult to interpret. In at least one of them, experimenter PK may have been a factor.

Overall, then, we do not have a clear picture of the psychology of PK. The little we have on personality and belief appears to be consistent with the ESP evidence. The altered states work does not appear to be so clear, but there is certainly a need for more — and more uniform — research. In this respect PK research does not show the consistent 'patterning' that we consider to be strong evidence in the case of ESP, at least not with respect to the same psychological factors. However, PK research is not without success stories, as the Schmidt/Jahn research discussed in Chapter 3 has already shown. We are now ready to present another success story.

The healing mind

The tradition of faith healing is an ancient and persistent one. Claims for 'miracle cures' are often extravagant and hard evidence is difficult to obtain. In essence, it is claimed that at least some individuals have the power to alleviate illness or cure the sick purely through an act of will, without using medication or even medical knowledge of any sort. From the point of view of a parapsychologist, any alleged power of the mind to change the physical world, even if that part of the physical world is another person's body, is a possible example of PK effects. But can the alleged powers of healers be investigated scientifically? Can we discover whether PK does, or does not, play a role in the cures claimed by healers?

To begin with, we need to be aware of the primacy of attitude and belief (or faith), or psychological factors generally, in the etiology of disease. Some startling medical evidence will show us that the claims of faith healing are hardly out of line with what we know of 'conventional' psychological effects.

In the *British Medical Journal* Dr. A. A. Mason reported the successful treatment by hypnosis of an intractable genetic illness. His patient was a boy suffering from a terrible skin condition known as ichthyosis ('fish skin'). The skin is hard, brittle, and splits easily, giving rise to suppurating wounds which easily become infected. There is no known effective cure, and children suffering from the condition usually die at a young age as a result of perpetual infections. Many different treatments have been tried, without success. Mason's patient had not responded to any of them.

Before he began hypnotic treatment, Mason was well aware that, should he succeed, skeptics would bend over backwards to try and attribute the boy's cure to something other than hypnosis. They would dispute the diagnosis and try to say that the cure was a long-term effect of previous treatments. Accusations of mistaken diagnosis bedevil many alleged claims for miraculous healing, but in this case the diagnosis was

An aerial view of Lourdes, France, on Ascension Day. Lourdes, the shrine of Saint Bernadette, is a place of pilgrimage for Catholics. Every year thousands visit the town in search of healing. Many depart healed in spirit, if not in body.

beyond dispute. People who turn to unorthodox therapies have usually tried what orthodox medicine has to offer first, so skeptics can always claim that earlier treatment has a delayed effect. Mason's solution to this dilemma was ingenious.

He hypnotized the boy and then gave the specific hypnotic suggestion that the hard skin would disappear from *one arm only*. This is exactly what happened. Now, it simply is not credible to claim that previous treatments just happened to affect only a specific part of the boy's body which the hypnotist then suggested should be cured! Clearly, the healed arm was an effect of hypnosis. Mason went on to clear up over 90% of the affected areas of the boy's body in this way, leaving only some small patches on his back. The inescapable conclusion is that hypnotic suggestion effectively cured this 'incurable' disease.

We should also mention Stephen Greer's remarkable research into personality and breast cancer at King's College Hospital in London. Greer and his research team established that certain personality patterns appear to predispose to malignant cell changes and early death. Factors such as the desire to fight the illness seem to make a huge difference to survival time, and a personality with much suppressed anger seems to predispose to early death, possibly through the mediation of the IgA (immunoglobulin) system.

The remarkable (and under-reported) work of the German researcher Grossarth-Maticek provides yet another pointer to the importance of psychological factors in disease. The population he chose to study lived in a village in (then) Yugoslavia and had very low social mobility — people were born, lived, and died in the same rural area. Hence, follow-up studies were easy to conduct. Using a vast battery of personality and medical tests, Grossarth-Maticek showed that so far as the genesis of lung cancer is concerned, the disease requires both a physical risk factor (smoking) *and* a psychological factor (anxiety coupled with an inability to express it, very similar to the neuroticism factor of Cattell and

Jesus restores the sight of a blind beggar. A competent opthalmologist would offer all sorts of medical reasons for such a cure. Was the healing 'will' that of Jesus or the beggar himself?

Eysenck). Smokers without this personality trait did not develop lung cancer, and neurotics who did not smoke didn't develop the disease either. The effects reported in this colossal, and admirably conducted and reported, long-term study with few equals in medical research are very clear indeed. Studying a range of illnesses, Grossarth-Maticek has provided excellent evidence that psychological factors are *at least as important* in the onset of disease as physiological factors such as blood pressure, cholesterol levels, and so on. There are also now many studies indicating how mental factors, like depression, can influence the immune system through changes in cortisol level, and in other ways.

There is much we could add to this. Just to give one example, bereavement has a powerful suppressive effect on certain white blood cells which lasts for several months, making the grieving person very prone to infection and disease (so the common wisdom that some people literally pine to death following the loss of a deeply loved partner may have some truth in it). The mind powerfully affects the body. This is, after all, why any clinical test of the usefulness of a drug must employ a *placebo* test, since doctors know all too well that placebos (inactive, harmless substances) can have a beneficial effect all of their own. Such is the power of belief and expectation.

A wounded pigeon is brought to an animal healer. With wild animals it is not easy to relate healing to any placebo effect. Pets and laboratory animals stay healthier and heal more quickly if they are treated with affection — there is trust and rapport between them and their keepers.

Of mice, plants, and enzymes

The difficulties involved in studying alleged claims of cures by faith healing, whether at Lourdes or by the efforts of the significantly more distasteful American evangelizing healers, are too great. Problems of mistaken diagnoses, possible delayed effects of previous treatments, the temporary nature of alleged cures, and so on are overwhelming. There are much simpler ways to go about investigating such matters. Bernard Grad, Professor of Psychiatry at McGill University in Canada, deserves special credit for developing a basic procedure which has developed into some of the most exciting research in the whole of parapsychology.

Grad inflicted small skin lesions, under anesthetic, on mice which were then treated by a faith healer, Oskar Estabany. The mice were divided into two groups, a control group (allowed to heal naturally, without treatment) and an experimental group, which Estabany treated. During the treatment Estabany was allowed to hold the cages in which the mice were living, not the mice themselves. This is important, because it is known that handling and stroking can influence the physical processes of healing. The wounds of both groups were then measured by laboratory technicians who did not know which mice were in the control group and which were in the experimental group. The possibility of recording errors influencing the reported difference between the groups was therefore ruled out. Finally, since mice are not notoriously susceptible to the effects of belief, if any difference was observed it could not be claimed to be a placebo effect!

In this experiment the wounds of the treated mice healed significantly faster than those of the control group. However, we cannot assume that this was due to PK. In a second experiment, in which the treated mice had their cages kept in insulated bags, they did not heal significantly faster than the control mice. So some form of very indirect physical contact cannot be ruled out.

However, in another of Grad's lines of research, Estabany showed an effect wholly independent of physical contact. Grad prepared two groups of plants grown in chemical solutions, either normal or saline (which would inhibit growth). Estabany was allowed only to handle the glass vessels which contained the saline solutions, but they

A Kirlian photograph of a young and healthy thistle plant; the 'aura' around the leaves would be discontinuous and weak if the plant were diseased. Do gardeners who 'talk' to their plants unwittingly exert PK?

were sealed from any direct physical contact. What Grad found was that saline solutions 'treated' by his healer depressed the growth rate of plants significantly less than 'untreated' saline solutions, yet chemical analysis of the saline showed no changes which could account for this.

Although these experiments were inconclusive, Grad went on to develop others which eliminated many of the problems of working with organic systems.

Estabany was again the subject in a remarkable series of experiments conducted by Sister Justina Smith, head of the chemistry and physics departments at Rosary Hill College, Buffalo, New York. These were designed to find out if Estabany could exert a PK effect on a very simple organic system, the activity of human enzymes. Enzymes are a major category of human proteins which serve many functions vital to life. In essence, they influence the rate of chemical reactions. Some speed up reactions, others inhibit them; the system is one of checks and balances. To give a simple indication of how important enzyme function is within the body, if only a handful of key enzymes in your body ceased their actions NOW, you would probably be dead before you got to the bottom of this page.

Smith tested Estabany for his ability to influence the activity of one enzyme in particular, the human digestive enzyme trypsin. Trypsin was selected for study because it is easy to prepare in a pure form, and the biochemical measures (or assays) needed to measure its activity are relatively simple. Smith found that Estabany was able to influence a trypsin solution by increasing the activity of the enzyme, without direct contact and with careful measurements being taken of such factors as temperature and magnetic field changes around the apparatus holding the enzyme (both of these factors are known to affect trypsin activity, so it was important to eliminate them as possible mechanisms for any influence Estabany had). No such changes took place, even though Smith calculated that the putative PK effect on the trypsin was similar in strength to that of a 13,000 gauss magnetic field.

Smith's experiments were partly replicated by Hoyt Edge, working with another faith healer. Here, the effects were less uniform, with the changes in trypsin activity varying in kind during a series of experiments. Is this surprising or disappointing? Interestingly, Edge found in one of his control studies that a magnetic field change which would be expected to affect the enzyme failed to do so. That is, the effect of a known and influential *physical* factor was not absolutely predictable or repeatable. Such a finding is worth keeping in mind when examining arguments about whether experiments in parapsychology are repeatable or not.

From these beginnings, several different lines of research into 'bio-PK' have developed. We can divide them broadly into three groups: research into PK effects on blood cells and chemical systems, PK effects on human body function, and PK effects on other creatures. All these lines of research are generating intriguing results.

Bug-zapping PK?

Many hazards lurk in modern food. Salmonella in chickens, listeria in cheeses, and botulism in cooked pork (a 1992 scare story) are making us rather wary of what we eat these days. Botulism is most definitely not to be taken lightly. Thus, the half-dozen or so experiments which have examined possible PK effects on small organisms (yeast cells, salmonella, and the gut-dwelling commensal *E. coli*) are of topical interest. In a recent review Gertrude Schmeidler located six such studies, all conducted by different researchers, all of which demonstrated significant effects on cultures of unicellular creatures by individuals attempting to use PK to influence their activity. Such studies appear to demonstrate, with a startling consistency, that the human will can inhibit or promote the growth of such organisms. Adding more recent studies, the success level remains very high and the precautions taken (measurements made by people unaware of which group of organisms was to be promoted or inhibited, elimination of physical contact between person and organism) appear to have been consistently good. This research suggests strongly that PK may be able to affect biological organisms of a simple kind. This has profound implications, for, under certain conditions, unicellular organisms are potent vectors of disease.

Effects on blood cells

Work with other cellular systems has examined how blood may be influenced by PK. In three experiments William Braud studied the disintegration of red blood cells placed in solutions with different salinity (salt concentration) to normal blood plasma. When red blood cells are placed in such solutions, they begin to disintegrate, a process known as hemolysis. Since a solution of red blood cells becomes increasingly transparent to light as the cells disintegrate, the rate of their destruction can easily be measured by the amount of light from a constant source transmitted through the solution, using an instrument called a spectrometer. In these experiments spectrometer readings were made by a technician unaware of whether or not a person at a distant location was trying to 'protect' the blood cells from destruction using PK (this is analogous to so-called 'distant healing', and obviously eliminates known physical mechanisms for the effect). In two of the three experiments the hemolysis was significantly slowed down by the distant person, and the three experiments overall showed combined results which were strongly significant.

Effects on blood systems have also been measured in a remarkable study by Snel and Van der Sidje in Bilhoven, Holland, using rats infected with the red blood cell parasite

Babesia. A healer was asked to attempt to strengthen the 'defenses' of the infected rats, and was given nothing more than photographs of the rats to work with — again, not a whiff of any direct physical contact. The healer lived 20 miles away from the rats and was not given any written material pertaining to the experiment, just the photographs of the creatures he was to help. Once again, measurements were made of these rats, and control rats not being given the benefits of 'distant healing', by researchers unaware of which rats were in which group. The results showed that the proportion of infected red blood cells was substantially lower in the treated group than in the control group for 14-day and 28-day measurements. The researchers also reported, intriguingly, that *all* the rats fared better than would normally be expected: 'Normally rats infected with *Babesia rodhani* do not survive as long as the animals

in our experiment.' It was as if the healer, in protecting the experimental rats, had helped all the rats in the study. After all, having only photographs to work with isn't much and (to our eyes anyway) all rats look pretty much alike (if they are of the same strain, which was true in this experiment). Perhaps the kindly healer wished to help all of them! Even so, the difference between the experimental and control group was significant.

Such results are startling. They imply a direct effect by human will on basic processes in the blood and within the immune system, and therefore on resistence to disease. They have obvious implications for healing.

A red blood cell (carries oxygen), a white blood cell (a lymphocyte, responsible for producing antibodies), and a blood platelet (essential for clotting and wound repair), all magnified 1,700 times. If PK can affect the cell lines that produce blood, it can affect every tissue, organ, and system in the body.

Influencing human body functions

A major body of research with human beings as PK targets has been conducted over more than a decade by William Braud and his co-workers at Mind Science Foundation in San Antonio, Texas. This long series of ground-breaking studies used a variety of different target systems for PK effects, but had certain features in common. Attempts were made by subjects to influence, by PK, some aspect of human behavior or activity taking place at a distant location. In different series of experiments Braud and his colleagues sought to discover whether people could influence the following: *electrodermal skin activity,* an index of autonomic nervous system activity and therefore related to anxiety and other emotional states — Braud's team conducted 323 test sessions in 15 different experiments using this one measure alone; *ideomotor reactions,* subtle involuntary changes in the muscular movements of arm, hand, and fingers associated with thinking; *muscular tremor,* a measure of more consciously-influenced movements in musculature; and *blood pressure.*

Braud and his team have also conducted other studies (such as the hemolysis experiments), but those we have mentioned are enough to be going on with. Some consistent features of these experiments must be stressed. First, the laboratory set-up is fully detailed by Braud, and seems quite clearly to fit our expectations of what sound experiments should be like. The physical separations of the influencers and target people are absolute. Measurements are made by technicians who are unaware of when attempts are or are not being made to influence the human targets. Comparisons are made between influence periods and non-influence periods, which are randomly selected, alternated, counterbalanced, and otherwise rendered unsusceptible to subtle artifacts. The physiological target systems chosen are specifically selected because they are typically fluctuating, labile systems which vary over short periods of time; this is important, for one would not expect to detect a subtle PK effect on a system which did not spontaneously change during normal human behavior (without anyone trying to influence it). And so on.

The overall importance of these studies is immense. Summarizing 655 test sessions from a wealth of experiments, the overall probability for the effects found is less than 1 in 30 thousand billion. The effects of human will on the behavior and unconscious activity of other people are clear-cut here, and findings are consistent across long series of studies. There is no question of one type of effect being plucked out of the air with statistics in one experiment, and a different one the next time around. The 15 electrodermal studies alone show a consistency of effect very, very clearly.

'Alternative' and 'complementary' medicine have had a raw deal from the high-tech scientific medical establishment. But for millennia medical practitioners have relied, wittingly or unwittingly, on the therapeutic power of the human will.

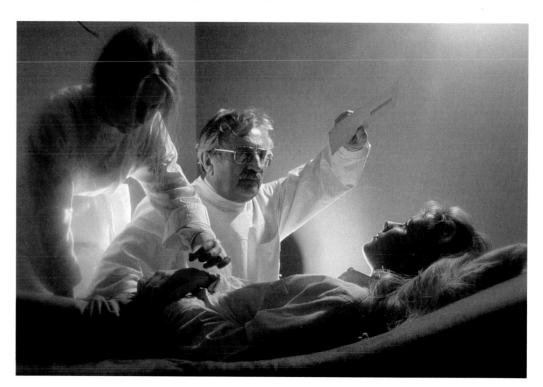

In his long summary review written with Marilyn Schlitz, his major co-researcher, Braud considers ten rival hypotheses to the PK theory, from equipment bias, statistical problems, and uncontrolled external stimuli to much subtler effects such as co-ordinated biological rhythms, placebo or expectancy effects, and others. Braud shows how each alternative explanation can be discounted and how, even in combination, they cannot explain the effects observed.

Overall, what this research appears to show is that humans can affect aspects of the body functioning of other humans by act of will alone. Both calming and stimulating effects have been observed. Effects on such factors as blood pressure, added to the evidence of PK effects on blood and enzymes, suggest strongly that PK effects in healing are entirely plausible.

We consider Braud's research program to be a remarkable, sustained body of excellent work. It is also important to note that while no other researchers have been able to produce such extensive bodies of evidence for bio-PK, this may simply be because no one else has had the time, facilities, and determination to so painstakingly construct a vital body of research. It is, of course, not true that Braud's spectacular work is without support;

the bio-PK experiments on unicellular organisms and in other areas support his conclusions. It is simply that, as a body of findings, this remarkable research is without peer. Given that there is support for key findings within it from other experimenters, it represents a formidable challenge to the skeptic.

PK: a summing up

This has been a long chapter. We hope the reader feels the journey has been worthwhile. From Home, and from the Schmidt/Jahn machine-PK work, we already had some formidable evidence regarding PK effects, but the evidence we have reviewed here adds to it in certain areas. The best of the poltergeist evidence, some core findings in metal-influencing PK studies, and the bio-PK research cannot readily be dismissed, even though the psychology of how people employ PK, and whether there are factors especially favorable to it, are not so clear. The results yielded by this research are remarkable, thought-provoking, and potentially of great practical importance. This is obviously so with the bio-PK research, but it is also true of the machine-PK research, despite the small size of the PK effects reported. Robert Morris, Dean Radin, and others have hypothesized that PK may be responsible for some computer failures, especially those associated with stress (time pressure, or a stressful, pressurized job) and that only a small effect would be needed to make many systems 'crash'. When one considers how many of the systems we take for granted rely on microchip technology, this is a possibility we have to take seriously.

In later chapters we will tackle some fundamental questions about psi. How does it work? Is survival after bodily death a hypothesis that can be investigated scientifically? However, an interesting detour comes first.

Thus far we have concerned ourselves almost exclusively with experiments in which individuals were consciously attempting to use psi or at least knew they were taking part in a psi experiment. From surveys of experience we know that this is virtually never the case in life outside the laboratory. Seemingly precognitive dreams or episodes of telepathy don't occur because people wish them to; they just happen, it seems. Surely this implies a discontinuity between laboratory research and real life.

Some research in the last 20 years has tried to bridge the gap between these two areas by examining the ability of people to use psi without making any effort to do so — indeed, in most cases, without realizing they are involved in a psi test at all. Such experiments have yielded some challenging findings very relevant to real-life psi, as we shall now see.

The parapsychology of everyday life

8

Many people who have had spontaneous psi experiences find it difficult to relate the results of scientific research to those experiences. 'What does all this research have to do with me?' they ask. Well, laboratory studies *do* cast light on real-life psi. They certainly point up some sources of error and confusion, and the laboratory phenomenon of psi-missing is, if you like, a clear experimental demonstration of what we might term in ordinary life 'bad luck'!

In real life psi just seems to happen. Those who have psi experiences do not set out to have them. There is no conscious intent involved. As parapsychologist Rex Stanford has pointed out, evolutionary considerations would seem to militate against the idea that psi occurs only when a person is consciously attempting to deploy it in some way. Stanford has pioneered the use of unconscious psi tests — or, better perhaps, non-aware psi tests. These are laboratory tests where people do not realize that they are, in some way or other, being tested for psi.

In addition to telling us more about how psi operates in real life, the test element in such experiments is reduced. People cannot become anxious about being tested if they do not know they are being tested. There are, of course, ethical considerations here. Is it right for an experimenter to deceive people about what is happening in the laboratory? Stanford is keenly sensitive to such issues, and has debated them extensively. In an 'unconscious' psi test there is *passive* deception, in the sense that the subject is not told everything about laboratory proceedings, but not *active* deception in the sense that the subject is being lied to. This is a key difference, and as the reader looks through the experiments we are about to recount, it should be clear that they are not in any way unethical.

Before we describe Stanford's experiments, however, we need to examine the theory behind them, since this was formulated in advance of most of the experiments and indeed guided and directed them. In this respect, Stanford's work is among the most elegant in scientific parapsychology. He recently published a lengthy re-evaluation and update of his model, cited in the Bibliography, and we urge anyone interested in this field to consult it. It is an erudite piece which could hold its own with review papers published in prestigious orthodox journals such as *Psychological Review*. We only wish more psychologists and other scientists would take the trouble to examine Stanford's writings.

Psi for everyone?

Stanford's working model of how psi operates in everyday life is called, rather intimidatingly, 'Psi-mediated Instrumental Response' (PMIR). As originally formulated, the essence of the PMIR model was as follows.

People use psi without being aware of it. They use ESP to scan the environment for useful and need-relevant information which cannot be obtained in other ways. Information which is relevant to need then tends to be acted upon, either in normal ways or — if nothing else will do — possibly by a PK response.

This model has three components: the notion of ESP as a scanning mechanism, the idea that psi operates in the service of needs, and the notion that psi detection of such need-related information can trigger responses which may include PK. These components need to be considered separately.

Opposite: In real life we may use psi more often than we realize, particularly when it comes to getting something we want.

Stanford swiftly revised his original model to eliminate the ESP-scanning theory. The notion of active scanning did not make sense, he came to believe, because the sheer amount of information processing involved would potentially be enormous. Even the notion that scanning would only operate to detect need-related events, rather than as a general sensing system, would not reduce the implausibility of the idea. Indeed, people would be swamped with psi-acquired information if the scanning part of the model was true! The brain could hardly function under such circumstances. Rather, Stanford placed a greater emphasis on the goal-oriented nature of psi; that is, psi works towards an end, and that end is the satisfaction of various needs.

There are problems with this notion. Goal-oriented theories of how people behave have a chequered history in psychology and are not very fashionable at the moment. The dropping of the scanning element of the theory certainly leaves something of a gap, for the selectivity of PMIR does not seem to be neatly specified.

At one time Stanford proposed a *conformance* model which sought to bridge this gap, but it is not an idea which is clear to us and neither has it been enthusiastically greeted in parapsychology. Discussing it would lead us into some abstruse side-paths, so for the moment we will look instead at some of the experimental evidence which might persuade us that this general line of thought is worth considering at all.

First, there have undoubtedly been many experiments in parapsychology in which some element of the test, not revealed to the subjects, definitely influenced behavior. We are talking about conscious psi tests here, but the point to grasp is that hidden elements of tests, detectable only by psi, definitely influence test scoring. As a simple example, psychologist James Carpenter tested high- and low-neurotic individuals with a standard ESP card test, but omitted to tell them that, for half of the tests, the sealed ESP cards (inside envelopes) were accompanied by pornographic pictures! Analyzing the results, Carpenter found that the high-neurotic individuals scored better on the ordinary ESP cards and poorly on ones with the extra picture, while low-neurotic people did the opposite. In other words, people responded differently to a hidden element of the test, depending on a key personality variable known to affect ESP test scoring. This, and other similar experiments, have shown that people don't just use ESP to sense what the experimenter tells them to, nor do they necessarily use it to do what they think they're trying to use ESP to do!.

In an experiment done in the late 1960s Stanford asked volunteers to listen to a tape-recorded account of a dream and then, later, asked them questions about it. This was not presented as being in any way a psi experiment. The camouflaged element of the experiment was that there were certain target answers and certain non-target answers. Stanford wanted to see if non-intentional psi would help his volunteers to answer the target questions correctly and the non-target answers incorrectly. For this to happen, psi would have to influence their memories of the dream account in such a way that accurate recall would be suppressed in favor of incorrect answers and poor recall would be boosted to provide correct answers. The results of the experiment showed very clearly that the way in which the volunteers' memories worked was affected by psi, even though they were unaware of being tested for psi.

Many experiments of a similar nature have been reported in the intervening years. To make order and sense out of them, let us tie them in to the major elements of Stanford's theory.

'Needful' psi

A key component of the PMIR model is the idea of 'need'. Stanford leaves this term undefined (and in some writings he uses the term 'disposition', which is probably a better word to use). This part of his theory uses knowledge which conventional psychology has acquired about needs and dispositions. While there are disputes about what these are and which have primacy, certain needs are obvious — food, drink, shelter, security, affiliative and socializing needs, and so on. What evidence do we have that need, however defined, is a crucial element in triggering psi?

One line of research which may be relevant here is a set of experiments, by William Braud, Stanford himself, and by Martin Johnson at Utrecht among others, which will be of keen interest to younger readers in particular. In essence, these experiments were variants on a single theme: students in an academic examination or test of some kind were supplied, covertly, with answer forms (either for essays or multiple-choice tests) for which answers or relevant information were supplied in a hidden pack below the form for some of the questions. Thus, information which could potentially assist the students (who obviously had a strong disposition to do well) was provided in a form which was shoved right under their noses. The results of these experiments generally showed fairly strong tendencies for students to score better on questions for which information was supplied in this covert manner. Was this need-related, ESP-focused acquisition of very helpful information? Does this kind of effect support the PMIR model?

Stanford himself is uncertain about some of these experiments. He notes, for example, that the ethics of some of them were questionable, and that in some cases there were technical problems which impaired the acceptability of their author's conclusions (to discuss these would require far more space than we have at our disposal, so we will simply accept Stanford's reservations). As one example of a finding which Stanford suggests does not truly make sense within the PMIR idea, Braud reported that the degree to which students appeared to extract information by ESP was inversely related to how well they scored on the questions for which they did *not* receive this hidden extra help. Braud suggested that this supported the PMIR idea. Students who had not revised well, or who were not very bright (and thus didn't score well on the non-ESP questions) would have a stronger need to use ESP and thus would be expected to show more evidence of ESP. This sounds reasonable, but as Stanford suggests, actually it isn't. Some students who do badly in exams are drop-outs or don't care much anyway. On the other hand, some of the real swots really do care — it's very important for them to succeed. So the picture is not clear-cut. A finding which seemed at first sight to support PMIR does not actually do so, in Stanford's opinion. Stanford also points out that students may have wondered what the sealed package below their answer forms was. Might they not have guessed that *something* was going on? Were these truly non-aware psi tests?

Obviously, if we had studies which clearly varied the strength of some salient need, and showed that ESP performance was related to the strength of that need, we would have better support for the PMIR theory. A word of warning, however: psychologists (and ordinary people for that matter) are well aware that, under conditions of excessive need, performance in tests of skill tends to deteriorate. Exactly how this occurs depends on the type of test, the conditions, and the need/drive in question, but the basic principle is that excessive need levels tend to produce over-arousal, stress effects, and impaired performance. So the relationship between need strength and ESP strength may not be a simple one; psychology gives us advance warning on that score (why do desperately impoverished people not manage to use ESP to win lotteries or football pools?). Keeping this in mind, let us consider one of Stanford's own experiments in a little more detail.

Stanford tested male volunteers with a simple word-association experiment, asking each volunteer to give the first word that came into his head in response to each of a set of words. If the volunteer produced an unusual (very fast or very slow) reponse to a randomly chosen key word in the test, he was invited to take part in a second

In an exam the need for answer-relevant information is very clear. Students who want to do well are strongly motivated to acquire extra information. If, as experiments suggest, ESP can be used unintentionally to access information hidden in the exam room itself, why should it not be used to gain information from sources outside it?

The floor of the Wall Street Stock Exchange, an information-saturated, psi-suppressing environment if ever there was one. There have been studies of psi being used, with some success, to play the stock and commodities markets.

'experiment'. The volunteers were not aware of the significance of a very fast or very slow response to the key words, so this was a test of non-aware psi.

The second 'experiment' simply invited the men to rate the attractiveness of a number of young women photographed in various stages of undress (for most men a pleasant enough way to pass a short period of time). Stanford reasoned that the prospect of doing this (sensed at a non-aware level) would motivate performance in the earlier word-association test. He also had half the men in the word-association test tested by a male experimenter and the other half by a female experimenter. Why? A woman doing the testing might encourage sexual thoughts or feelings and so produce a stronger ESP effect.

What happened? Very fast and very slow responses to key words were especially marked when the female experimenter was doing the testing! The only way the volunteers could have chosen the 'right' responses in the word-association test was to use unintentional ESP. ESP told them which response would obtain a pleasant reward. The strength of their need to obtain that reward was manipulated by the sex of the experimenter.

More studies of this kind are badly needed. Stanford's study has not been replicated by other researchers as yet, so while this result is a tantalizing and intriguing one, we cannot be certain of its reliability until other researchers have added their findings to it.

Using PK to satisfy needs

What about the PK side of the PMIR model? We have some evidence that ESP can be used to detect need-related information and that need strength may be related to its use. Is there any evidence that PK can be used to satisfy a need if normal channels of doing so are closed? In terms of the PMIR model, if the only way PMIR can achieve its goal is by using a 'paranormal response' is that what will happen? In the experiment described above, a non-paranormal response (word association) was sufficient to satisfy the need, but in one of Stanford's most remarkable experiments this was not so.

Forty men, tested individually, were given a short conscious PK test with a Schmidt machine at the start of their testing. Afterwards, they were told that they would be taking part in a psychology experiment on the co-ordination of movement. This consisted of a 'pursuit rotor tracking' test, which involves keeping a small pointer or some similar indicator in the middle of a track which moves slightly from side to side. Stanford set the movement of the track to be slow, so that the task would be very tedious. Each volunteer was told to expect 45 minutes of this boredom.

Meanwhile, unknown to the volunteers and at some distance from them, Stanford had set up an REG which produced ten pulses at 10-second intervals, divided between six different channels. This machine ticked over while each volunteer was trying to concentrate on his pursuit rotor tracking. If, at any time, the machine produced at least seven out of ten pulses in one of the channels (a very unlikely event — we know exactly how often this will occur by chance), a signal was relayed to another experimenter to go and release the volunteer and take him off to another room. Here, as you might have guessed, he was shown pictures of scantily clad young women.

In a nutshell, then, an experiment has been set up in which people are being bored out of their wits. If a machine, in a distant place, does something very unusual and strange, they will escape from their boredom and do something much more pleasant. If the machine behaves normally, they are condemned to 45 minutes of boredom. So the need here is the need to escape and avoid being bored. The volunteers *can* escape if the machine behaves strangely but, since they don't even know the machine is there or that it has any bearing on what is happening to them, they must use ESP to find out. Since the probability of the machine behaving strangely is small, their only way of escaping is to use PK to bias the machine. So the experiment very neatly corresponds to the PMIR model: ESP detection motivated by need, PK response in the service of that need.

The results of this experiment were clear-cut indeed. The volunteers as a whole performed only slightly above chance on the first stage, the conscious PK test. On the non-intentional PK test, however, they scored well above chance. If chance alone had been at work, some 7.2% of them would have escaped; in the event, 20% did so. This gives quite strong support to the PMIR theory. It is also interesting that the men scored better on the non-intentional PK test than on the intentional one. Perhaps psi effects in real life are often stronger than those that can be elicited in the laboratory.

Was this an accident waiting to happen from the moment the driver decided not to take his usual delivery route? Or did ESP tell him that something worse was going to happen on his usual route?

'So *that's* why I did it...'

Stanford's model also has anecdotal support. The PMIR notion suggests that full-blown recognition of information detected by ESP may be the exception rather than the norm. Instead, ESP may influence behavior in such a way as to satisfy some need without a person ever realizing that anything untoward has happened. Waking up in the morning and thinking 'That was a precognitive dream!' or seeing an apparition of a person at the time of his or her death may be tip-of-the-iceberg cases only. Psi may be much more common.

Let's take two simple examples. A friend of one of the authors was in the habit of taking walks around Cambridge, always following a

favored and scenic route. On one occasion he was mulling over making some wine at home, and pondered this during his exercise. For once — and this was something he never did — he changed his usual route, his thoughts playing on other matters of no particular consequence, not really watching where he was going until he ended up...outside a wine shop. As it happened, there were some crates of empty bottles there which were about to be thrown away, and a swift enquiry allowed him to carry off a good haul of empty bottles which he then used for his wine-making. Coincidence of course. Or was it 'luck'? Isn't 'luck' another term for the effective use of psi?

Stanford himself gives another example. He and his wife were driving home from the opera one evening and, at one point in their journey, needed to turn off a major expressway in order to get home. Just before the turn, Stanford felt a very strong urge not to make it; he wanted to carry on along the expressway into the area of a neighboring bay and watch ducks and geese. Although Stanford and his wife are enthusiastic bird-watchers, this urge was clearly irrational since it was nearly midnight! Stanford wondered whether this might not have been PMIR at work, so he decided to take the turnoff, which he had an irrational urge *not* to do. Wondering whether need-related PMIR had tried to steer him away from some danger on the road, he drove slowly and with excessive caution. Sure enough, not far along the turnoff there was a major road hazard.

Now, in both these cases what *was not* consciously recognized was the factor relevant to need. Our friend did not suddenly think 'Wow! Free wine bottles at the wine shop!' and head off in that direction, and Stanford did not sense the nature of the road hazard. Instead, what was detected by ESP triggered a response which helped the individual get to, or away from, what was need-related (approach to the desired wine bottles, avoidance of the road hazard). As Stanford points out, if he hadn't deliberately bucked his urge to take an alternative route, he would never have known about the hazard. How often does psi steer us away from dangerous situations?

The details of Stanford's theory contain many predictions about just how this indirect type of effect is most likely to occur. Reviewing all the postulates of the theory is beyond us here, but here are a few examples which will bring out more of the flavor of it.

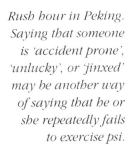

Rush hour in Peking. Saying that someone is 'accident prone', 'unlucky', or 'jinxed' may be another way of saying that he or she repeatedly fails to exercise psi.

Stanford suggests that what ESP can trigger in the way of thoughts, impressions, and behavior will be similar in kind to what other unconscious, or more accurately *pre-conscious*, detections can also trigger. In experiments, this means that ESP effects should show a similarity to the effects of *subliminally* perceived stimuli. Subliminal stimuli are ones which are displayed for such a short time (perhaps one-hundredth of a second or so) that they are not consciously recognized, but which nonetheless can affect our thoughts, memories, and behavior.

Testing this notion is not at all simple, for the reason that the study of subliminal perception in psychology is a real minefield. However, Stanford has surveyed the results of a handful of good experiments (conducted by other experimenters) which have compared people's performance in very similar subliminal and ESP tasks and found that overall there *is* a relationship between the two. That is to say, people who score high on subliminal testing also score high on ESP testing when the nature of the testing is very similar for both modalities. The correlation is weak, but it is beyond chance limits, which lends support to Stanford's theory. There seems to be some definite continuity between how we react to stimuli below our level of conscious awareness and how we react to those which are only accessible by extrasensory means.

Stanford further suggests that there are particular types of response which may be more successful than others as vehicles for PMIR, responses which are in some way 'primed' and ready to be triggered by ESP. From real life, Stanford gives the example of a person who dialled a friend and obtained a wrong number — finding someone in distress on the other end of the telephone, and in need of medical help. The person was able to summon such help. The mistake made was a simple one-digit change. Such mistakes are 'primed' in that they are moderately likely to occur. Such 'ready and available' responses may be the most likely to be triggered by PMIR. This claim has some support from word-association tests with hidden ESP components, although given the technical nature of the findings and the need for further research we won't go into the details here. Once more, the fine-grain detail of Stanford's theory holds up well in some subtle and sophisticated research.

'...and why I didn't'

Stanford's theory also contains a range of predictions about why there will be limits to PMIR, some of which we have already touched on. First, circumstances may effectively box people in and prevent PMIR from occurring. Consider a person who has booked an expensive plane flight and, shortly beforehand, gets a strong urge to travel by train instead, or do something that will prevent him catching the plane. Let's assume that the plane is going to crash and that PMIR is screaming at him not to catch the flight. However, having spent a large sum of money and probably needing to get to his destination at the required time, that person is highly unlikely to cancel. Even if he is very uneasy (strong PMIR), he'll rationalize his feelings as pre-flight nerves. Other factors may have boxed him in still further — checking train times to get to the airport and making arrangements to get a taxi to get to the rail station well ahead of time may leave PMIR little chance for generating some kind of 'mistake' which might save his skin. One can see how circumstance may simply not allow the right kind of response to manifest itself.

Commuter routines and tight schedules may override responses to ESP-acquired information.

There are many other psychological factors which might have the same PMIR-

'Five minutes to spare...'. A lifestyle governed by the clock is not conducive to psi.

dampening effect. Need strength is one we've already noted; if a person is too needy, PMIR might malfunction, even generating the equivalent of psi-missing in everyday life. Need conflicts and personality factors might also have inhibiting effects. A neurotic man, for example, might use PMIR to engineer an encounter with a pretty woman but not in such a way as to bring about the real possibility of sexual involvement; he is too anxious about sex to want it in a wholehearted way.

Further factors suggest themselves. Elements of rigidity in behavior will inhibit PMIR; unvarying routines and prefigured plans will prevent PMIR-influenced changes (Stanford gives the droll example of someone saying: 'Don't talk to me about going with you to the art exhibit; I have been planning for six months to take my dog for a shampoo today'). Strong preoccupations will also inhibit PMIR; if you're on Chapter 33 of a 35-chapter thriller, with the dénouement beckoning, nothing is going to drag you away!

These are commonsense suggestions, and while there is experimental evidence in support of some of them, their greatest force is felt outside the laboratory. After all, the PMIR theory was designed to dovetail laboratory and real-life psi events.

Brain, bias, and lability

Stanford's model throws interesting light on evidence we have already visited. For example, it offers an alternative understanding of why altered states of consciousness, such as hypnosis, dreams, and the ganzfeld, may enhance psi. Rather than attributing psi effects to a reduction of internal and external 'noise', Stanford offers an explanation in terms of spontaneity and lability (openness to change). William Braud has elaborated on this view.

Stanford suggests that a characteristic of altered states is that they undo the many factors that seem to inhibit psi generally. People in altered states are not preoccupied with what they have to do there and then, or right after the experiment, or next week; they are not boxed in by circumstances which prevent psi expression. What altered states seem to do is reduce a specific factor known as *stereotypy*. This technical term is fairly easily illustrated. In simple ESP card-guessing experiments, people tend to have certain characteristic biases when giving responses. They rarely repeat the same symbol on successive guesses (this *alternation bias* is very strongly ingrained with people in a wide variety of psychological settings), they tend to balance guesses across symbol types, and they tend to show slight preferences for certain symbols over others, notably the circle (if playing cards were being used, the Ace of Spades would be guessed more than one time in 52!). There is evidence that such biases and rigidities are reduced and weakened in altered states of consciousness. Stanford suggests that it is this, rather than noise reduction, which may explain their psi-boosting effects. He himself analyzed ESP card experiment results and found that subjects who showed one particular stereotyped bias (making fairly even numbers of guesses for different symbols) showed less evidence of ESP than those who made responses of more unequal, spontaneous patterns.

It may be that the Honorton noise-reduction model and Stanford's spontaneity model are not incompatible. Honorton's model was couched in terms of external (world) noise and body (muscular, visceral) noise; Stanford's model might add additional understanding of what occurs in the brain. Stanford himself has conducted some highly technical ganzfeld ESP experiments in order to try and resolve the two models. These did not yield strongly consistent results, and the later experiments tended to show only chance effects. Without any independent replication, it is difficult to know what to make of them. The issue is still unresolved.

In the PMIR model we have a subtle and sophisticated account of how psi may function in everyday life. It makes predictions which have been moderately well supported by experiments — although, alas, we must once again say that much more research is needed. It attempts to draw together laboratory psi and psi in the real world. And it offers many avenues for future exploration. But now we must leave such prospects behind and address the fundamental question: 'If psi exists, how does it work?'

The physics of psi

Sceptics often maintain that psi is impossible because it is incompatible with known physical laws. This view, of course, rests on the belief that physical 'laws' are true, 100.000% true, and true for all time. This belief, set against the history of scientific thought, is no more than a vulnerable assumption. Moreover, as we shall see, there are models which propose that psi is, at the very least, compatible with what is currently known in terms of physics. First, however, let us review what parapsychologists would consider is known with some confidence about psi from the physical standpoint.

At the heart of our knowledge, alas, is a mystery: we don't know how psi works. On the other hand, experiments have produced effects which cannot reasonably be explained as chance or artifacts (we shall review the case for this statement thoroughly in our final chapter) and which, according to the rules of scientific method, must be accepted as genuine anomalies, real effects. We can measure the strength of these effects, as well as the influence on them of other measurable factors such as personality, belief, and altered states of consciousness. We find that these effects can be strengthened through such procedures as the majority-vote procedure (as Ryzl used with Stepanek) or the more exotic 'PK bit sampling' procedure ingeniously devised by Dean Radin. We find that working models of these effects, Honorton's noise-reduction model or Stanford's PMIR model, have scientific coherence and produce testable predictions. Psi can be affected, positively, negatively, and without conscious awareness, by human intention. There are some ways, however, in which psi appears difficult to construe as any kind of human sense (precognition being an obvious example). If psi were like a signal, as the noise-reduction model in particular implies (and as the affinity with subliminal perception does too), what known source of energy could be responsible for transmitting it?

The cybernetic model

Let us begin by considering a working model which scientists have used to describe human perception and action: the cybernetic model, the human machine, the brain-as-computer. In such a model, information reaches the brain through the senses. This information is conveyed to us by some physical carrier signal (such as light rays, which set off chemical changes in the retina). The brain then decodes that information (psychologists differ on the degree of activity the brain shows in interpreting or *constructing* the meaning of such information, and obviously the brain filters out a lot of incoming information too). If there is some need to act on that information, or on information stored from previously apprehended signals, the brain organizes and despatches messages along the nerves appropriate to the action it wishes to undertake: information flows from brain to skeletal muscles, organs, glands, hormone systems, and so on. Although this is simplistically put, the human organism is seen as a receiver of information, conveyed by a physical transmission medium, which processes the information and acts upon it as appropriate.

Is it possible to examine psi as a function of this putative human machine? Although Rhine claimed that psi was 'non-physical', meaning that one couldn't examine psi as part of this robot-man, it was he who coined the term *extrasensory* perception, and what a value judgement *that* term involves! We are conditioned by language to think of ESP as some special, extra kind of *perception* and to a lesser extent to think

Opposite: The Cockcroft-Walton generator at the Fermi National Accelerator Laboratory in Chicago. If even a millionth of the money spent on investigating the behavior of sub-atomic particles had been spent on investigating ESP, many of the phenomena described in this book would be better understood.

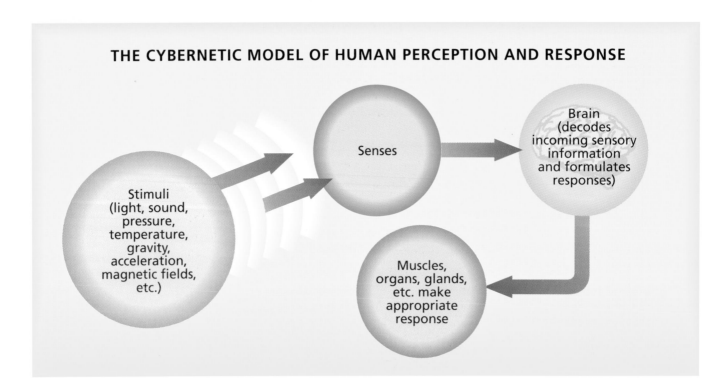

THE CYBERNETIC MODEL OF HUMAN PERCEPTION AND RESPONSE

Stimuli
(light, sound,
pressure,
temperature,
gravity,
acceleration,
magnetic fields,
etc.)

Senses

Brain
(decodes
incoming sensory
information
and formulates
responses)

Muscles,
organs, glands,
etc. make
appropriate
response

of PK as some special, extra kind of *action*. Our first instinct with ESP is to think of it as a perceptual process and to look for some kind of physical transmission medium for it, something analogous to the light rays which bring information to our eyes. It is ironic that this is, in a sense, opposite to Rhine's intention in coining the term 'extrasensory perception'.

The wiring of the human computer. These are neurones (nerve cells) in the cerebral cortex of the human brain. The yellow blobs are cell bodies, which communicate with one another via a tangle of connections called axons and dendrites.

Now, there are some sound reasons for considering that it may not be possible (or, at least, it is extremely unlikely) for *any* known physical carrier to mediate ESP effects. Rather than bore the reader with the results of some spectacularly under-achieving research that tried to pin down the effects of electromagnetism on psi, let us get down to basics. Take, for example, experiments on what is termed 'blind PK'. In these experiments people wish for a high score on the target face of a thrown die, *but they are not told what this target face is*. They simply have to wish for the right outcome, whatever that may be. Hence, by the cybernetic model, the only way they can find out which face to wish for is by using ESP. Since ESP is hardly as reliable as simply being told which face to aim for, it is clear that by the cybernetic model one would expect scoring rates to be lower in blind PK than in other PK tests with dice. This has not been the case.

As the thoughtful reader will probably have realized, the experiments discribed in the last chapter go further. In non-intentional psi experiments, people do not know they are being tested for psi. Considering matters from the cybernetic model standpoint, an experiment where someone has to use ESP to figure out *anything* relevant to the psi test and then use PK to influence matters would not be expected to be very successful, since so much has to be done. Yet, if anything, the strength of psi effects in such studies is greater than in comparable forced-choice psi tests where people know exactly what they're supposed to be doing.

There is a possible escape route here if we want to retain the cybernetic model with its signal-carrier element. Perhaps some other factor compensates for the expected reduction in blind PK and non-intentional psi experiments. Perhaps, for example, the fact that people don't know they're being tested, or can do nothing more than give themselves up to hoping for the best in some vague wishful way in blind PK tests, means that they are not prone to test anxiety. And anxiety is unfavorable for psi. Could this factor balance out the increased difficulty factor of having to learn what the test goal is with ESP?

This is a weak argument and can be readily refuted by considering one of Schmidt's many machine-PK experiments. When asked to bias the output of an REG, subjects were actually shown the mixed output of two different REGs. One of these was a simple binary device, another a much more complicated machine which sampled many pulses and in effect took a majority vote of the most common pulse type before deciding which binary output to deliver. The scoring rates on the outputs of both machine types were the same. In other words the scoring rate appeared independent of the complexity of the system PK was affecting. This is wholly unexpected from any cybernetic model and since the psychological conditions were the same for the two machines we cannot claim that anxiety or any other such factor was operating with respect to one machine and not the other.

So the cybernetic working model of perception and action has some problems when faced with psi, and there are further characteristics of psi which cause further difficulties, as we shall now see.

Psi at a distance

Actually, to be mischievious, let us start with something which does *not* cause a problem for a physical signal-carrier model of psi, although some skeptics have erroneously claimed that it does. To summarize many experiments, there is no evidence that increasing the distance between a person and the object or event he is attempting to sense via ESP has any effect on scoring rates. The most dramatic demonstration of long-distance ESP remains, of course, the remarkable ESP experiment carried out by Apollo astronaut Ed Mitchell in which, despite the scores of thousand of miles between him and the subjects he attempted to send telepathic messages to, results suggestive of ESP were obtained.

To be sure, very few systematic comparisons of psi over varying distances, eliminating the effects of psychological expectancy, have been conducted. The most notable exception

was a large study by Karlis Osis, of the American Society for Psychical Research. In these experiments, Osis made sure that telepathy test percipients had no knowledge of the location of senders (who were up to 1,000 miles distant), thus removing any effect of belief (people might have *expected* to score lower with increasing distance). As it happened, there *was* a small, but significant, decline of ESP scoring with increasing distance in this study, but the effect really was small. There have been quite a few successful studies with distances of 100, 1,000, or more miles separating sender and receiver.

Is this a problem for the signal-carrier model? Not at all, and skeptics who have asserted that it is are simply wrong. Just think of your radio. With a powerful enough signal, detection does not vary much over hundreds of miles, and with a suitably sensitive radio, using the right fine-tuning and signal-optimizing technology, attenuation of signal detection with distance is minimal. The independence of ESP from physical distance factors is not a problem! But other findings do present significant difficulties for a physical-carrier model of psi — and, of course, if PK effects are independent of distance (and there is enough evidence of long-distance PK for us to wonder about this), then a physical basis for the active effects of PK would be difficult to imagine.

Physical properties of targets

Research shows that the physical properties of targets used in ESP tests have little or no effect on scoring rates (independent of any psychological factors associated with physical differences). There have been successful reports of ESP being used to detect targets on microfilm, for example. From the earliest days of ESP testing, success was reported with a procedure known as the DT (Down Through) test, in which people guessed the order of 25 ESP cards in a sealed pack. The cards are stacked one on top of the other. It is hard to imagine any kind of sensing, or physical carrier signal, which would not be subject to considerable confusion with such extreme proximity of targets.

Turning to PK, there are similar problems here. In dice PK experiments, for example, scoring rates remain unaffected by the weight of the dice, or by the materials from which the dice are made. Add in the 'complexity independence' of Schmidt's two-machine experiment, and one can see that the problems for partisans of the signal-carrier model are accumulating very swiftly.

The time barrier

Of all psi phenomena, precognition is the one which causes the biggest headaches. More than one physicist has been known to state that telepathy is really no problem for his way of thinking, but precognition is another kettle of fish altogether. If an event precedes its cause in time — if the information exists in the future — then it seems highly unreasonable to look for any physical carrier signal as a basis for precognition. While we have no sound comparisons of precognition over varying time intervals (available evidence from experiments is rather scrappy), the fact that precognition exists at all is a bad enough headache. Unless...

Unless what appears to be precognition is actually PK. Instead of predicting the order of ESP cards in a pack at some future time (for example), might it not be possible to use PK to bias that order when the cards are shuffled or otherwise randomized? Rhine, in his own precognition research, was aware of this problem and devised a 'weather key', a random determination of targets which would be triggered by a temperature variable at a distant location some time after the guesses were made. It was actually suggested that perhaps the subjects in these precognition experiments were using PK to influence weather systems hundreds or thousands of miles away, but this is a fairly mind-boggling notion.

While such an alternative view is possible, we are inclined to reject it because of spontaneous cases of precognition. What of the numerous precognitions of the Aberfan

Opposite: Edgar D. Mitchell moonwalks on the hilly uplands north of Fra Mauro Crater in January 1971. His attempts to send telepathic messages to earthlings 238,900 miles away met with some success. As many experiments on earth have shown, distance does not seem to be a barrier to ESP.

Inset: Mitchell (left) with Apollo 14 mission commander Alan B. Shepard Jr. (middle) and command module pilot Stuart Roosa (right) shortly before take-off.

disaster, or that of the Flixborough explosion? Admittedly, we stated that such cases cannot provide proof of precognition, but then neither can science itself (just better evidence). To explain away precognition by invoking weather-changing, disaster-causing PK really does look like swallowing the camel while straining at the gnat. It is not logically absurd, just wildly implausible. If precognition exists, it presents insuperable problems for any model of psi which involves energy-carrying signals as a transmission medium.

Towards a new definition of psi?

Fortunately there are new theories which do not appear to suffer from some of the problems associated with the cybernetic model. These theories have been developed by physicists, and they lean heavily on the models and ways of thinking of quantum mechanics. At this stage, two warnings are in order.

As we have noted, skeptics like the psychologist C.E.M. Hansel have asserted that psi is not possible because it contradicts the laws of physics. We are psychologists, but we do not feel qualified to make such categorical assertions about physics. We frankly admit that we cannot evaluate the finer points of some of the theories we are about to discuss. What we can do, however, is examine their logic (do they make some kind of sense?) and consider whether they are scientific models (do they make testable predictions?).

The second warning is that, despite the fact that we shall concentrate on the logic of these ideas and not get bogged down in technicalities, this chapter will include some sections which are rather hard going. This is because we will be dealing with ideas which are, at times, strange to the point of perversity. At times, theories and models in sub-atomic physics are so Alice-in-Wonderland that telepathy seems almost banal by comparison (a point some physicists have actually made explicit). If some ideas seem peculiar and contrary to common sense, that's just the way it is in physics! As Einstein said: 'Quantum theory reminds me a little of the system of delusions of an exceedingly intelligent paranoiac, concocted of incoherent elements of thought.' Mercifully for us, the logic may be weird, but it is not incomprehensible. In what Paul Davies has referred to as the 'quantum madhouse' there is method.

A fuzzy world

Let us begin with a brief, and simplified, explanation of how physicists think about the Universe. For a long time the *atom* was believed to be the basic building-block of matter. Exploration of the sub-atomic level did not begin until quite recently, in historical terms. Evidence of it is around us in the form of nuclear weaponry, Three Mile Island, and Chernobyl. At school many of us were taught that the atom is composed of three different subatomic particles. The atoms of different elements are composed of differing numbers of *protons* (positively charged particles in the nucleus of the atom), *neutrons* (similarly located particles carrying no net electrical charge), and *electrons* (much smaller, negatively charged, flighty little particles which orbit the nucleus and are only 1/1800th the size of the much larger protons and neutrons therein). Different elements — the oxygen we breathe to survive, metals such as iron or aluminum, and so on — have atoms composed of different numbers of these subatomic particles. Now, as younger readers will be aware, further progress has shown that there are sub-sub-atomic particles, the hadrons and leptons, of which the *quark* (with its own subspecies) is the most notable case, giving a definite Russian-doll feel to the whole business. We'll eschew the sub-sub-atomic levels, however, since they are not germane to our argument here.

The atom with its constituent particles is easily visualized as looking rather like a miniature solar system, with the neutrons and protons imagined as a sun and the electrons as orbiting planets. Unfortunately, that neat view is nothing much like the truth.

Improbable as it may seem, certain aspects of the ways in which electrons behave show that to view them as *particles* leads to some unfortunate absurdities. It is now accepted that electrons sometimes behave as if they were particles and sometimes as if they were *waves*. To put matters more precisely, it is sometimes more useful to conceive of electrons as particles and sometimes more useful to think of them as waves.

The next problem is that in old, classical physics particles had definite properties. They had precise velocity and precise position rather, to use a famous analogy, as if the Universe were a giant billiard table. However, from the viewpoint of quantum mechanics (which with Relativity theory remains the basis of modern physics in most respects) this is not so. Before a measurement is made — before a system is observed — the properties of a particle are *indefinite*. It is the case that the particle covers, or fluctuates over, a *range*

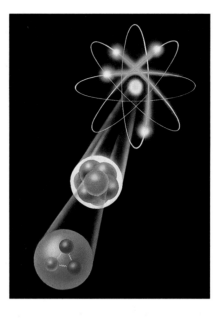

This is the neat and tidy 'particle' view of the universe. Visualized here is an atom of beryllium (only three of its five neutrons shown) with its four orbiting electrons. The protons (red) and neutrons (blue) in the nucleus each consist of three quarks. Protons have two 'up' quarks (dark blue) and one 'down' quark (green), while neutrons have one 'up' and two 'downs'.

of positions (or velocities) simultaneously. The particle's properties are fluctuating, or *fuzzy*. An analogy given by the physicist Evan Harris Walker is that of a person standing in the doorway of a house with one foot inside and one outside: he is both inside and outside the house simultaneously. Similarly, our electrons are in many places, and have many velocities, at the same time.

This 'fuzziness' of a particle in quantum mechanics is described by a *wave function*, which is a function of time and the particular properties of the particle being measured. If we are dealing with a particle which has a velocity fluctuating around an average (mean) value of 3 cm/second, for example, the wave function might look something like that shown right.

What this wave function means is that when we observe the particle (make some measurement of its velocity) we are *most likely* to observe that mean value, 3 cm/second. But we may also observe other velocity values; the further away from the mean they get, the less likely they are to be observed. This is the principle of scatter again. This is very reminiscent of psi testing and its statistical basis, of course, and indeed quantum physics might be said to be fundamentally statistical in character. Just as statistical theory produces precise equations with which to predict the chance average and scatter of scores in psi experiments (using ESP cards or falling dice or random event generators), similar equations can predict the values along the wave function of a particle.

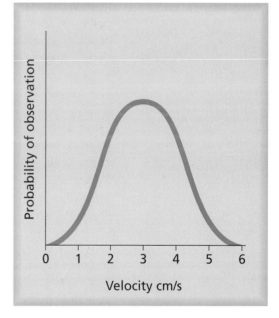

Indeed, if we make measurements on a large number of particles of the same type, with the same wave function, we find that our distribution of values looks like that of the wave function for the single particle as noted above. However, our series of measurements has the quality that *any individual observation is random*. That is, we cannot predict which value we will observe for the velocity of any individual particle, and in this respect the system is truly a random one. This, of course, is the property of nature which Schmidt and others have exploited by building their random event generators around just such a random process, the emission of electrons during the radioactive decay of Strontium-90.

Another key point to grasp here is that the particle we measure only acquires a *precise*

Any particle observed at a precise moment has a range of possible velocities which can be expressed as a wave function with a normal distribution curve.

It is the act of observation or measurement which gives a billiard ball or a sub-atomic particle a precise velocity and position. What this implies is that the observer can affect the event being observed.

velocity when we measure it. Before that time, it has no precise velocity at all, but fluctuates over a range of velocities. When we examine how we make our measurements, matters get still stranger.

The measurement problem

Let us consider an electron travelling in space, whose velocity we are about to measure using a recording meter. Common sense tells us that when we make a measurement, the meter needle shows a precise value. Unfortunately, this need not necessarily be so. The detector and the meter are themselves composed of large numbers of atoms and can thus be described in terms of a *many-particle wave function*. This odd way of looking at things is unfortunately a logical extrapolation of the logic of physics. If the velocity of the particle is indefinite (an axiom), then the position of the meter needle must needs be indefinite too. Just as the velocity of the electron is fluctuating and fuzzy, so the needle must fluctuate over a range of different possible measurements. Yet this is absurd. The needle is in one place, the observer sees a discrete value.

The measurement problem in a nutshell. The velocity of sub-atomic particle A is about to be measured at point B. Since the velocity of A is indefinite and the detector at B and the meter at C also consist of sub-atomic particles — also with indeterminate features — how can we make a single, definite measurement?

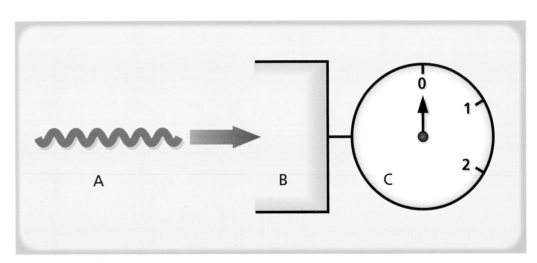

Evan Harris Walker paraphrased a famous paradox (that of Schrodinger's Cat) to express the problem here. With our meter we are trying to measure the velocity of an electron. Imagine the meter needle is attached to a hammer which is just above the head of an unfortunate rat, so that if the needle moves in one particular direction (one side of the distribution) the hammer hits and kills the miserable rodent. The velocity of the electron is indeterminate, which means that the position of the meter needle is fuzzy, i.e. the needle occupies many positions simultaneously. Our only conclusion seems to be that the rodent will be simultaneously alive (half of the possible needle positions) and dead (the other half) until the measurement is made and a discrete position for the needle is observed. This seems ludicrous, yet this 'measurement problem' remains a thorny one. The problem is this: How does a fuzzy system become a discrete measurement when observed?

Here there are differences of opinion within physics. The most popular view remains that of Nils Bohr and his colleagues. Their 'Copenhagen interpretation' asserts that macroscopic systems (such as measurement devices) cannot be considered in the same way as microscopic systems (electrons, etc.) and so cannot be discussed in quantum terms. Stripped down to basics, what this view says is that the act of measurement just happens and is not capable of deeper analysis. It just *is*. One cannot account for individual measurements, and one can only speak of the aggregate of many measurements, of the statistical whole.

There are problems with this view. First, certain physicists (notably von Neumann) have actually done a respectable job of describing measurement systems in quantum-mechanical terms, and there is no doubt that under certain conditions (especially at temperature extremes) macroscopic events become flagrantly describable in such terms. The other problem is that the Copenhagen interpretation effectively posts a sign saying 'No further understanding beyond this point'. This is not a view which is likely to hold sway indefinitely. There is a whiff of Rutherford's tutor in it.

There are alternative views. The Everett-Wheeler theory is the most extraordinary, for it postulates that the 'collapse of the wave function' (how we move from a fuzzy range of possible values to one discrete observed value in the act of measurement) doesn't happen at all. The suggestion is that all possible measurements are actually observed *somewhere*. In our universe only one possibility is observed, but in an infinite number of alternative universes an infinite number of variously varying doppelgangers of ourselves are observing all the other possible outcomes. We cannot know of them, but they exist, and the infinite number of universes grows by an infinite (or incalculably large) number with every passing second

The idea that psi emanates from alternative selves living in indefinitely multiplying other universes is entertaining but hardly testable.

This model has been taken sufficiently seriously to be discussed in learned scientific journals, but as one commentator has observed: 'Although this is a complete and consistent picture, it is a rather unsettling one, with no means to test its validity.' It is a bizarre irony that John Wheeler, a physicist associated with this model, has had the audacity to petition the American Association for the Advancement of Science to exclude the Parapsychological Association from its ranks, begging the AAAS (unsuccessfully) to throw out the 'weirdos from the workshop of science'. In the course of his campaign Wheeler made a groundless attack on the integrity of J.B. Rhine, which he later

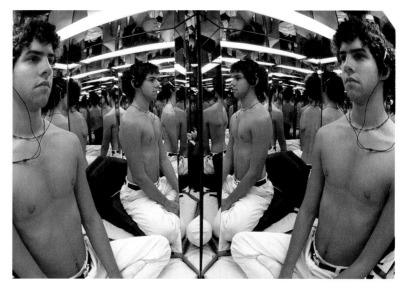

apologized for. Yet one would be hard put to find anything as bizarre in all of parapsychology as the 'many universes' theory!

From our viewpoint, the many universes theory does not seem to offer much relevance to psi, simply because as an almost wholly untestable notion it does not help us to advance our knowledge or understanding of psi. However, a third category of explanation for the collapse of the wave function (sometimes referred to as collapse of the *state vector*) is of more interest. Many physicists have pondered that there must somehow be 'hidden variables' in the quantum system which are required to give the full description of it which might resolve the measurement problem, and which are responsible for the collapse of the wave function. What are they? Many years' search for them at the physical level having proved unsuccessful, the suspicion began to be entertained that they might be found in the operations of human consciousness itself. In 1961 American physicist Eugene Wigner proposed this in a speculative manner, and in 1967 ventured the idea more seriously. This school of thought remains a heterodox one in physics, but it is a point of view which is proposed by a reasonable minority of theoreticians.

There are reasons for thinking that some affinity with parapsychology might be found here. After all, any set of ideas which accepts an important role for the observer making the measurement, and a possible role for the consciousness of that observer, would appear to open the door to psi events. In this connection, we can look at a further strange aspect of measurement. Imagine two particles, bound together by some inter- or intra-atomic binding force. Now, imagine this dyad being split up by an explosion, such that the two particles fly off in opposite directions. Imagine further that we place detectors (measuring devices) to measure their velocities as shown below.

Action at a distance. The two-particle dyad AB is split by an explosion, and A and B fly off in opposite directions. If the velocity of A is measured at X, by the law of conservation of momentum the velocity of B will be known also, without needing to measure it at Y. In collapsing the wave function of A by the act of measuring its velocity, the wave function of B is also collapsed.

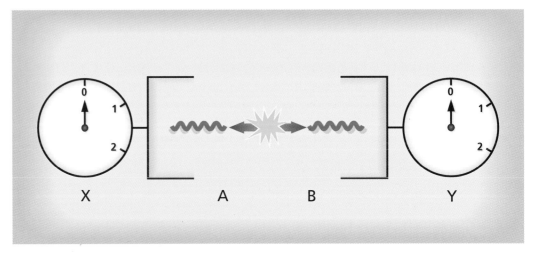

When particle A is observed we will 'see' a finite velocity (say, 4 cm/second). The state vector for particle A has been collapsed in the measurement process. But the law of conservation of momentum states that, under these conditions, particle B will have a momentum equal and opposite to that of particle A. Thus, a measurement of the velocity of A also collapses the state vector of particle B, since once A has been measured we know exactly what the value of B will be. This is *action at a distance*. The 'distant collapse' of the state vector of B by an observation made at a spatial distance from it (and that distance can be of any value within this paradox) illustrates the problem that the quantum-mechanical state vector is *non-local*, i.e. not confined to a small region of space. Such distant collapse will occur when an observer deals with two (or more) systems which have interacted in the past (and are therefore said to be 'correlated systems'). In our example, the correlation was caused by the particles having been at one time bound together.

This is the famous Einstein-Podolsky-Rosen (EPR) paradox and its implications are simple, but profound. An observer can affect an event taking place at almost any distance away from him, in principle. If an observer has any influence on the observation made at A, he has an equal effect on the state vector of the correlated, distant system. Thus, collapse of the state vector is *spatially invariant* (i.e. distance doesn't matter). In certain treatments of this paradox the state vector collapse can have features of *temporal invariance* into the bargain (that is, just as space doesn't matter, time doesn't matter either). We are dealing with observation effects which are not limited by space or time constraints. Now, all this has a definite echo of psi events, thought of in a different framework to the everyday common sense and intuition most people employ.

This is perhaps as far as many physicists who do not find parapsychology problematic are prepared to go. They would suggest that (a) quantum mechanics is an uncertain enough business to prevent anyone calling psi events impossible, and spatial and temporal invariance do indeed appear to allow psi events to occur, and (b) the classical 'measurement problem' in quantum mechanics may well require a better understanding of the observer before it is better resolved, and perhaps consciousness may play a part in this (although this is where many such physicists tend to grow uneasy). Certain physicists have, however, gone further. Nobel laureate Brian Josephson has stated that, if psi events had not been reported, an imaginative theoretician could have predicted from quantum theory that they should occur! Olivier Costa de Beauregard has gone further still and stated that the most fundamental axioms of quantum mechanics demand that psi events *must* occur as a result of the spatial and temporal invariance elements of the EPR paradox.

These claims would be interesting enough, but Evan Harris Walker in particular has gone further and generated a theory which is part good physics, part plausible intuition, and part fairly wild speculation, but which makes some clear predictions about psi phenomena. It is also undoubtedly the case that the quantum-mechanical (QM) models of psi help us to understand some puzzling psi effects in new and simple ways, and have also generated at least one entirely new type of truly mind-boggling psi effect. The experimental impact of these theories is intriguing. Let us pursue Walker's line of thinking (which has also been developed, with variations, by several other theoreticians) a little further and then mention some intriguing findings which suggest that his theory, extravagant as it may seem, is capable of producing fresh and startling insights.

Consciousness and the physical world

Walker's theory attempts to deal with the three crucial variables in a psi experiment: the observer, the observation, and the observed system. In his model, they become Consciousness, Feedback, and Randomness. How?

First, Walker has a theory about interactions between the physical brain and the (physically unmeasurable) Mind, or Consciousness (Walker often uses the term 'will' here, but this carries certain connotations which are unhelpful at this stage). Randomness enters the picture because the brain, with its staggering complexity, contains many random or quasi-random processes or elements of processes. Consciousness is capable of producing powerful effects on the function of the brain by collapsing the state vectors of these processes. Thus, the Mind/brain interaction is, for Walker, symmetrical with the Mind/quantum system interaction. It is just that one occurs within the body and the other occurs outside it.

This might seem bizarre. We are not accustomed to think of our brains as random event generators (unless, perhaps, when we dream or have over-indulged in alcohol). However, Walker's model postulates only a few such basic processes, most notably QM 'electron tunnelling' at the synapses (junctions) between nerve cells. This is plausible enough, given the physical constraints of the synaptic system (at least, it is not clearly implausible). Further, we might take note that scientists such as Sir John Eccles, winner of a Nobel prize for his work on central nervous system function, has similar ideas so far as Consciousness-brain interactions are concerned. By affecting just a few random brain processes, a cascade of subsequent effects can be generated through neural connections, and Consciousness can create powerful changes in brain function. We are not entirely certain that Walker says anything about this process other than the fact that it happens, but we are entitled to ask if it has implications for psi.

Feedback is simply shorthand for the way in which Consciousness is coupled to the observation act, in terms of information flow from the observation to the Mind. In variants of the QM model of psi, this factor exerts a crucial effect on limiting psi events (no feedback, no psi event can be triggered). We will discuss this further below.

Finally, it is of course essential to Walker's theory, for technical reasons, that Consciousness should be capable of operating non-locally. That is, it can interact with a physical system which it is observing, and is not simply confined to the brain itself.

Consciousness and the physical world. The act of observing a measurement may not be confined to seeing the value registered on the measuring device. Random processes in the brain may interact not only with sub-atomic events in the measuring device, but also with the events being measured.

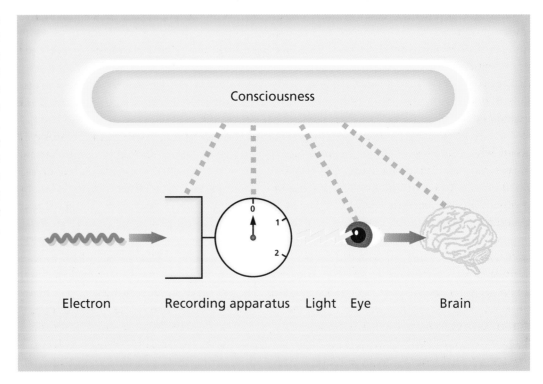

This is the basic nature of the model, then. Consciousness can influence random events directly both within and outside the body, by playing some key role in the collapse of the state vector(s) of those events in the act of observation. Now let us see what specific predictions and tests follow from this model.

Observing and influencing

Almost all QM models of psi make a simple prediction: if one does not observe a system, then one cannot affect it. If Consciousness is not linked to state vector collapse through a role in the act of observation, it will not be influential on that collapse. In the case of psi experiments, this means that if a person does not see anything of the results of an experiment, that person cannot use psi to affect the results. This prediction leads to a re-interpretation of some old experiments, clears up some apparent problems about psi, makes clear predictions, and generates some thorny paradoxes into the bargain.

Re-interpretations Just who does produce the psi in successful experiments? The obvious answer, of course, is that the subjects do. QM theories state that this may be so, but if the subjects do not see the results, then they *cannot* have produced the significant results. As an example, we might consider the long-distance ESP studies of Karlis Osis we referred to earlier. Since the subjects never got details of the results, but the experimenters did (through checking and scoring the test results), the theory suggests that the subjects could *not* have produced the psi. It must have been the people who got the feedback — the experimenters!

However, matters are not so simple. Consider again Rex Stanford's PMIR experiments. Here, subjects may not have received feedback concerning the key responses they made in the secret psi tests, but they *did* receive information deriving from the *consequences* of those responses (e.g. if successful, they got a rewarding experience). The key issue here becomes this: What exactly is a measurement and how exactly does feedback operate? Generally, QM theories suggest that optimal feedback is a guess-by-guess, target-by-target replay of the whole experiment, nitty-gritty detail. However, weaker feedback can take the form of summary scores for the person's test, or even a wink from an experimenter as if to say 'well done'.

QM theories do contain a number of clearly specified predictions about scoring rates in psi experiments as a function of the type, and amount, of feedback produced, but they tend to do this in a simple mathematical way, defining information in mathematical terms. This is fine, but it may not actually account for all sources and pathways of feedback in experimental settings. Without getting bogged down in mathematical equations, the point to note here is that the feedback postulates of QM theories make specific assertions about who can trigger psi events and, in the case of existing data, they suggest that psi events may not have been caused by the people to whom they are attributed. Since isolating the true psi sources in experiments is obviously important for being able to control and replicate the effects, QM theories hold out the hope of more repeatable experiments in future.

Walker has also been able to re-interpret the results of some complex early dice-PK experiments in terms of his particular version of the QM model. The interest here is that the results were obtained some years previously by a Swedish engineer who had his own theory of what should happen in these studies! The *placement effects* in these experiments were subtle and complex and we do not want to get bogged down in the technical details (for interested readers, the Bibliography has the relevant sources). We wish simply to note that QM theories have been productive in offering alternative understandings of data we thought we understood first time around.

Explanations QM theory is able to explain some experimental findings which have long proved to be extremely puzzling for parapsychology. A classic example here is the so-called *checker effect*.

In a series of three classic ESP experiments Robert Brier and Sarah Feather (Rhine's daughter) observed that the person who checked (scored and tallied) the results of a card-guessing experiment strongly affected the results. Different checkers found quite different patterns of scoring, despite the fact that the subjects in the experiment knew nothing about the checkers (or vice versa) or about the results of the experiments.

This puzzling phenomenon has subsequently been exhaustively analyzed by researchers following in the Feather-Brier tradition at the Foundation for Research on the Nature of Man. The reason why these effects must be taken seriously is that they have proved to be remarkably consistent across series of experiments. They are not after-the-fact, *post hoc* findings of questionable statistical value which have been dredged up from old data. And an especially disturbing aspect of the checker effect is that it appears to exist even when some considerable time — even years — has elapsed between collecting the data (recording guesses and targets) and checking the results.

From a conventional viewpoint, we have to go through some strange mental contortions to explain such an effect, How can a future analyzer of the results, utterly unknown to the subjects in an experiment, who looks at the data weeks or months ahead affect the ESP test performance of the subjects when they make their responses? In Walker's theory, however, there is no problem with this. It follows from the temporal and spatial invariance aspects of the measurement issue in QM. Future observers of an event can play a role in the collapse of the state vector because there is temporal invariance in that process. A thorny problem for conventional analysis is no problem at all for QM models (although they may differ as to how far future observers can play a role as vector-influencing agents, as we shall see later).

Predictions Here we come to one of the great triumphs of the QM models. The temporal invariance element in state vector collapse has inspired the experimental investigations of a unique phenomenon, *retro-PK*.

Let us explain what we mean by this term by considering one of Schmidt's remarkable and beautiful experiments on this theme. Schmidt arranged for an REG machine to be triggered so as to generate a series of binary random numbers which were stored on magnetic tape and not observed in any way, by anyone, at the time. Hours or days later, Schmidt arranged for subjects to listen, over headphones, to series of clicks which appeared in either the left- or right-hand channel, depending on the output of the binary REG for each pulse. They were asked to concentrate on wishing for a higher frequency of clicks in one ear than the other (which would happen if the REG output was biased to one channel rather than the other). Since the nature of the clicks was determined by the output of the REG, to succeed in their task the subjects had to use PK to influence the output of the machine *in the past*, at the time when it was actually generating the pulses stored on the magnetic tape.

The results of this experiment showed strongly above-chance scoring and retro-PK results have been reported subsequently by Schmidt and by several other researchers. The retro effect appears to be well documented now, illustrating how the QM models have had the classical scientific merit of predicting entirely new and hitherto unsuspected experimental results. This kind of experiment would not have been dreamed up from other models of how psi might work.

Walker's model (and, we believe, most QM models) makes a further prediction. If the psychological states of the subjects in these experiments had been measured at the time when the REG was triggered and again at the time of feedback (when they actually heard the clicks, in the Schmidt retro-PK experiment), then only their psychology at the latter instant would have been important. It would not be difficult to use manipulations of, say, anxiety levels, to test this prediction. We are not aware of this aspect of QM theory having been satisfactorily tested, and yet we have another clear prediction here which surely requires testing, and could be done quite easily.

Paradox Just as the spatio-temporal invariance element of QM models has become one of their great insights and strengths (as in generating the retro-PK experiments), it is also their Achilles heel (however, this is an importation of the quandaries of quantum theory itself rather than a unique problem associated with applying QM models to parapsychology). The difficulty is this: If future observers can affect a past event (as in the checker effect and the retro-PK experiments), then where is the limit? *Which* observers? Where does this process end?

Let us consider another ground-breaking experiment by Schmidt. In a later retro-PK study he played some of the target pulses *four times over* to his subjects without their realizing it. On those particular targets they scored much higher than on target clicks heard (observed) only once. Thus, multiple (cumulative) effects of later observations exist. This opens the door to the 'divergence problem': more than one act of observation (and by implication more than one observer) can play a role in collapse of the state vector.

QM models have a variety of solutions to this problem. One strategy is to allow feedback a key role. The reason why readers of journals, for example, have little effect on the results of experiments reported in them is that they get very little feedback, perhaps just a statistical summary. Without fine-grain feedback, they can exert very little in the way of effects. Walker himself argues that there is a spatio-temporally invariant 'coupling' of observers of events such that future observers are highly constrained in their roles in collapsing the state vector (we must be honest and state that we are not convinced that we fully follow the logic of his account). Grappling with the divergence problem has proved to be a nasty headache for QM theorists of psi. We would not wish to claim that these models are without significant problems. Yet there is further support to be found for them.

Ghost and machine: the machine

Randomness is, for Walker, the key feature of the human machine. Synaptic electron-tunnelling within the brain, and QM randomness in events influenced by psi outside the body, are crucial random phenomena. Without such randomness, there can be no psi.

This part of the model suggests that PK cannot influence 'pseudo-random' events. A pseudo-random event generator is one which uses an algorithm (a mathematical equation) to generate a string of events which have the semblance of randomness. Walker argues that the output of such pseudo-random generators cannot be affected by PK. Experimental results suggest that random events may be more readily affected by PK, but that pseudo-PK may also influence random event generators. Why? Because pseudo-random events have to be triggered in some way; specifically, the algorithm has to be given a starting point, often referred to as a *seed number*, to kick-start the sequence it generates. Since that seed number is derived randomly, it is susceptible to PK influence! As yet, there does not appear to be a technique for making the derivation of the seed number algorithmic so that a 'true' pseudo-random event generator can be generated (or at least parapsychologists have not yet used such a procedure). Walker's model makes an absolutely testable

A small section of the 16-mile-long circular tunnel used to accelerate electrons and positrons at CERN, Geneva. Technology like this enables physicists to study processes where PK effects may be fundamental.

prediction here, and we look forward to the time when it can be tested. The important thing is that, *in principle*, the model is testable.

Walker's theory also predicts that the complexity of the processes involved in random event generation is not an important factor (under some circumstances more complex systems may actually allow greater scope for collapse of state vectors, as in the case of multiply tumbling dice or the Jahn random mechanical cascade, which produce a greater number of truly random events). This prediction is again supported by Schmidt's work with simple and complex REGs.

Incidentally, this randomness postulate also helps us to dispose of an old skeptical argument about PK, as voiced by Hansel. Why, he asked, could PK not be used to

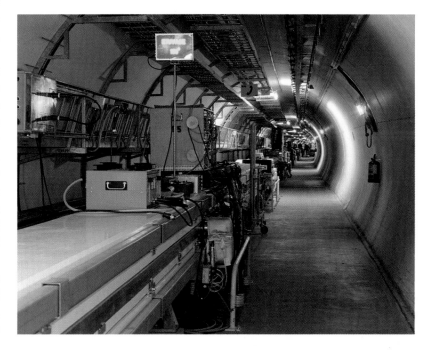

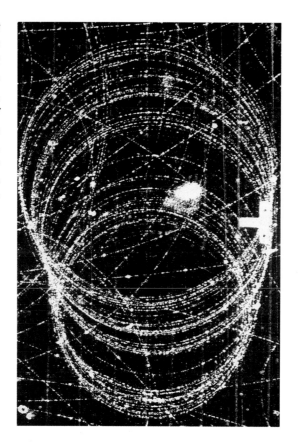

A lone electron traces a series of spirals in a cloud chamber at Lawrence Berkely Laboratory, California. Do patterns of randomness in the sub-atomic realm and in the world at large generate the phenomena we call psi?

generate a force which could be detected by a simple balance? Why use dice? The answer, according to Walker, is obvious: the dynamic system (dice tumbling, REG firing) is much easier to affect than a static system without many random QM events (the static balance). Dynamic systems have inherently greater randomness and thus are easier to influence. This does not mean that 'macro-PK' effects, such as levitations of static objects, are impossible or never happen, simply that they will be far rarer, and much more difficult to elicit, than PK in dynamic systems. This element of Walker's theory also accords with William Braud's notes on the dynamic nature of target systems being a crucial variable in bio-PK research. It further shows that, while earlier researchers thought that the physical characteristics of targets in PK experiments did not affect the results, they simply were not looking at the right characteristics. If they had studied static versus dynamic, labile targets, they would have found a difference (Walker would say that they did so, but did not realize the significance of their observations).

Just as this thesis disposes of Hansel's question, it also ties in with Stanford's suggestions about why altered states of consciousness are favorable for psi. The 'de-structuring' of the brain induced by such altered states (reflected in hallucinations, odd and bizarre imagery and thinking, and so on) should be reflected in an increase in the frequency of truly random events in the brain according to Walker's model, and thus greater scope for Consciousness to influence internal state-vector collapse. There is a definite affinity between the physicist and the psychologist here.

Ghost and machine: the ghost

And so to Consciousness itself, once ridiculed by philosopher Gilbert Ryle as 'the ghost in the machine'. A highly effective ghost in Walker's opinion.

For Walker, the goal of Consciousness is a key element. What does the observer want to see? What does he wish for, what is his disposition (as Stanford would say)? This parameter influences the collapse of the state vector. This is a purely psychological level of inquiry, since one can only find out by asking the observer (or possibly by manipulating his desires or disposition).

However, and this is where matters get interesting, Walker's theory proposes a definite limit on the ability of Consciousness to influence physical systems. Most QM theories have some form of feedback-related limit, as we have seen, but Walker has also proposed a limit on the amount of information (in a mathematical sense) which Consciousness can 'feed into' a physical system. While the details of his derivation do not concern us here, what is of interest is that his postulates about the 'channel capacity' of Consciousness as an influencing agent produce some specific and testable predictions.

The most important of these is the prediction that the 'signal to noise ratio' in psi experiments will be independent of the base probabilities for success or failure. Let us consider some of the experiments we have already reflected on. In a Schmidt experiment with a binary REG the 'base probability' for success is 50%, 1 in 2, because there are two alternative possibilities for the REG output. In ESP card-guessing the base probability for success is 1 in 5, 20%, since there are five different possible card symbols. For dice PK experiments the base probability is 16.67%, 1 in 6, there being six possible outcomes when a die is thrown. In short, the 'base probability' is the chance average (mean) we discussed in our first chapter. Walker asserts that, other things being equal, there is no reason to suppose that Consciousness will feed different amounts of information into any of these systems rather than another. The signal/noise ratio (as measured statistically and reflected in odds-against-chance values and more sophisticated assessments) will be the same for all values of the base probability.

So what? Well, this prediction is quite different from other models of how psi might work. Consider, for example, an appealing model of psi which states that psi works on a few trials in an experiment, and when it does it collapses the state vector to create the desired outcome. How often it works is moderately constant across time, for example, on 10% of occasions (a high value, actually, but let us use this as an illustration). If this were so, we would find that the signal/noise ratio should change dramatically as the base probability changes.

Why is this? Consider a binary REG experiment. Psi works 10% of the time (in 10 out of every 100 trials a hit is scored). However, in the other 90 trials chance success is 45 hits. So the overall scoring rate is 55 hits in 100, which is 1.1 times the success rate expected by chance. Now imagine a situation with an REG which divides pulses across 10 different channels. Psi works in 10 trials out of every 100, giving 10 hits. Of the other 90, 1 in 10 (nine) will be hits by chance alone. The overall scoring rate will be 19 hits in 100 trials, which is 1.9 times the success rate expected by chance, a far superior level of performance (and a much higher signal/noise ratio).

The all-or-none model predicts that the signal/noise ratio, and the anti-chance odds for the experiment, will depend on the base probability. Walker's model states that there will be no such relationship at all. The evidence we have suggests that Walker's model is more accurate, although we cannot entirely discount psychological factors here (people may be more discouraged by psi tests in which the base probability for success is low, since they gain few successes as a percentage of total trials and lose motivation). At any rate, what is truly important here is something almost unthinkable not so very long ago: precise mathematical statements about how psi should operate.

A continuing controversy

Let us try to summarize the good and bad points of the difficult, counter-intuitive QM models of psi, and consider where they may be headed.

The good points of the QM models are clear. They are logically sound. The physics behind them is unusual in terms of the interpretation of state vector collapse, but not absurd. The models make testable predictions, and they make sense out of some puzzling findings in parapsychology. They have generated at least one entirely new line of research and offer many further avenues for exploration.

Difficulties remain nonetheless. The theory is counter-intuitive, but in part this is because some of the associated problems (such as the divergence problem) are direct importations of problems in physics (a point which has escaped some of Walker's critics). The relevance of QM models to spontaneous psi events is, of course, most unclear, but then explaining such events is not the primary task of QM theorists.

There remain further contentious problems with these theories. We do not know whether consciousness is *sufficient* to collapse the state vector. What appears to us to be a

QM theories suggest that Consciousness, or Mind, may be independent of the body it inhabits.

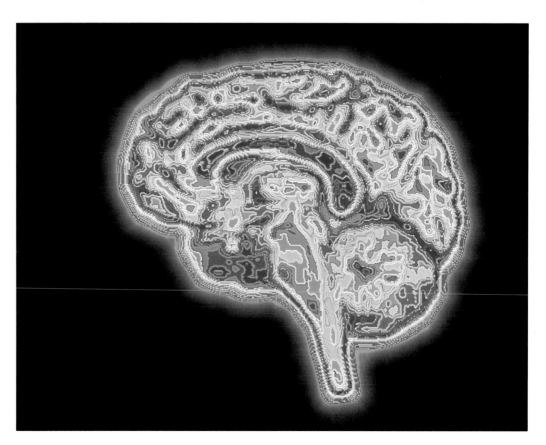

pivotal experiment reported in 1989 by Edwin May suggests that consciousness may not, after all, be *necessary* for collapsing the state vector (this is an absolutely crucial issue, and we are startled that no replication of this experiment in physics appears to have been performed). And it remains the case that most physicists are still tied to the Copenhagen interpretation of the measurement problem which, despite the assertions about the nature of measurement systems and their interactions with QM events, is at heart an empty non-answer, simply an assertion of an unanalyzable block to further understanding.

There are two broad ways of considering Walker's model and the variant QM-inspired models of other theoreticians. One can consider them as precise formulations which can be experimented on easily and pronounced true or false. This is not the most pragmatically sensible viewpoint. A more intelligent and productive approach is to consider whether these models are useful. Do they produce testable predictions? Do they explain what we already know? Do they lead us down new avenues of enquiry? The acid test of a theory is whether it suggests new experiments and generates worthwhile research. In this respect QM models do have something to offer parapsychology. We do not suggest that these models are *true* (we think that is a meaningless way of looking at them). We consider them *useful*. And in that sense they are respectable science.

In this sense they differ fundamentally from John Hasted's speculations about psi events being explicable in terms of the Everett-Wheeler multiple universes theory in physics. Hasted suggests that psi events occur when there is some psi-mediated communication between parallel universes, such that events improbable in one are somehow 'gated' in from another where they have become actualized outcomes. Now, this is not in accord with basic theory in physics (where different universes are interdicted), nor does it appear to lead to unique and testable predictions. Thus, we see that certain QM models (such as Walker's) have definite superiority to others.

Are QM theories going anywhere? This is where life gets interesting. They have not, in recent years, inspired many new experiments. In part this is undoubtedly because the experiments they have inspired are often complex, strange, and even counter-intuitive. Most parapsychologists have a training in psychology and are not comfortable with the strange ideas of QM models (which derive in large part from the strangeness of physics). For this reason many parapsychologists have preferred to continue with more traditional lines of enquiry. Two other factors also come into play here. First, while QM models state that psychological factors in the observer are of key importance to collapsing state vectors (and thus for the occurrence and nature of psi), they relegate such factors to the domain of psychology (quite rightly so). Hence, parapsychologists have tended to stick to the psychological domain; that is their training, after all. The second factor is that dramatic progress in parapsychology has been achieved by other means in the last decade, through a procedure known as *metanalysis*, which we will be reviewing in the final chapter. Just as Braid and Elliotson were unlucky in that hypnotic anesthesia fell into disuse because something better came along (chloroform), QM models have suffered because an alternative line of breakthrough now seems to be on the cards.

We will return later to the issue of whether parapsychology is science or pseudo-science, a point we began to develop in asserting that QM models are 'respectable science'. In our next chapter we will step outside the boundaries of science and explore a subject which preoccupied the very earliest pioneers of parapsychology. It is a subject we feel we cannot ignore, and one which many readers will have wondered about themselves: life after death.

Life after death?

So far, our main concern has been with the growing body of scientific evidence that has sought to pinpoint the anomalies we term psi and provide clues as to how psi might work, when it might work best, who uses it most efficiently, what it might be able to accomplish, and so forth. Yet we have ignored 'the big question', the question that fired the imagination of the first systematic psychical researchers: Do human beings survive physical death? For those nineteenth-century British researchers, faith in an afterlife was not sufficient. Driven by a triumphant materialism, and by the evolutionary theory and scientific atheism of their age, they were determined to find evidence, rather than mere surmise, of survival after death.

While parapsychologists are certainly not all motivated by religious considerations in their interest in survival (as some critics have erroneously claimed), there are several reasons why we are going to consider this issue, despite the fact that it requires us to go beyond the boundaries of scientific method and experiment. The first reason is historical; survival after death was important to the earliest psychical researchers. That does not mean that they, or researchers today, were not dispassionate and honest in their enquiries in this area, just that we do not feel it appropriate to disavow the history of the field. Second, the issue is relevant to the experience of many people. It is also something which many people consider to be important, otherwise mediums would not receive the steady supply of clients they do. And thirdly, we feel that the best of the evidence we are going to present is capable of scientific *consideration* and is of very high quality. We cannot run away from facts because we do not care for them. As it happens, we are not certain that we *do* much care for the implications of reincarnation research, personally speaking, but we are not prepared to ignore or deride the evidence on that score.

Various strands of evidence

The existence of psi appears to imply that Mind can operate outside the body. This is most obvious in the case of PK, where human will appears able to affect distant objects and events. If you like, consciousness is *non-local*, it is not confined to the physical limits of our brains. Logically, then, we should seek further evidence of detachment of Mind from Body. Our first port of call is the out-of-body experience (OBE for short), also referred to as astral projection, astral planing, or astral travelling by the more occult-inclined writers on this topic. We can leave purported astral realms out of our considerations, and concentrate first on what it is like to have an OBE. Here is a typical, although very brief and undetailed, account of an OBE from an eight-year-old boy: 'Such a funny thing has happened. I was just lying in bed reading when I felt I was rising into the air. I seemed to go near the ceiling. Then I looked down and could see myself lying in bed. I came slowly down. I called out...'.

Do such events really occur, or are they are just hallucinations? If Mind can leave Body in this way, then might it be able to leave it permanently, and retain its integrity and coherence, after the death of the body? This possibility is most sharply focused with one special variety of OBE, the near-death experience, or NDE. NDEs have been reported by people who sense their minds apparently leaving their bodies when very close to death (or indeed during brief episodes of clinical death, from which they were resuscitated).

Opposite: Belief in some form of life after death rests upon the widely accepted idea that Mind and Body are somehow separate, that the body is merely a vehicle for the spirit.

Our next step will be to look at events which are said to suggest the operation of Mind after death: apparitions, communications from mediums, and evidence for 'past lives' from so-called 'hypnotic regression' and direct study of people who appear to have been reincarnated from previous lives.

Can there be a final scientific verdict on the issue of survival after death? There is a thorny problem here. A medium may give detailed information about someone who is dead, for example, and we can consult documents and interview witnesses whose testimony convinces us, beyond reasonable doubt, that the information given by the medium is both accurate and could not have been acquired by other than paranormal means (let's assume this for the sake of argument). But this does not *prove* that the dead person has somehow survived to pass this information on. After all, if *we* can verify the information given by the medium, it means that either there is documentary evidence for it (which could, in theory, be tapped by clairvoyance) or memories and information residing in the minds of those who knew the deceased (likewise accessible, by telepathy). In theory, the medium may have been using exceptional psi powers — so-called 'Super-ESP' — to gather information from those sources. This impasse will be discussed in more detail later, but *in theory* Super-ESP is a viable alternative to the survival claim.

Despite this, and the fact that much of the evidence we will survey does not come from scientific experiment, we can still come to reasoned conclusions about survival after death. The frame of mind we need to adopt is that of a French 'examining magistrate', who collects and analyzes all the evidence relevant to a case. We can use our rationality, and our sense of plausibility and reasonable doubt, to decide how strong the case looks. We cannot have a final scientific verdict, but we can have a provisional, reasoned, rational one.

An artist's impression of the 'astral' body leaving the physical body. People who say they have had OBEs typically report looking down on their body (never up) and floating freely in space.

Out-of-body experiences

'I was very tired, physically exhausted, but my mind was rather active. I lay down on my bed to rest for a while in the late afternoon. I felt an odd prickly sensation in my limbs and then a buzzing sound.... I was conscious of some kind of pressure around or in my head and then I felt as if I was travelling along some dark tunnel, very fast...this ended and I looked around me to find myself seemingly floating a few feet up in the air in my bedroom. I looked down and found my body underneath me. For some odd reason I was especially taken with an odd cobweb pattern on the top of my wardrobe.... I got a little scared by this and I willed myself to go back to my body. I got pulled back as if along some kind of cord or thread and it seemed to me, though I'm not certain, that I re-entered my body through my head. I gave a slight start and sat up. It was completely unexpected. When I regained my wits I checked the wardrobe top.... The odd cobweb pattern was there alright.'

Such OBE experiences are not uncommon. While estimates from surveys differ depending on how questions are asked, it seems that some 10–20% of the general population may have had at least one such experience and a small minority report repeated OBEs. So this is not a freak phenomenon confined to the 'astral travelling' community by any means.

Is ESP being used during an OBE? For example, in

the case above, the person 'saw' something not visible from a normal standpoint, thus raising the possibility of a 'dislocated' Mind perceiving something paranormally.

Charles Tart has reported an interesting experiment which sought to verify precisely this kind of effect. A practised 'OBEr', a woman, lying in one room with an EEG wired up to her, was able to read a five-digit number placed on top of a wardrobe in another room. Karlis Osis has reported an even more ingenious experiment, with an OBEr in one room and a unique type of ESP target in another. This apparatus created and displayed optical targets which were visible *only to someone standing directly in front of the machine.* The subject in the experiment unfailingly reported the correct target in test sessions where he rated himself confident of success (at a rate well beyond chance limits).

The Osis experiment is particularly neat, for one is tempted to think that something of the man's mind must have been positioned before the apparatus in order to see the optical effect. However, the logic is false. If ESP can detect microfiche targets and succeed in DT (Down Through) ESP-card tests where symbols are stacked one on top of the other, we know that the naive model of ESP as a localized sense is erroneous. Osis's results may show quite normal ESP effects. Indeed it could be argued that OBEs are nothing more than simultaneously occurring hallucinations.

This general conclusion is reinforced by two experiments reported by John Palmer, in which he successfully induced OBEs in volunteers. In the first experiment he employed a rotating spiral visual field. In the second he used ganzfeld conditions and instructed his subjects to have an OBE which would enable them to find out about a target picture being seen by another person in another room. In the first of these experiments the overall scoring was below chance, and the people who had OBEs showed significant psi-missing. In the second experiment exactly the reverse happened (above-chance scoring, and significantly above-chance for those who successfully experienced OBEs).

The point here is that these results are *exactly* the same as those obtained by Palmer in ordinary ganzfeld and altered-states experiments where no OBEs were invited or reported. The strongest ESP results came from those subjects who were most strongly affected by the altered state of consciousness. This suggests that the OBE is in itself an irrelevance. It is of note only as a marker of a strongly altered state, which can be measured in other ways in any event. What *really* counts is the altered state itself, although to be fair, those subjects in Palmer's experiments who reported OBEs had a rather different quality of experience to that of most spontaneous OBErs. Have experiments with seasoned and experienced OBErs provided any greater insight into this phenomenon?

A formal laboratory OBE experiment. The volunteer is wearing colored glasses and listening to an induction tape. The quality of experimentally-induced OBEs seems to be different from that of spontaneous cases.

In 1976 parapsychologist Robert Morris reported an experiment with practised OBEr Stuart Harary. Morris suggested that a good test of whether *something* left Harary's body during OBEs would be to test a human or animal monitor which might respond to that something. Harary's pet kitten was chosen for the job. The kitten was placed in an enclosed space in a separate room while Harary attempted, during randomly selected periods of time in experimental sessions (half of the time, in fact), to 'travel' mentally to it. During the time when Harary was OBEing (as it were), the kitten sat quietly and appeared comfortable and happy. It never miaowed. During the other half of the test sessions, the cat appeared restless and miaowed 37 times. Interestingly, when this experiment was repeated with another cat with whom Harary had no rapport, no significant effects were found.

So, did the little creature sense something of Harary's mental presence, which quietened and comforted it? One experimenter reported a shadowy apparition at one instant during one of the time periods when, unknown to him, Harary was having an OBE. But Harary could have been using PK to influence the cat and the experimenter, so the case remains unproven. The same possibility applies to more recent studies by Osis, in which success in the optical-target test was accompanied by signals coming from strain gauges (as in Hasted's metal-bending studies) located nearby. This could have been concurrent ESP and PK.

John Palmer has suggested that a stronger case for OBEs might be made if it could be shown that the psi effects associated with OBEs were somehow different in kind from psi effects reported without OBEs. It is some time since this suggestion was made, but we are not aware of any evidence of this type having been presented. Monitoring brain wave activity during OBEs has not been helpful, with discrepant results from different experiments.

At present we have no good grounds for deciding whether the OBE is a purely subjective phenomenon or not. However, since OBE reports have been associated with strong psi effects in experiments, it may be that the OBE is a good indicator of a psi-conducive state.

Light at the end of the tunnel

Early chroniclers of OBEs noted that a significant proportion of them were induced by strong fear, stress, or injury, although they tended to play down this fact, fearing that such cases might be more likely to be explained away as hallucinations than as 'natural' OBEs. In the last 20 years or so, however, great interest has been shown in the stress-induced OBE. Raymond Moody is generally regarded as one of the pioneer researchers in this field, having collected several hundred case reports of near-death experiences, NDEs.

Here is a fairly typical example of an NDE as reported to one of us (the numbers refer to some of the characteristics of NDEs as listed on page 156). 'I find this very difficult to explain, hard to express myself...there are certain qualities I find it hard to convey (1).... 'I was in a car accident [details given]. I was dimly aware of much activity going on around, and people shouting, but I can't remember much of that (2). I felt strangely calm, very tranquil, as if little mattered to me any more (3). I slowly became aware of travelling as if down a long chute of some kind (5), moving along, a blur around me. I don't think I had any idea of what I was [sic]. In the distance, though, I saw a light...a globe of light. It moved towards me slowly and when it drew close it was so brilliant, pure light, but not dazzling (9).... This light, I simply cannot describe what it meant...it wasn't God or Christ or anything like that, but it was someone, some agent or force.... I got an astonishing feeling of the complete benevolence of this light. Behind it were what I suppose I would have to call buildings of some kind, all lit up (12)...there were other lights around, I suppose now I would say they were spirits or something but I don't remember any of them as people I'd known.... The light suddenly made some motion to me. It pointed, or rather it seemed to orient itself in some way down.... I realized that I was going to return to myself, to my body, and live.... Although it sounds bizarre, I must say I'm not sure I was altogether pleased. The light was so full of everything good that I think I almost wanted to stay. But it faded...eventually I came round (15). I had been very severely injured in the crash.'

Now this person had never heard of Moody or his work, and yet the parallels between his experiences and many of those described by Moody are striking. The major component missing in this account as compared with the prototypical NDE, is what Moody terms 'The Being of Light' (9) who frequently directs (non-verbally) the attention of the person to his or her life and its past events with a wordless question such as: 'What have you done with your life? Are you prepared to die?' Moody's respondents said that such questions were never accusatory; they felt aware of the Being's infinite and unqualified love for them. As a result of their experiences, Moody's respondents claimed that they had lost all fear of death, although they had no wish to die. The huge majority of them treasured the experience, and its impact on their subsequent lives was very powerful and very positive.

Pointers to survival after death are given by meetings with dead people who have been known to the person having an NDE, and also by the fact that an NDE does not appear to be terminated by actual clinical death (in one of Moody's cases, lasting for many minutes before resuscitation). The content of an NDE may even have an imagery familiar from the visionary writings of mystics; some people report having seen a 'realm of bewildered spirits', beings whose purpose in life was not fulfilled or who committed suicide. The Review may include an apparent revelation of the consequences of one's actions. Moody, pondering on the perpetrators of Nazi atrocities, wrote that their actions would have resulted in 'countless individual tragedies...innumerable long lingering deaths, and fast brutal ones...in awful degradations, in years of hunger, tears, and torments for their victims. If what happened to my subjects happened to these men, they would see all these things and many others come alive, vividly portrayed before them. In my wildest fantasies, I am totally unable to imagine a hell more horrible, more ultimately unbearable than this.' One can perhaps see the origin of notions of Heaven, and Hell, in these experiences.

Naturally, Moody sought for normal explanations of NDEs. A severely injured or stressed person is inevitably affected by powerful physiological changes such as depleted oxygen supply to the brain, sensory isolation, and the like. Some of the characteristics of an NDE are by no means unique to it. The sensation of travelling along a chute or tunnel is one encountered in epileptics, migraine sufferers, and sometimes when just about to fall asleep (one of us can confirm that anesthesia at the dentist also elicited the effect). Drugs and anesthetics may indeed elicit some of the simplest phenomena associated with NDEs, although there are abundant cases of NDEs from people who were not under the influence of drugs or anesthetics at the time of their experience.

Psychiatrist Ronald Siegel of Los Angeles has penned an extensive critical review of NDEs, claiming that they can be explained in terms of strong psychological needs and wishes combined with medical trauma. Most of the characteristics of NDEs, he asserts, are also reported by people taking LSD and other hallucinogens. This may be missing the point, however. If there is some continuity between OBEs and NDEs, why should we expect the latter to be different in kind from certain experiences of the living and healthy? Also, save for some extremely dubious claims about hellish experiences publicized by religiously committed writers, negatively toned NDEs are much less common than aversive hallucinogenic experiences. This does not really square with the stress-generated response theory.

The wish-fulfilment element of the theory also runs into a problem. The phenomenology of an NDE (the nature of the experience in itself) appears to be quite independent of a person's cultural background. Whether people believe in angels and spirits, Christ, Vishnu, or Buddha does not appear to make any difference. Indeed stereotyped accounts of Heaven and Hell are very rare in NDE reports. Social class, education, and economic status do not correlate with the frequency or nature of NDEs either.

Demons torturing souls in the double mouths of Hell, an illustration from a fifteenth-century French manuscript. Apocalyptic and terrifying visions of other worlds are more likely with LSD and other hallucinogenic drugs than with NDEs.

CHARACTERISTIC ELEMENTS OF NEAR-DEATH EXPERIENCES

1. Ineffability
Very difficult to convey all aspects of the experience in words.

2. Knowledge of others
Some people appear to perceive the speech and actions of those around them when they are deeply unconscious.

3. Calmness
Strong sense of tranquility and peace.

4. Buzzing sound
Auditory sensations, described as buzzing, 'ringing of a loud bell', 'a whistling sound, like the wind'. Frequently experienced as unpleasant.

5. The Dark Tunnel
Sensation of rapid movement along a 'dark tunnel', 'a long cave', 'a valley' (origin of the term 'Valley of the Shadow of Death?').

6. OBE aspect
Sensation of possessing a body apart from the physical one. Frequently great surprise is expressed about this.

7. Meeting others
Encounters with 'spirits' of people one has known who have died.

8. 'Bewildered spirits' (unusual)
Reports of seeing people who are dead and bound to some object, person, or habit; they appear in conflict or torment; they appear more humanized than other 'spirits'.

9. The Being of Light
Appearance of a personal being, composed of brilliant but undazzling light, radiating intense joy, love, and warmth. Strongly ineffable. Frequently seen as a guide or emissary.

10. The Review
The Being of Light directs attention to the past life, to actions performed and to their consequences, wordlessly. This is done to evoke reflection, not to 'judge' the person. 'He (Being of Light) was trying to show me something in each one of these flashbacks. All through this, he kept stressing the importance of love.... There wasn't any accusation in any of this, though.'

11. The Vision of Knowledge (unusual)
Brief glimpses of a quite separate realm of existence in which all knowledge seems to co-exist in a timeless state. Very strongly ineffable.

12. Cities of Light (unusual)
Sometimes described in almost Biblical terms as Heaven; rivers like glass, buildings of crystal; all suffused with light.

13. The Border
A body of water, or a line, a gate, a fence, a door, or a gray mist; to cross it means to accept Death.

14. Rescue or Reprieve (unusual)
Belief that the Being of Light or some other agency pardons one or saves one from Death. In such cases the person is frequently afraid for another person still alive on earth — a spouse whose heart may be broken, a child who may not be brought up as the person would wish.

15. The Return
Often disappointing at the time, especially in cases where people have been resuscitated after clinical death.

16. Effects on later life
Very strongly positive. Loss of all fear of death, occasional reports of acquiring greater sensitivity to people (including developing psi abilities), strong sense of purpose. Reduced anxieties about life.

17. Telling others
Frequently met with incomprehension or dismissal; people learn not to discuss NDEs too readily.

'God the Father', from the Isenheim altarpiece by fifteenth-century German artist Mathis Grünewald, is strongly reminiscent of the Being of Light encountered by many NDErs — ineffable, radiant, timeless.

From time to time someone with little or no experience of the field offers a suggestion about NDEs. Carl Sagan, for example, opined that the universality of NDEs may have something to do with the experience we all share, birth. The 'tunnel' could be the birth canal, and the OBE element a reliving of the birth experience. This notion (which received wholly uncritical support in certain quarters) may have been influenced by such practices as 'rebirthing' and similar New Age therapies, but it falls apart on even cursory scrutiny. The birth canal is not at all like a tunnel. The mental capacities of newborns are not such that they could remember the birth experience in a way which could explain the great depth and detail of NDE sensations and imagery. It has also been found that NDEs are reported equally frequently by people who have had 'normal' births and those born by Caesarean section. This rather shoots down the notion that the tunnel effects reported during NDEs are an echo of experiences in the birth canal.

Attempts have been made to extrapolate what is known of characteristic organization patterns of the visual cortex of the brain to the tunnel imagery of NDEs. For example, an increase in cortical excitability might generate 'stripes' of activity in the visual cortex which would generate the appearance of concentric rings or spirals, thus creating a tunnelling effect. Because the number of neurones devoted to a unit area is higher in the center of the visual field, the appearance of a central focused light might be created. These speculations may account for the crudest elements of the simplest NDE phenomena, but they do not even begin to account for at least 95% of the complex phenomenology of NDEs, and there is no reason to believe that such simplistic 'explanations' will make any progress in this direction.

The cardiologist's research

'I must admit that when I first read *Life After Life*, I felt these experiences were either fabrications by persons who had taken advantage of the author, Dr. Raymond Moody, or were embellishments by Moody himself to produce a best-selling book. Five years and 116 interviews later, I am convinced that my original suspicions about this were wrong, for many reasons.'

This is a paragraph from a quite excellent book, *Recollections of Death*, by Atlanta cardiologist Michael Sabom. What distinguishes Sabom from many other medical men who were equally skeptical of Moody's reports was that he was prepared to look at the issue (and he had a clear and precise methodology for doing so worked out in advance). He admits that he did not expect to find any of his patients speak of an NDE or anything like it. Nevertheless he went about his interviews with people who had recovered from serious heart attacks or similar life-threatening events (such as arresting during major surgery) with great care 'as if a routine medical history were being taken'. He notes that one of his earliest interviews was with a woman who said to him afterwards: 'You seemed to be out mainly to disprove the experience as much as anything when I talked with you the first time.' Yet Sabom found that, while his patients were initially reluctant to mention the fact that they had had an NDE and were even fearful that doctors would dismiss their experience as absurd or hallucinatory, a startling proportion of those who had had a close brush with death seemed to have had an NDE. In broad terms, Sabom's findings corroborate those of Moody, Kenneth Ring, Russell Noyes, and other NDE researchers, but we consider Sabom's work to be the finest in the field.

Sabom's book is meticulously documented, with an exhaustive tabulation of his five-year study findings. He devotes considerable space to considering possible explanations for NDEs in terms of conscious or subconscious fabrication, psychological phenomena such as depersonalization and autoscopic ('self-seeing') hallucination syndromes, the effects of prior expectations (finding, startlingly, that a significantly higher percentage of people who did *not* experience NDEs had some earlier awareness of their existence), drug-

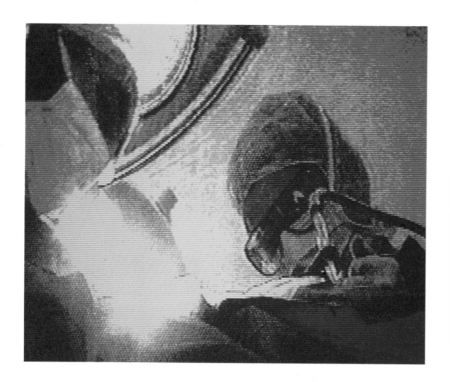

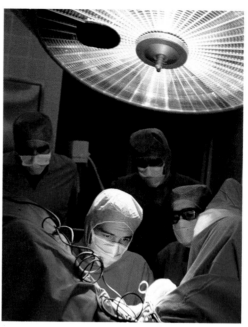

Some patients undergoing major surgery seem to be aware, at some level, of remarks made by surgeons and nurses, but the level of awareness of patients who report NDEs on the operating table seems to be of a higher order. Small details of equipment and procedures are noted with precision.

induced effects, temporal lobe seizures, the release of brain chemicals known as endorphins, acidosis (excessive carbon dioxide levels), and so on. He does a fine job of illustrating the weakness of all these explanations, both individually and in combination. Perhaps Sabom's distinctive contribution, however, is an ingenious investigation he made into the accuracy of NDErs' accounts of being aware of their environment at some stage during their near-death crisis.

Sabom interviewed many people who reported being aware of events around them during their crisis, in the manner of an OBE. People who had suffered heart attacks and had been given CPR (cardio-pulmonary resuscitation) often described events which occurred during the resuscitation, while they were wholly unconscious of course. Sabom refers to such cases as 'autoscopic NDEs', literally NDEs in which one sees oneself. From interviewing these people, Sabom was able to elicit very specific recollections of events pertaining to resuscitation. Such cases were by no means rare; Sabom was able to document 32 cases of this kind.

What he then did was to interview 25 cardiac patients who had *not* experienced any NDE or reported any OBE during resuscitation, but who were (as he put it) 'seasoned cardiac patients with an average duration of known heart disease exceeding five years'. These 25 people were matched to the autoscopic-NDErs for age, sex, race, and other variables. Sabom then invited these 'seasoned cardiac patients' to observe the cardiac monitors to which they were attached, the appearance of cardiac defibrillators used in CPR, general equipment in CPR technology, and the general procedures of the cardiac ward. Sabom even made sure that his control group were regular TV watchers — the reason for all this being that he wanted to find out if the *specific* details of the recollections of his autoscopic-NDErs could be accounted for by general prior experience (such as TV exposure to medical dramas) and/or specific exposure to life on a cardiac ward.

Sabom found that his control group subjects made characteristic errors when invited to give an account of what CPR procedures were like; 20 of the 23 who gave some such account made at least one major error. The most common one was believing that mouth-to-mouth resuscitation is a means of giving artificial respiration to people who have suffered cardiac arrest. Other mistakes included various misconceptions about how the throat and windpipe are kept open during CPR, misconceptions of how cardiac massage is given (e.g. thinking that a blow to the back or stomach was used to start the heart beating), misconceptions of how the defibrillator is used (the idea that the pads had suction cups on their bases, for example), in fact misconceptions about almost every aspect of CPR procedure. By contrast, the accounts of the autoscopic-NDErs contained no such significant errors. Thus it seems that Sabom's autoscopic NDE patients were not making educated guesses about CPR procedures, as he originally suspected. This gives credence to the suggestion that, in some way, they accurately perceived what was happening to them during resuscitation, despite being unconscious. While there is some slight evidence of awareness under anesthesia without any autoscopic NDE, the accounts of people who have been aware of what is happening to them at such times are typically more fragmentary, and much less frequent, than the autoscopic experiences Sabom documented from his NDE patients.

The NDE is a more baffling, and puzzling, phenomenon than the OBE. It is not easy to account for the nature of the experience in terms of known physiology. Psi may be involved in the accurate accounts and recollections people give in 'autoscopic' cases where they are able accurately to describe what has been happening around them during times of deep unconsciousness. If it is not psi, it is a sensory acuity which in itself would be a source of marvel, an acuity hitherto not recognized or understood by psychology. The few reports that exist in which people who have died allegedly describe the process of death are similar in some ways to NDE accounts.

Finally, we have arrived at the point where we must consider possible cases of communication not from people near death who return to speak of it, but from those who have indeed passed to 'the other side'...if there is one.

Apparitions: the quick and the dead

Are ghosts, or apparitions, purely hallucinatory? Many people believe that they have 'seen a ghost' — the experience is as old as records of civilization. Here is a fairly typical sample.

'I was working in a large girls' boarding school in Kent. I was 29 years old and in excellent health, good eyesight, and of a normal and non-excitable disposition.

'One night I was going downstairs, carrying an Aladdin Lamp [sic], turned fairly low...and as I reached the top of a long straight staircase I saw what appeared to be the figure of an elderly man walking down the staircase in front of me. He was five or six steps down when I saw him. His back was turned to me, his hair was grey, and one hand was on the banister rail.

'I stood still and watched him go down until, on reaching the bottom of the staircase with his hand on the newel post, he disappeared. There was no sound of footsteps although the staircase was not carpeted. He seemed to be wearing a long dark garment.

'I knew at once he was a "ghost" but was only conscious of extreme interest. The house was very old, reputedly haunted, and there were of course a great many people living in it, although I suppose most of them were asleep at the time.

'Although I lived there for four years this was my only experience of the kind in that house, and although other people occasionally saw "ghosts" these were not the same as the figure of the old man.'

Now, there are some good reasons for considering that this experience may well have been a hallucination. First, *observing conditions were bad* — it was dark and the observer had only a dim lamp to see by. Second, *the house was reputed to be haunted* — remember Cornell's 'ghost' in our first chapter? Expectancy and belief affect perceptions. Third, *other people saw different 'ghosts'* — while some difference between observers is to be expected (as questioning different witnesses of a car accident will swiftly confirm, even though their differences do not mean that no accident took place!), we are told that other people did not see the old man. Finally, there is nothing in this tale to suggest anything other than hallucination.

So, in what circumstances might an apparition be reasonably considered to be something other than a hallucination? We suggest four different factors and types of case where such a summary dismissal is not so easily made.

Collective apparitions Several people independently see the same apparition in the same place at the same time, giving similar accounts.

Hauntings Repeated observations of an apparition by different people at different times in the same place.

Crisis apparitions Apparitions of the dying which appear to a living person close to the time of death.

Informative apparitions Apparitions which give information to the person seeing them which he or she could not otherwise have known (crisis apparitions are a special instance of this, of course).

The first two categories are not very common, although there are enough cases available for our scrutiny. Here is a typical example of a haunting: 'I had lived in Trondheim for four years and left the city in 1938, but have often visited the city since that time. I was much interested in the construction work done at the cathedral. 'One sunny morning I went into the cathedral. I walked along the north passage.... Looking across towards the south hall, I noticed a nun sitting quietly in one of the many niches along the wall.... I wondered what she was doing there at this time of day. I thought I would talk to her as I came closer, but when I was just six or seven feet away from her, she faded away and I saw her no more! I must say I was puzzled, but walking into the west end of the cathedral I stopped and talked to one of the women cleaning the church and said to her: "I thought I saw a Catholic nun over in the west end, sitting in a niche, but when I came near she disappeared. How could that be?" "Oh," answered the woman, "we often see her." And this I have verified by others.'

Such cases, when observations are made in good conditions (a sunny day and daylight in the cathedral) and when independent witnesses have been interviewed by researchers and details checked, cannot be so easily dismissed as hallucinations.

Crisis and informative apparitions are of greater interest, however. At least, crisis cases seem to be moderately common and there is some possibility of verifying their accuracy. If a person reports seeing an apparition of someone at the time of death at a distant place, then it is possible to investigate the case by interviewing witnesses. If the link is verified, then one can arrive at some judgement about it, taking into account the kind of problem which we discussed in our first chapter — obviously, the death must be an unexpected one to have any evidential value, and so on.

The most important work in this area, to this day, remains the late nineteenth-century work of the pioneers of the British Society for Psychical Research. In a way, research was easier then. If, in 1893, one dreamed of a relative dying in a foreign land, one might mention it to others long before any news could be confirmed. Today we have telephones

Eight mystics form a circle in the ruins of Alexandra Palace, London, destroyed by fire in 1980. They concluded that there were 'a fair number of ghosts around' and that the elements of earth, air, fire, and water were out of balance. Experiments by Gertrude Schmeidler showed that some psychics are able to sense the nature and location of alleged ghostly presences to a higher-than-chance degree.

The 'phantom nun' of Borley Rectory in Yorkshire was thoroughly investigated by the Society for Psychical Research in 1929, but no good evidence was found. Rumors of haunting seem to predispose people to see apparitions.

and fax machines, instant communication. Finding independent witnesses to crisis and informative apparations is that much harder since news travels so fast.

The monumental *Census of Hallucinations* gathered by the early SPR workers involved asking some 17,000 people about their experiences of hallucination (including apparitions). Some 2,300 people said they had had some form of hallucinatory experience, and after eliminating those which appeared to be dreams, or might have been due to drugs, fever, and the like, the researchers were left with around 1,700 cases for further investigation. Of these, around 80 involved apparent crisis apparitions where a 'ghost' appeared within 12 hours of the time of someone's death. Extensive checking and questioning pared this number down to 32 cases where death could not have been expected from actuarial or circumstantial considerations, and where there were (in virtually every case) independent witnesses. 'Strong' cases thus formed some 1.5% of the total census. From the Registrar-General's tables of the day it was found that the odds against a person dying on any given day were some 19,000 to 1. On the face of it, the rate of 'crisis apparitions' appears to have exceeded this number very substantially.

Unfortunately, the methods used by early researchers are not truly acceptable to us. Too many assumptions were made, and too many subjective judgements about the strength of cases. There are too many uncertainties here for the data to be summarily judged with statistics. However, it is an uncomfortable fact that the actual rate of coincidence between experiencing an apparition and the death of the person involved exceeds the chance odds by some 250 to 1. Even if the judgements behind the statistics are open to question, this is a very high ratio.

If we accept, for the sake of argument, that apparitions may not be explicable solely in terms of hallucinations, visual illusions, and coincidence, does this favor some kind of 'survivalist' interpretation? Or could 'Super-ESP' explain the results observed? After all, a crisis apparition could be a telepathic awareness of someone's death *plus* a strong hallucination generated in response to that stressful telepathic understanding (this is a fairly tenuous, but not logically absurd, hypothesis and some researchers have advanced it).

One example of how research may be able to progress on this front is an ingenious experiment by Gertrude Schmeidler and her colleagues. After investigating allegedly haunted houses, they compiled lists of what 'ghosts' had been seen doing in the places in the houses where they had been seen. Small groups of psychics were then asked to visit the houses and check off 'correct' actions and locations from a list which contained both true and false items randomly intermixed. Schmeidler found that the some of the psychics were able to pinpoint to a significantly better-than-chance degree which ghost had done what and where, as it were. Schmeidler also tested a group of skeptics in exactly the same way and found that their reports worked out exactly at the chance level. This is interesting. If apparitions were attributable to visual illusions in shady parts of the houses and so on, one might have thought that the skeptics would sniff out such places and score better than the psychics (or at least better than chance), but this was not so.

Of course, Schmeidler's psychics may have been using simple ESP rather than sensitively picking up the 'vibes' of the building, as some of them put it. But at least they seem to have picked up *something*, which gives us something firmer than the shaky tales one often finds in this area of research

Is there anybody there?

In Chapter 2 we examined the career of D.D. Home, a physical medium — one in whose presence PK effects appear to occur. Where survival after death is concerned, however, our concern is with *mental mediumship*. Mental mediums convey information which they claim to have obtained, paranormally, from the spirits of deceased people. As we have noted, it is always possible that such information might be obtained via Super-ESP. However, the first thing we need to decide is whether there is anything here worthy of our attention at all.

The vast majority of mental mediums are inoffensive people whose sincerity it would be uncharitable to question, but who produce a great deal of waffle which no seasoned researcher takes seriously. Their services can be comforting to the relatives of a recently deceased person and many of them charge no fee, or only a token fee. They are not commercially oriented charlatans exploiting the gullible for profit. On the contrary, many are kindly and well-meaning. This is not to say that anything more than self-deception is involved in their performances. It does not take much practice to learn 'cold reading' (to give quite an effective performance as a 'medium') with nothing paranormal being involved at all. This technique uses general statements which fish for information which is later fed back to the person giving it (amazingly, people often forget that they gave the information in the first place), and — among other ploys — simply being alert to the information people give away about themselves by their age, sex, race, style of speaking, choice of words, clothes, jewelry, and so on. Educated guesswork and following leads from fished-for information can produce an extremely convincing piece of 'mediumship' so far as the sitter is concerned. Being aware of such problems, let us review some of the better evidence.

The 'Golden Age' of mental mediumship roughly spanned the years 1880–1940. During this period, six female mental mediums, all of high reputation, were particularly thoroughly investigated, and some intriguing reports and evidence amassed. Since then, there have been no well-documented cases. Why is this? Skeptics would say that modern researchers are highly alert to the tricks and self-deceptions of mediums and so the 'evidence' has

merely evaporated. There are alternative explanations, including the fact that researchers these days simply do not have the time, money and/or patronage to investigate mediums in depth. In any case, the objections of even the most hardened skeptic would be muted compared with those of arch-skeptic Richard Hodgson, the Australian-born researcher who first studied the great, and arguably the most remarkable, mental medium of all time, Mrs. Leonore Piper. In fact the details of Mrs. Piper's career are far more revealing and of considerably greater value than a shallower general survey of mediumship.

The remarkable Mrs. Piper

In 1884 Mrs. Piper was a quite unexceptional housewife living in Boston, Massachusetts. Unexceptional, that is, until she visited a faith-healing medium, slipped into trance, and received a 'message' for another sitter at the seance. She then began holding seances for her friends, during which a 'control spirit', a Frenchman calling himself 'Dr. Phinuit', became a regular *dramatis persona*. Phinuit was the intermediary between Mrs. Piper's sitters and the 'spirits' with whom they wished to communicate. Rumors about these sittings reached the ears of the psychologist William James, who was curious enough to attend one of Mrs. Piper's seances in 1885. Later, James despatched other researchers to Mrs. Piper, introducing them with pseudonyms. Many expressed the view that Mrs. Piper had given them information, often of a quite personal and intimate nature, which they did not consider she could have obtained by normal means. One, however, wrote to James describing Mrs. Piper as 'that insipid prophetess' — she was not a woman of great education or erudition, and did not pretend to be.

*Right: Mental medium
Mrs. Leonore Piper,
who refused to be
debunked.*

In 1887 Richard Hodgson arrived in Boston to take up the post of Secretary to the American Society for Psychical Research. Naturally he attended some of Mrs. Piper's seances. From his own letters and those of others, Hodgson emerges as a fairly obnoxious individual, highly intelligent but also belligerent, insensitive, and vituperative. A less likely dupe of charlatanry it would be difficult to imagine. Yet he eventually became convinced not only that Mrs. Piper had psi ability, but that her trance messages proved survival after physical death.

Born in 1855, Hodgson had read Law at Melbourne and then Moral Sciences at Cambridge, and was a founder member of the British Society for Psychical Research. In 1884 the SPR sent him to India to evaluate the medium Madame Blavatsky and the Theosophist cult she had originated. Hodgson's report was devastating; he regarded Blavatsky as a fraud and most of the

Theosophists as pathetic dupes (it can hardly be said, whatever one thinks of Theosophy, that his report was balanced, fair, or objective). In other investigations, he zestfully rubbished the credibility of witnesses at seances held by physical mediums, in which activity he was helped by his apparently considerable abilities as a conjurer. In short, Hodgson's forte was hostile-aggressive debunking. Although he lacked fairness and balance, no one could possibly have accused him of credulity.

Working with other researchers, Hodgson approached Mrs Piper's case in his typically meticulous manner. Complete verbatim records were kept of the large majority of seances and whenever circumstances permitted, and signed testimonies were taken from other seance participants. *Proxy sittings* were also organized, a key element in testing mental mediums. A proxy sitting is one in which a sitter is sent along and asked to request information on behalf of another person, who is not present, and whom the sitter does not know. The crucial point about this is that the medium cannot pump the sitter for information (since he or she knows nothing relevant) and cannot try to learn anything by inference (since the object of the medium's attention is not present or known to her either).

In 1889 Hodgson exported Mrs. Piper to England. There, too, many proxy sittings were held. On arrival at the house of the researcher Sir Oliver Lodge, Mrs. Piper's baggage was checked for any information she might have collected in advance about potential sitters at her seances. Indeed, Hodgson even hired private detectives to follow her and her family to make sure there was no secret research being conducted at libraries, registry offices, or with friends of sitters to flush out information which 'Phinuit' might then offer at seances. In this respect the researcher's job was much easier a hundred years ago than it is today. Now, with so much information about all of us stored on computer, a medium with a pet data snooper could learn a great deal about seance sitters without ever stepping out of line herself.

To resume our narrative, at the time of Mrs. Piper's visit Lodge had a house full of newly-employed servants who could have told her almost nothing of value even if she had been able to slip the leash and interrogate them (with all the risks of detection which that would have incurred). Seances were held with individuals chosen 'in great measure of chance' by Hodgson. In some cases he selected them only after Mrs. Piper had gone into trance, precluding her from collecting any information about them in advance. In one sitting, for example, Lodge presented Mrs. Piper with a watch belonging to an uncle of his whom he had known but slightly in his later years. 'Uncle Jerry' announced himself, named his brother, and claimed ownership

Mrs. Piper acquired a huge reputation on both sides of the Atlantic. Her 'confession' to the New York Herald *on 20 October, 1901 — 'I am no telephone to the spirit world' — should not be taken too seriously, however. The editor knew how to sell newspapers.*

of the watch. Lodge replied that he would need information (not known to him) about Jerry's early life to validate this claim, which he would then check with the surviving brother. 'Uncle Jerry' obliged. As Lodge wrote: ' "Uncle Jerry" recalled episodes such as swimming the creek when they were boys together, and running some risk of getting drowned; killing a cat in Smith's field; the possession of a small rifle, and of a long peculiar skin, like a snake-skin, which he thought was not long in the possession of Uncle Robert [the surviving brother].' These facts were then, according to Lodge, 'more or less completely verified'. It is perhaps the nature of these facts which is intriguing. They are the kind of childhood memories which are odd enough to ring true.

However, what Lodge did *not* report was that these correct and sometimes very specific and unusual items of information were interspersed with generalities and erroneous comments. A reading of the full transcripts and records of Mrs. Piper's seances suggests that a goodly proportion of correct and specific information was given, however. One could perhaps dismiss this as coincidence. Our evaluation is that, when an individual appears able to provide substantially correct information *repeatedly,* this argument begins to wear thin. Although the Lodge sitting was not a proxy sitting, it approximates to one; information was given which really does appear not to have been known to anyone present (Lodge had to make postal enquiries to check the information given by Mrs. Piper).

Coincidence can be more plausibly ruled out from an experiment conducted with Mrs Piper after her return to America. 'Phinuit' had now been largely displaced by 'G.P.', ostensibly the spirit of a young man, George Pellew, who had died in an accident in 1892. G.P. correctly recognized, from a total of 150 sitters, the 30 he had known when alive, and *only* those 30. Clearly this cannot be a chance event, and if Mrs. Piper was responding to some very subtle cues from the sitters she saw while in trance, this prodigious level of accuracy seems truly extraordinary. A less quantifiable point, but one we cannot dismiss, is that G.P. behaved in slightly different ways entirely appropriate to each of the 30 individuals; his demeanor and style of conversation were, his friends claimed, exactly as they had been towards them when he was alive. During G.P.'s control, Hodgson had virtually complete supervision of seance proceedings and created and kept full and complete records.

What is remarkable about Mrs. Piper is that every researcher who studied her at first hand for a reasonable period of time, no matter what his initial attitude, became convinced that she had paranormal powers. The records of her seances run to several thousand pages, so we have only been able to take the merest dip into the evidence. What we have here is a mountain of material which defied, and still defies, disbelief. Hodgson, and other skeptics almost as hostile, was totally convinced by Mrs. Piper. Indeed, Hodgson went further than believing in Mrs. Piper's paranormal powers; he believed that her mediumship proved survival after death. This belief is thought to have rested on evidence he did *not* publish (so much for the claim that only negative results and evidence don't get into print) — it was rumored that Mrs. Piper gave him information of an intensely personal nature concerning a deceased woman. Did this influence his judgement?

What conclusions can we draw about Mrs. Piper? Having waded through a fair slice of the Piper archive ourselves, the only conclusion we can come to is that something remarkable was going on. Coincidence, cold reading, other stratagems of charlatanry, self-deception — none of these even begin to explain Mrs. Piper.

A case for Super-ESP?

Was the information Mrs. Piper gave communicated to her by the spirits of the dead? Or by Super-ESP? Some of Mrs. Piper's control 'spirits' seem to have been more like secondary personalities of the woman herself (G.P. was unusual in that historical evidence of his existence was available) than non-corporeal survivals of dead individuals. Perhaps these *alter egos* made it easier for her to enter an ESP-conducive state. Perhaps they were a measure of her having entered that state.

However, the Super-ESP hypothesis is difficult to square with some intriguing evidence presented by Alan Gauld, whom we have already mentioned in connection with his work on poltergeists. Gauld studied cases in which the information given by 'spirits' about their lives on earth could be verified by consulting historical sources. Gauld was fortunate enough to find an archive of material gathered 20 years previously by a group of amateurs who had held seances over a long period of time and kept and filed copious notes. In this archive Gauld unearthed several cases in which 'spirits' unknown to the participants gave information about their lives which, although subsequently proved to be correct, was originally published *incorrectly* in contemporary sources! In such cases, there can be no question of one of the seance sitters having inadvertently read about the dead person and regurgitated the information in the seance. For the Super-ESP explanation to work here, one would have to say that the medium eschewed clairvoyance or telepathy as a means of accessing the incorrect evidence in favor of using precognition to learn the correct version, which is really straining things a bit far.

Here is an extraordinary example of this type of case, involving one 'Harry Stockbridge', a pseudonym used by Gauld to protect the identity of the family of the young man in question. The 'spirit' of Harry Stockbridge (who was unknown to any of the participants) arrived at the seance unannounced and uninvited and gave the following details about his life (the results of Gauld's researches are given in brackets).

'Second Loot attached Northumberland Fusiliers. Died Fourteenth July, Sixteen.' (A second lieutenant in the Northumberland Fusiliers, named Harry Stockbridge, was killed on 14 July, 1916. The date of death is *incorrectly* given in the War Office official lists.)

'Tyneside Scottish.' (Stockbridge was originally in a Tyneside Irish battalion of the Northumberland Fusiliers, but at the time of his death had been transferred to a Tyneside Scottish battalion, a fact which does not seem to have found its way into print.)

'Tall, dark, thin. Special features large brown eyes.' (Verified by relatives and by a photograph, but not, so far as could be discovered, mentioned in any printed source.)

'I hung out in Leicester.' (True.)

Asked what were his likes and dislikes: 'Problems any. Pepys reading. Water colouring.' (He studied mathematics and physics at university. His university career is referred to in print, but not his subject of study ['Problems' presumably refers to mathematical puzzles and the like — authors' note]. Relatives could not answer for sure on the latter points.)

Asked if he knew a 'Powys Street' about which a sitter had dreamed: 'I knew it well.' (It later transpired that there was a street of this name not far from this birthplace.)

Now, at some points it would be nice to have more detail. More could have been said about Powys Street, for example, and it would have been better if the 'spirit' had actually said 'mathematical problems' or even 'number problems'. But the source gives name, date of death, appearance, regiment, battalion — these are specific and were all checked and found to be correct, even when unpublished or published in error. Coincidence seems an unlikely explanation. Fraud would be incredible. Are we really expected to believe that an amateur seance group went to great lengths to scour records, and even dig up unpublished information, just to deceive a researcher whose appearance on the scene 20 years *later* they took no steps to invite and could not have foreseen? And if they had worked from records (the first obvious port of call), why were the errors in those records not carried over into the seances? Fraud is unbelievable here. Psi effects seem the most plausible, and parsimonious, explanation.

Spirits for the Modern Age

Some semblance of mediumship still continues in 'channelling' and similar practices, but there are probably good psychological reasons why the age of the great mediums seems to have passed. Just as 'Philip' was dreamed up in order to catalyze PK effects, so the 'control spirits' of mediums (whether 'Dr. Phinuit', 'G.P.', or the Red Indian wise men so much in vogue with modern Caucasian American mediums) may really be little more, in most cases, than psychological props for the medium.

Rex Stanford and others have made the point that psi events (especially powerful ones) are *ego-alien*. That is, we are not truly comfortable with them, so our chances of exerting psi effects are stronger if we can somehow manage not to feel responsible for them. This was part of the reasoning behind Stanford's non-intentional psi experiments. If we can 'blame' psi effects on something else, on some kind of scapegoat, our psi capacities may be liberated. 'Spirits' represent that 'something else'.

If we follow this line of argument, which is not implausible, it would go some way towards explaining why great mediums are a thing of the past. Spirits were culturally acceptable in Mrs. Piper's day; the spiritualist craze was in full swing. Today their acceptability has declined. Many people think the traditional image of the medium and his or her control spirit passé, banal, even disreputable. Our culture has changed, and it may be that other forms of psychological prop are now more potent, more powerful. Let us dip a toe in some dangerous waters by considering what these may be.

Two props suggest themselves. One would be 'unidentified flying objects', UFOs. UFOlogists have reported many cases of alleged spontaneous psi among people who claim to have been contacted by UFOs or even (as is increasingly popular) abducted by their occupants. In keeping with the times, it is easier to attribute psi effects to a man-in-black from a distant galaxy than to a discarnate spirit. Claimed contacts with extraterrestrial objects and beings have not been evaluated with psi testing in a formal way, but this is a possible

A modern computer-designed, computer-printed astrological birth chart. Some astrologers are capable of making accurate statements about clients, but are the charts they draw up merely psychological props which facilitate the use of ESP?

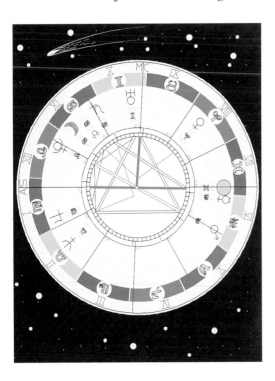

avenue for exploration. Another possibility concerns astrology. There is little scientific evidence to show that *traditional* astrology has validity, but there are studies which suggest that astrologers may be able to give more information from birth charts than coincidence and cross-matching would allow. Astrologers might have the ultimate psychological prop for the psi they use to make their readings, namely a system which is in theory scientific and testable. One could hardly imagine a better psychological prop in an age of science. If this is so, there may be individuals with interesting psi test abilities among astrologers. Getting to test these hypotheses will not be easy, since UFOlogists, parapsychologists, and astrologers are often wary of each other, but our suggestion is certainly testable and some day someone will make the attempt, we hope!

We turn now to a final line of research relevant to the issue of survival after death: the study of reincarnation. Clearly, if a strong case could be made for reincarnation, one would logically be forced to accept some kind of survival beyond death. In the first edition of our book, we considered two lines of evidence, 'hypnotic regression' to past lives and alleged reincarnation in children. This time round we will confine ourselves to the latter, cutting straight to the heart of the matter and the best evidence available.

Reincarnation studies

In 1977 the prestigious *Journal of Nervous and Mental Diseases* published two papers on the subject of reincarnation by psychiatrist Dr. Ian Stevenson, then based at the University of Virginia. That such a journal should have given space to such an unusual topic is a mark of the esteem in which Stevenson's work is held, even by skeptics.

There are two good reasons why this research is much more powerful than 'hypnotic regression to past lives' with adults. First, Stevenson's cases concern young, in some cases *very* young, children; allegations that 'past lives' are constructed from mostly forgotten snippets from newspapers, books, magazines, films, and TV programs are simply not plausible with respect to two- or three-year olds. Second, Stevenson's researches have largely been conducted in developing countries where sources of communication of this kind are not plentiful. In short, a 'regression' from a literate and observant Western adult poses far more problems than cases involving young children from semi-literate cultures.

The characteristic quality of Stevenson's work is its sheer, even intimidating, professionalism. Through one of his many contacts, he hears first details of a case of possible reincarnation. Almost without exception, the case concerns a very young child (in around half of his cases, two years old or younger) whose utterances and behavior suggest that he or she has had a past life. Off Stevenson goes to study the case at first hand, to Alaska, Lebanon, India, Sri Lanka, Brazil, and so on. He speaks fluent French and German in addition to English, and in other cases uses trusted interpreters to interrogate witnesses. Witnesses are almost always interviewed at least twice to check for reliability, and for any given case Stevenson uses at least two interpreters, and sometimes more, to check testimony and the accuracy of interpretation. He possesses a vast library of tapes from these interviews. Documents, registers, and archives are checked for corroboration of testimony. Stevenson's books contain abundant, fine-detail reporting of his research.

We will consider first a case of considerable evidential value which Stevenson was able to investigate before the two families concerned met. There was thus no danger of the testimony of the child's family being contaminated by the testimony of the family of the deceased person of whom the child appeared to be a reincarnation.

Stevenson arrived in Lebanon in 1964 (when it was still possible to visit Lebanon in some kind of safety) after being told by a young Lebanese, who had assisted him in a Brazilian investigation two years earlier, that there were many cases of reincarnation in his country. Among the Druse (Druze) people, who belong to a minority Islamic sect, belief in reincarnation is strong. Indeed, reincarnation is a fundamental tenet of their religion. However, many Druses express considerable skepticism about particular alleged individual instances of reincarnation; they are not gullible people.

As Stevenson set out to find his Lebanese contact, he learned of a case in the village he had come to visit, Kornayel, some ten miles east of Beirut. It transpired that the father of the child concerned was the cousin of the man he had come to meet. On his first evening, Stevenson made complete written notes of his interview with this man, Mohammed Elawar, and his wife. On this occasion only an untrained interpreter was on hand; for four further days Stevenson used two other, trained, interpreters. On a second visit five months later (with another interpreter) Stevenson rechecked much of the material he had gathered on his first visit and added new information.

On his first visit Stevenson was told how Mohammed's son Imad had been born in December 1958. The first word he spoke was 'Jamileh'. Although his parents did not know it, this was the name of the mistress of Ibrahim Boumhazy, the man whose reincarnation Imad appears to have been. As soon as he could string sentences together, Imad started to speak about his past life. His father scolded him for telling lies, but Imad persisted. At the age of two, he spontaneously recognized a neighbor of Boumhazy's in the street. He also gave many details about Boumhazy's house, his relatives, and his life. Nonetheless the Elawar family did not feel moved to do any checking. Mohammed, the father, had once attended a funeral in the town of Khriby, where Boumhazy had lived, but had not met any member of the Boumhazy family.

The two villages, Kornayel and Khriby, are only 20 miles apart, but the people of the region (at that time) tended not to travel very much and members of the Elawar and Boumhazy families were adamant that they had not met. After collecting all the information he could about Imad, Stevenson set out for Khriby to collect as much information as possible from the Boumhazy family.

After this, Stevenson took Imad and his father to Khriby, where Imad was introduced to the Boumhazy family. He recognized many of them spontaneously, addressing them in the correct manner. The Boumhazys were astonished at the way Imad *behaved*, which is not a trivial element in these cases. This five-year-old child behaved, the family said, just as Ibrahim had.

An imam (priest) on his rounds in a Druse village. Although reincarnation is part of the Druse doctrine, individual cases are regarded with considerable skepticism.

Some of the statements made by Imad about his past life, including intimate details and precise observations about his home and relatives, are listed opposite. The sheer wealth of information given, and its very specific nature, seems to rule out coincidence as an even remotely plausible explanation. Of 57 statements checked by Stevenson, 51 were correct and verified.

The case of Imad Elawar is one of many investigated and scrupulously reported by Stevenson. Given a body of such cases, what explanations other than reincarnation can we offer for them?

Coincidence No-one has ever suggested that coincidence is a plausible explanation, and neither do we.

Faulty memory In the Imad Elawar case, both families were adamant that they had not met. Thus, conversations between them could not have yielded information which they then unwittingly regurgitated. Casual, indirect, and forgotten contact cannot explain the huge wealth of specific and correct comments made by Imad. In other cases, researchers have been able to verify that the family of the dead person has had no contact at all with the child's family; sometimes the exact identity of the child's past life was not known at the time of research. Problems of memory are irrelevant here.

In many of the cultures Stevenson's cases come from, communication and social mobility are very restricted. Most people live and die within a very narrow domain. Casual leakage of information is much less likely than in our media-saturated, highly mobile Western societies.

Fraud One might reasonably ask why two Lebanese families (totalling 17 people interviewed) would *want* to conspire to fool a researcher who would then publish his findings in a foreign country. There was nothing in it for them. Some aspects of Imad's reincarnation were clearly embarrassing to them (a five-year-old reminiscing about good times with his mistress, for example). It is also impossible to 'coach' children this young (and younger — half of Stevenson's cases concern children aged two or under) to go along with a fictional story in a plausible and consistent way.

There are other cases where fraud is not credible, cases in which the child claims to be the reincarnation of a murderer or criminal, for example. In some cases the family of the child has clearly gone to some lengths to keep the child's utterances quiet and make sure the neighbors didn't get to hear of them.

REINCARNATION: THE CASE OF IMAD ELAWAR

For each item listed below there was at least one informant and one corroborator. In many cases there were two or more informants and corroborators. Information from Imad Elawar was obtained in advance of Stevenson's visit to Khriby, Lebanon.

Information given by Imad Elawar

1. His name was Bouhamzy and he lived in Khriby.
2. He had a woman called Jamileh.
3. She was beautiful
4. She wore high heels.
5. He had a brother 'Amin'.

6. Amin worked at Tripoli.
7. Amin worked in a courthouse

8. There was someone called 'Mehibeh'.
9. He had brothers called Said and Toufic
10. He had a sister, Huda.
11. A truck ran over a man, broke both his legs, and crushed his trunk.
12. He (Ibrahim) was a friend of Kemal Joumblatt.
13. He was very fond of hunting.

14. He had a double-barrelled shotgun.
15. He also had a rifle.
16. He had hidden his gun.

17. He had a brown dog and had once beaten another dog.
18. His house was in Khriby; there was a slope before it.
19. There were two wells at the house, one full and one empty.

20. They were building a new garden when he died.
21. There were apple and cherry trees in the garden.
22. He had a small yellow car and a minibus.
23. He also had a truck.
24. He used the truck for hauling rocks.
25. There were two garages at his house.

26. The tools for the car were kept in the attic.
27. He had a goat, and sheep.
28. He had five children.

Stevenson's comments

1. The first name (i.e. Ibrahim) was never used.
2. Correct: Ibrahim's mistress.
3. Jamileh was famous in Khriby for her beauty.
4. Correct, and very unusual amongst Druse women.
5. Amin was a close relative. Close relatives are sometimes referred to as 'brother'.
6. Correct.
7. Amin was an official of the Lebanese government. His office was in a courthouse.
8. Cousin of Ibrahim Bouhamzy.
9. Ibrahim had cousins called Said and Toufic (see note 5).
10. Correct..
11. All details correct for Said Bouhamzy (see note 9)..
12. Ibrahim was a friend of this Druse politician and philosopher.
13. Ibrahim was passionately fond of hunting. Imad frequently asked his father to take him hunting.
14. Correct.
15. Correct.
16. Correct. Presumably refers to the rifle, which was an illegal possession in Lebanon..
17. Ibrahim had a brown dog, which had once fought with another dog which Ibrahim had beaten.
18. Correct.
19. Correct. These were not spring wells, but concrete concavities used for storing grape juice. During the rainy season one became filled with water, while the shallower one did not, since water evaporated from it. Hence one was full and one was empty.
20. When Ibrahim died, the garden was being rebuilt.
21. Correct.

22. Both correct.
23. Correct.
24. Correct.
25. Almost correct. Ibrahim kept his vehicles in the open, outside two *sheds*.
26. Correct.

27. Correct.
28. Quite wrong: he had none. Said (see note 9) had five sons.

Stranger and stranger

Another researcher, Antonia Mills, who travelled to India on three separate trips between 1987 and 1989, has documented 26 cases of reincarnation among Moslem families in sects where reincarnation is definitely not an encouraged belief. She has also documented ten cases of reincarnation where either the child was Hindu and the previous personality Moslem, or *vice versa*. Hindu-Moslem relations vary in different parts of the Indian subcontinent, depending on local history, but as a rule Hindus and Moslems do not intermarry and in some towns and cities live apart in separate quarters or districts. In some provinces religious differences are an excuse for widespread inter-community violence and murder. It is not believable for a moment that any Moslem or Hindu family would want to cook up a reincarnation in which the child was previously of the other religious group. Nor is it possible to imagine a high-caste Hindu family wanting to fabricate a reincarnation of a low-caste person. Nevertheless such cases are among those reported by Stevenson.

Are birthmarks or birth defects physical carry-overs from previous lives? Reincarnation researcher Ian Stevenson has found some support for this suggestion. A large port wine stain, for example, could represent extensive burns sustained at the time of death.

Let us venture a little further into this especially intriguing area. Stevenson has reported many cases in which not only is there a great deal of psychological evidence pertaining to reincarnation, but also physical evidence. Specific birth marks and birth defects have been reported as being closely related to the cause, or effects, of death of the previous personality. For example, a pattern of blotchy birthmarks on a child's back may correspond to exit wounds from a fatal gunshot in a previous incarnation. There is also one report of an albino being reincarnated as an albino. Stevenson has one or more books in press on this subject as we write, and having seen some of his evidence in illustrated lectures we await publication with considerable anticipation. The frequency of different types of birthmark can be estimated from medical statistics, so it should be possible to show just how unlikely such match-ups are (the anti-chance odds are likely to be astronomical). Given the objective nature of these marks and defects, coincidence and fraud are wholly excluded even as theoretical possibilities, and mistakes of testimony are irrelevancies.

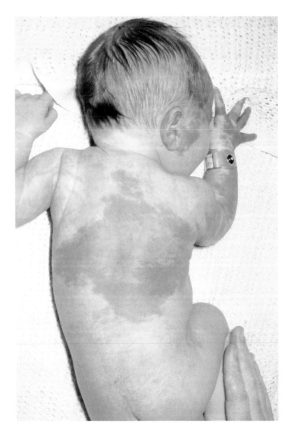

In 1991 researcher Jurgen Keil, who worked with Stevenson in experimental studies with Pavel Stepanek two decades earlier, reported his first reincarnation studies from Burma, Thailand, and Turkey. Keil, based in Tasmania, makes it clear that his research was not motivated by a strong belief in survival: 'I regard a belief in the finality of death as reasonable.' While he modestly refers to his research as 'a limited field study replication', his 16 investigated cases of reincarnation include several in which families clearly attempted to keep the matter confidential (one family requested anonymity, fearful of the attitudes of foreigners and of their own peers if the facts leaked out). The quality of documentation and correspondence in these cases is good, and we hope this is the beginning of further extensive field confirmations of Stevenson's findings.

We can only speculate about the frequency of reincarnation (in some cultures reincarnation is regarded as universal, but conscious recollection of it is considered rare). There are some indications that violent death may be involved in a far higher percentage of reincarnations than one would expect, so that a 'wrongly terminated life' may be likely to result in a conscious reincarnation. There also appears to be a tendency for a relatively short time (a few weeks or months) to elapse between death and reincarnation. However, this may simply imply that in cases with longer intervals between death and reincarnation, the reincarnated person is less likely to spontaneously recall a past life. Reported cases are by no means confined to cultures with a belief in reincarnation, though many are reported from such cultures probably because the people involved are less reluctant to disclose them to researchers. There are, indeed, a handful of Western cases. Finally, children who appear to be reincarnations do not become chronically maladjusted adolescents or adults; the majority seem to gradually lose the vivid memories of their past lives as they mature.

The case for survival

It will be clear to the reader by now that, in respect of survival of physical death, we consider the evidence compiled by Stevenson, Mills, Keil, and a few others to be superior to any other (save for aspects of the Piper mediumship). Having read many hundreds of pages of Stevenson's writings, and seen the beginnings of independent confirmation, we cannot in honesty force ourselves away from the view that something of truly great importance is being revealed to us here. One of us (Sargent) would like specifically to note that reincarnation is a possibility he is very uncomfortable with. Looking at projected world population statistics, at the degradation of the environment, and at recent European history, he does not find the notion of having to return at some future date enormously appealing. But such personal, emotional bias cannot be grounds for rejecting the evidence, no matter how unpalatable its implications may be.

We consider that virtually anyone, reading Stevenson's research and cautious interpretations, would have at least to agree that there is something astonishing here. We urge readers to consult the Bibliography and find out for themselves.

While the Super-ESP hypothesis remains a theoretical explanation for the reincarnation evidence, one final telling point should be made. As Stevenson himself notes, Super-ESP could perhaps account for the *information* reported by the children. However, why Super-ESP should collect information so exclusively about one other human being and not manifest itself in any other manner is hard to explain. Even worse, Super-ESP can hardly account for the *behavior* of the children. In Imad's case, what impressed the Boumhazy family most was that the child behaved as their own son had done. Recognition of similarities between the personality of the dead person and the child is sometimes quite spontaneous by family members. Alan Gauld has studied many of the older psychical researchers in great detail, and knows more about them than anyone could possibly expect to learn by ESP, but he is also sure that not for a moment could he accurately *impersonate* them. Reincarnated children do this at an age when their role-playing skills and abilities are often poorly developed. This is not a point to be dismissed lightly.

Antonia Mills discusses a case in which a Hindu-born child, Naresh Kumar Raydas, was adamant that he had been born a Moslem, the son of an old Fakir by his second wife. From the age of two the child performed *namaz* (Moslem ritual prayer) when he felt he was unobserved by his own Hindu family. He would follow the old Fakir, begging alms and praying for people as a Moslem would. When finally taken to the Fakir's family, he identified his siblings and discussed his death (being killed driving a cart) with his mother (he had a birthmark which corresponded to the crushing wounds suffered by the dead son, Mushir). Before he met Naresh, the Fakir did not believe in reincarnation, but when discussing the case with Mills he shook with emotion. As Mills reports: 'Unable to sleep, at midnight he prayed, "Allah, what is this mystery?" '

Whether one wishes to pray to a deity or believes there is nothing there to pray to, the mystery surrounding these children is one which cannot be ignored.

11

Psi, science, and the future

We consider that the experiments and facts summarized in this book constitute a strong claim for genuine anomalies in the realm of human ability. The case is persuasive. Human beings do seem to use sensory abilities beyond their 'conventional' senses. They do seem to influence distant events and objects through acts of will alone.

Nonetheless, many scientists find it hard to accept the methods and findings of parapsychology. They either ignore the evidence available, make superficial comments about it, claim that it is all due to erroneous experimental methods or mass fraud, or simply assert that the effects are impossible and cannot occur. There are at least two reasons for this. One is historical. Parapsychology still carries with it memories of mediums, dubious materializations of ectoplasm, and assorted kinds of charlatanry. Scientists are wary of subject matter so controversial. However, this is not a rational basis for dismissing parapsychology as a science. A dubious past hardly disqualifies a science! After all, chemistry had its origins in alchemy and astronomy in astrology — Kepler, among many other early eminent astronomers, dabbled in and was highly sympathetic to astrology.

The other reason is of more general importance. Science often handles true innovation very badly. One has only to consider the mixture of fury, rage, and vituperative criticism ladled out to the pioneers of vaccination, the theory of continental drift, hypnotic anesthesia, and many other genuine advances in knowledge to realize this. At heart, science is all too often a deeply conservative process. The suggestion that scientists are simply being very cautious, wisely reluctant to accept new evidence prematurely, fails to explain the irrational emotion displayed by many scientists when faced with evidence of genuine anomalies.

In this final chapter we delve a little deeper into the irrationality of science when confronted with such evidence. While the thrust of what we have to say is harsh, the harshest judgements are those made by members of the organization which betrayed basic principles of scientific enquiry.

The 'Starbaby' scandal

There exists in the United States an organization calling itself the Committee for Scientific Investigation of Claims of the Paranormal, or CSICOP for short. While the Executive Council of CSICOP has, in fact, few scientists, it has assiduously courted distinguished scientists as members, giving itself the appearance of a scientific organization, an appearance which it exploits to the full when its members go 'ghostbusting'. Interestingly, CSICOP as an organization does not undertake any research of its own. The reason for this is simple: it once did, and the results of that research merit a special place in the history of science.

Between 1976 and 1980 a group of CSICOP's senior Council members investigated the findings of the French researchers Michel and Françoise Gauquelin. The Gauquelins' data, collected over decades, show that certain special groups (distinguished scientists, artists, sports champions, etc.) tend to be born with certain planets in certain positions (sectors) of the sky. One of us (Eysenck) has long been interested in, and has made a special study of, this remarkable work and can testify to the excellence of its method. The CSICOP group

Opposite: Arab astrologers chart the heavens in a sixteenth-century illustration to The Travels of Sir John Mandeville. *Astronomy grew out of astrology, just as parapsychology has grown out of gee-whizzery.*

investigated one particular finding, the 'Mars effect' for sports champions.

One member of the CSICOP group, the statistician Marvin Zelen, did not accept the Gauquelins' claims about the frequencies of planets in different sectors of the heavens (there are astronomical technicalities which affect expected planetary frequencies), so he proposed a 'challenge' to the Gauquelins. The 'Zelen test' involved comparing a small group of 'Mars effect' champions with a very large 'control' group of non-champions, born in the same locations and at similar seasons. Next, Zelen (with CSICOP Chairman Paul Kurtz and astronomer George Abell) collected a new sample of data for sports champions to test the claimed Mars effect.

The results of the 'Zelen test' were absolutely clear-cut. The Gauquelins' statistics were correct. Their sports champions showed the Mars effect and the 16,000+ control sample did not — they showed exactly the theoretical frequencies for the placement of Mars which the Gauquelins had claimed. The Gauquelins were wholly vindicated by this finding.

The Mars effect. The Gauquelins showed that more sports champions are born when the planet Mars is close to the eastern horizon (Rise) or directly overhead (Culmination) than at other times of year. The left hand scale and blue line represent data from the Gauquelins; the right hand scale and green line show data from an independent survey.

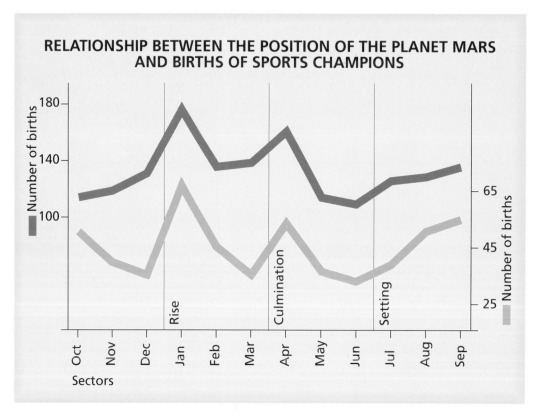

After that things got muddier and more confused. KZA (Kurtz, Zelen, and Abell) started finding all kinds of reasons why the results of the Zelen test didn't please them. They began to chop up the data for sports champions in ways which were not part of any pre-agreed statistical analysis, dropping female champions on the bizarre grounds that 'women have not had the same opportunities men have had to pursue sports', dividing up the Gauquelins' sample of champions in *post hoc* ways in an attempt to discredit their Mars effect, collecting their own sample of champions without an agreed written protocol for doing so and erroneously claiming it disproved the effect, and so on.

Many of the issues surrounding KZA's research are technical, and it would be too time-consuming to go through them all here. The reader who wants to know how CSICOP operates must check the reports cited in the Bibliography. To prove our point about CSICOP we will quote the reactions of skeptics among CSICOP's own membership.

The first to break ranks was Dennis Rawlins, a CSICOP ex-Fellow, who remains highly

What makes sports champions? Physical prowess, yes, but also a relentless will to win. The differing frequency of champion births through the year is real enough, but it is tempting to look for explanations a little nearer home than the planet Mars. Might time of conception or the first trimester in utero be just as significant as time of birth?

skeptical about the Mars effect but who nevertheless felt that the KZA research was being conducted along illegitimate lines. Very simple errors were being made, despite Rawlins' best efforts to point them out. His attempts to circulate his comments on the problems of the research were systematically suppressed by CSICOP, which refused to allow him to speak at meetings and denied him access to their own journal while continuing to publish misleading accounts of the research findings and conclusions. Although Rawlins repeatedly warned KZA about the errors in their research, he was ignored — and then suppressed. Finally he was dropped from the list of CSICOP's Fellows. The cover-up had begun.

When other CSICOP members began to hear of Rawlins' treatment, some of them (to their credit) started making enquiries about his criticisms. When they did so, they found themselves barred from publishing what they had learned in CSICOP publications (which continued to carry misleading accounts of the research). One of those so excluded was Richard Kammann, a professor of psychology who has co-written very critical papers of his own on the subject of parapsychology. Kammann's final account of the treatment he received from KZA and the CSICOP organization is staggering. If the reader is motivated to read only one of the many books and papers in our Bibliography, read Kammann's.

Kammann researched the entire affair from start to finish. His conclusion was that KZA had 'persisted in offering to the public a set of demonstrably false statistical arguments against the Mars effect in spite of four years of continuous and steadily mounting criticism of their illogic.... The striking feature of all these fallacies was not just their unmooring from the anchors of logic but their unsinkability in four years of competent statistical bombardment by Michel Gauquelin, Elizabeth Scott, Dennis Rawlins and Ray Hyman.' Scott, a statistician, and Hyman, a psychologist, were both involved with CSICOP at the time. 'Like the other Fellows of CSICOP,' Kammann continues, 'I couldn't accept that Dennis Rawlins was the single honest and correct person on a nine-man Council consisting of men of such stature and reputation as Martin Gardner, Professor Ray Hyman, the Amazing Randi and Kendrick Frazier. After seven months of research, I have come to the opposite conclusion. CSICOP has no defense of the trio's Mars fiasco and has progressively trapped itself, degree by irreversible degree, into an anti-Rawlins propaganda campaign, into suppression of his evidence, and into stonewalling against other critics.'

Kammann also lists the ways in which he, like Rawlins and anyone else who criticized CSICOP from within, was subjected to ridicule, suppression of criticism, denial of access to publications, and prolonged stonewalling. His article is as damning an indictment of CSICOP as one can possibly imagine, because his skepticism and integrity were not in question and he was, at the time, a CSICOP member. Another CSICOP member, the Dutch journalist Piet Hein Hoebens, has said that he regards Kammann's account of the KZA affair as 'an eminently fair, highly readable and — given the circumstances — remarkably restrained statement from a distinguished skeptic who has gone to almost incredible lengths in his attempts to help CSICOP free itself from its Martian predicament.'

But not even KZA could go on stonewalling forever. After publication of a long summary review by the wholly independent British scholar Patrick Curry, and seven years after the Zelen test had first been proposed, *The Skeptical Enquirer* (CSICOP's house magazine) finally published a 'Reappraisal'. In this, KZA admit their *post hoc* dabbling with the champions sample from the Gauquelins was wrong and that they should have agreed a protocol for their own research with the Gauquelins (to determine what predictions the Gauquelins would have made for the data). But it was a grudging and mean-spirited retraction, with no apologies to Rawlins (whose name was deleted from the list of those who were 'involved in [our] experiments'), no apologies to the Gauquelins for the baseless insinuations made about the trustworthiness of their data, and no recognition of most of the criticism from CSICOP's own ranks.

The reason we have detailed this shameful affair at some length is that CSICOP — despite having abandoned research of its own, possibly mindful of Curry's judgement that the KZA debacle 'must call into question any further CSICOP involvement in research on the Mars effect, and possibly other "paranormal" areas' — has continued to flourish as an organization and uses its influence to attack any area of science which it dislikes, and to harass and suppress researchers in controversial areas of science. A recent, infamous, example of this was the Amazing Randi's extraordinary behavior in the laboratory of French researcher Jacques Benveniste. Benveniste published biochemical findings which appeared to support homeopathic medical theories in the highly prestigious *Les Comptes Rendus de l'Académie des Sciences*, the journal of the French Academy of Sciences. An investigating team was despatched by the journal *Nature* to investigate these highly controversial findings, and Randi was one of the investigators. Benveniste's laboratory literally became a circus while Randi was there. Rather than bore the reader with the details, we will simply note that this time even *The Skeptical Enquirer* published articles questioning the validity of the investigation, accusing it of 'careless criticisms', 'squander(ing) credibility', and 'preconceived bias'. Randi, during a public lecture on the affair, 'mimicked the Gallic mannerisms of Benveniste and made highly derogatory comments about "French science". Many in the audience were offended.'

Quite simply, CSICOP is not a scientific organization. The preponderance of conjurers and media people in its higher echelons show it to be a propaganda movement, dedicated to 'ghostbusting' and to extirpating 'irrational' beliefs. Unfortunately, due to its expertise in media manipulation and the sympathetic attitude of many academics who vaguely feel that 'ghostbusting' is a good idea although they remain blissfully ignorant of the facts, CSICOP members have had a baneful effect on parapsychology and retarded its development, until recently that is.

To his great credit, the psychologist Ray Hyman is that rare bird, a CSICOP member who is prepared to look at the evidence and attempt to assess it in something resembling a judicious and fair manner. His dialogue with Charles Honorton, over ganzfeld research, has enabled parapsychology to make a real breakthrough in recent years. It has been a difficult road, however, and the skeptics have abandoned fallacious criticisms only slowly.

The ganzfeld controversy

In 1982, at a conference in Cambridge to mark the centenary of the British Society for Psychical Research and the 25th anniversary of the founding of the Parapsychological Association, Hyman presented a version of a subsequently published paper criticizing published experiments on ganzfeld ESP. This body of research is recognized as perhaps the strongest that parapsychology has to offer, but Hyman made many criticisms of it, on statistical and experimental grounds. His assertion was that flaws in experimental methods made the whole body of research untrustworthy.

Jettisoning the support that ganzfeld studies give to the ESP hypothesis this would be a real blow to parapsychology. So Honorton and Hyman began a dialogue to try to thrash out their different views of the research, pooling ideas and comparing their evaluations of individual experiments. In December 1986 they published a joint communiqué of agreed findings and recommendations for the future.

The first major point here is that Hyman abandoned his statistical criticisms of the ganzfeld experiments as a body of evidence. While a few individual experiments may be untrustworthy on statistical grounds, Hyman finally accepted that statistical errors could not possibly explain the vast odds against chance for the findings of the experiments as a group. Nor was it plausible to assert that the published experiments were lucky breaks and that there are many unpublished, unsuccessful experiments lying around. One can calculate how many such unpublished experiments would have to have been conducted to make published evidence worthless, and the number runs into many hundreds. Given how long these experiments take to conduct, and the handful of experimenters available within parapsychology to conduct them, everyone agrees that this is not a credible skeptical stance. Hyman's statistical criticisms were untenable (obviously so even on first reading of his paper), but it took him some time to retract them. Nonetheless, one must give him credit for being prepared to change his mind.

Hyman's second set of criticisms concerned the experimental methods used in ganzfeld research. Were 'sensory cues' completely eliminated? In a few free-response experiments, the judges had not been given duplicate targets (fingerprint clues can be left on originals). Was the random determination of targets correctly conducted? Such matters cannot always be decided as simply and objectively as the statistical, number-crunching element of Hyman's criticisms. There is abundant room for the operation of a critic's own prejudices when it comes to deciding whether an experimental method is sound or not. A piece of research from conventional psychology illustrates this tendency very neatly.

In this study the researchers wrote up a (non-existent) experiment on astrology and submitted copies of the article, reporting chance results, to ten leading academic journals. They also submitted copies of the article, this time reporting results favoring astrology, to ten other journals, the two groups of journals being matched for prestige and for the percentage of submitted papers they accept for publication. Every journal given a 'positive' paper rejected it, the referees (commentators who evaluate articles for publication) often criticizing the methods used. Nine of the ten journals offered the 'negative' paper accepted it for publication, their referees often praising the same methods of research that had been damned by the other referees! Clearly, appraisal of the excellence or otherwise of an experimental method is strongly influenced by whether one cares for the results or not.

Ray Hyman, by playing devil's advocate for the skeptical viewpoint, triggered research that made evidence for ESP even more convincing.

At the time of Hyman's criticisms, one of us (Sargent) had reported seven ganzfeld experiments. Hyman classified only one of them as having good random determination of the target. The one 'good' study gave the results closest to chance and was the least favorable to the ESP hypothesis. Since all seven experiments used exactly the same randomization procedure, it is obvious and demonstrable that Hyman's judgement was influenced by his own biases. Either all the experiments were good or they were all bad; it is logically incoherent to classify them differently.

Fortunately, it is possible to transcend such personal biases, at least to some degree. Here we enter a new area of statistical analysis called *metanalysis*. While the term may sound forbidding, the logic behind it is very simple.

In our first chapter we explained the notions of *chance average* and *scatter* in relation to individual experiments, and guesses or trials within experiments. What metanalysis does, in essence, is to consider each individual *experiment* as if it were one 'guess' or 'trial'. *In metanalysis the experiment becomes the unit of analysis.* In any statistical science, what we look for are the characteristics of the *distribution* of experimental results. In particular, we are interested to know whether the average value of the distribution pattern is different from the average value that would be expected by chance alone. Applying metanalysis to ganzfeld experiments, what we find is a normal distribution pattern with an average value of 38%, clearly different from the 25% average that one would expect by chance.

The debate intensifies

This statistic alone confirms what we already knew: the results of ganzfeld experiments cannot be attributed to chance. However, because of the more powerful statistical nature of metanalysis, we can go a great deal further. For example, we can get a measure of what is technically known as *effect size*. This is not conveyed simply by the 38% figure. Effect size depends, among other things, on how many trials are included in individual experiments. If huge amounts of data are collected, findings which are statistically significant may actually be vanishingly small. Effect size is a good index of how *practically* significant a finding is, as opposed to its purely *statistical* significance. When considering effect size, we are not only asking 'Is this due to chance?' but also 'Does this really matter?'

With the ganzfeld data, the effect size is large, unquestionably an important, practically significant finding. Robert Rosenthal, the psychologist who has done more than anyone else to implement the broad use of metanalysis in psychology, has shown that the effect size obtained in ganzfeld research is larger than that obtained in several major areas of research in conventional psychology.

Metanalysis also enables us to assess how important details of experimental methods are. Groups of judges can assess experiments in terms of 'flaw counts', giving yes or no judgements for a variety of key elements in the experimental methods used. With training, judges can come to a very high level of agreement on flaw counts, working independently and regardless of their skeptical position. Flaw counts include such factors as whether aspects of the experimental method were fully described, whether data recording was wholly objective (e.g. machine recording, or photographing the fall of dice in old PK dice experiments), whether duplicate targets were used for judging (in free-response experiments), and so on. By using clearly specified elements of experimental methods in these analyses, it is possible to eliminate global, subjective decisions about how 'good' or 'bad' experiments are, and to achieve simpler, more reliable judgements about them. There are no perfect experiments to be found anywhere in science. The question is, does the quality of an experiment have any relationship to the effect size which is found for it? If there is a negative relationship, it means that the best conducted, 'blue riband' experiments have weaker results than ones with poorer method. That would suggest that, after all, ESP might be 'Error Some Place'.

This argument has taken much longer to resolve than the simple, statistical one, but it has finally been agreed, in the case of the ganzfeld research, that there is no significant relationship between flaws in an experiment and apparent evidence for ESP in the results. This is now agreed, after independent reviewers have analyzed the evidence, in addition to Hyman and Honorton. Allegations that ganzfeld results are artifacts of sloppy experimenting simply do not hold water.

We can go further with metanalysis. Are there differences between the results obtained by different researchers? We can take the aggregate research findings of each experimenter and conduct a metanalysis on those. We can take the results of different experimenters and see if they show *homogeneity* (everyone gets much the same results). In fact analyses show a small degree of *heterogeneity* — some experimenters consistently get better results than others (this has nothing to do with whether their experimental methods are good or weak). This does not mean that some experimenters are less honest or trustworthy than others! As Rosenthal notes: 'That different investigators may obtain significantly different results from their subjects is well known in various areas of psychology.' He goes on to recount an eyelid conditioning experiment in which one set of researchers obtained results in the predicted direction 94% of the time whereas another group did so only 62% of the time. Indeed, the heterogeneity of findings in parapsychology is far less than in much of psychology. Actually, if one ignored all the results obtained by the two experimenters who have reported more ganzfeld research than anyone else (Honorton and Sargent), the remaining results would still be hugely significant. The findings do not depend on the contributions of one or two individual researchers. We edge closer to the 'repeatable experiment'.

There is more, much more, that metanalysis tells us. For example, even though the mean (average) success rate of ganzfeld experiments is way beyond the limits of chance, metanalysis predicts that some experiments will yield results that are within the limits of chance. Indeed, in the case of experiments with small sample sizes, a majority would be expected to do so. Metanalysis tells the researcher exactly how many trials he should conduct in an experiment if he wishes to be pretty certain of finding a statistically significant result, and that number is *far higher* than in many of the experiments which have actually been conducted! Metanalysis shows us that many 'failures to replicate' ganzfeld results *should* have failed; they simply did not test enough subjects.

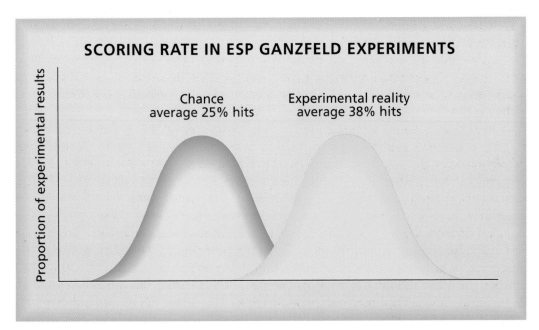

SCORING RATE IN ESP GANZFELD EXPERIMENTS

Proportion of experimental results

Chance
average 25% hits

Experimental reality
average 38% hits

Using metanalysis it became clear that the distribution of results in ganzfeld experiments had a much higher average value than chance would have predicted.

Statistician Jessica Utts, who like Rosenthal and others has viewed parapsychology as a great testing ground for metanalysis (which bids fair to raise all of psychology into new areas of understanding), has provided a further, mind-boggling finding from metanalysis. Using Hyman's own collation of ganzfeld experiments, Utts took out all those which reported statistically significant findings (in the distribution of experiments, these are the ones at the top end of the range). If the effect size is big, there should still be a visible bias even in the remaining experiments towards the true effect (38%) rather than the chance average (25%). Utts computed that, if the 13 'failures' were pooled together, *as a body of experiments they showed a statistically better than chance ESP effect.* Many failures are actually successes which don't quite make it — this is only seen when evidence from different experiments, and from different experimenters, is pieced together.

We consider that the metanalyses sprouting up within parapsychology have given a dramatic impetus to the subject. They come as close to proof as science will allow that there are genuine anomalies in the findings of many thousands of experiments, conducted over many decades, which cannot possibly be explained away as bad, inept, or fraudulent science. The breakthrough is here at last. The interest in parapsychology being shown by 'outsiders' such as Robert Rosenthal, Daryl Bem, and Jessica Utts is a sign of this. But we would be foolish not to expect rearguard action from those whose biases do not allow them to change their notion of how the world works.

An official appraisal

Psi is part, although an elusive part, of human functioning. Many organizations, including the U.S. military, are interested in optimizing human performance, particularly in conditions of high stress.

In December 1987 the National Research Council (NRC) of the American National Academy of Sciences released a report, *Enhancing Human Performance*, which included a summation of progress in many areas of psychology, including parapsychology, prepared for the U.S. Army. The Committee Chair stated that 'perhaps our strongest conclusions are in the area of parapsychology.... The Committee finds no scientific justification from research conducted over a period of 130 years for the existence of parapsychological phenomena.'

If this were true, it would be a damning indictment. However, a quick glance at the names of those who wrote the NRC report and assessed parapsychology opens our eyes: Ray Hyman and James Alcock, both CSICOP Executive Members. No parapsychologist, nor any 'neutral party', was involved.

The NRC report is a curious document. It actually excludes some premier research from consideration, and the authors have confessed in public that they cannot justify having excluded it (or even remember why they did). While Hyman had already accepted that his original statistical criticisms of ganzfeld ESP research were invalid, and that a number of different experimenters have obtained very successful results with the technique, neither of these points was made in a very critical review of this research. The NRC report also used the kind of 'slur-by-association' strategy heavily relied upon in CSICOP publications: it devoted almost as much space to some experiments on 'plant psi' as it did to ganzfeld research. The plant research was allegedly witnessed at a 'parapsychological laboratory', when the authors knew very well that the researcher involved had never had any affiliation with scientific parapsychology and that his claims had been debunked by parapsychologists. Further, and this is astonishing, this was the *only* direct investigation made by the authors.

The NRC report on parapsychology has been wholly discredited by a number of criticisms far fiercer than ours. At times it verges on incoherence. How can the authors reconcile their claim that there is no evidence for psi with their statement that, with respect to superior psi experiments, 'We do not have a smoking gun, *nor have we demonstrated a plausible alternative*'? This is utterly baffling. Indeed, the NRC now mails out copies of its report with the front page of a highly critical review of its parapsychology section attached. Someone somewhere in the NRC is clearly very embarrassed about the whole affair.

Indeed, there is a sinister element to the NRC report. A background paper on parapsychology and metanalysis, by Robert Rosenthal and his co-worker Monica Harris, undertook a comparative analysis of the six areas of research covered by the NRC report (neither of these researchers is in any way involved in parapsychology research and neither has taken any public position on parapsychology). A major conclusion they reached from flaw analysis was that parapsychology had a far, far superior standard of experimental method to the five areas of conventional psychology. Their paper was not referred to in the NRC report's section on parapsychology, since this conclusion did not suit the skeptical authors, but it was referred to in other sections, dealing with research in psychology. John Swets, chairman of the NRC, actually telephoned Rosenthal and asked him to withdraw the parapsychology section of the paper. To his great credit, Rosenthal refused. Unable to rid themselves of this irksome appraisal and rather than attempt to criticize Rosenthal's contribution, the authors of the parapsychology section of the NRC report simply tried to pretend that it did not exist.

It is simply disgraceful that a *bona fide* article by a very distinguished psychologist was treated in this way. When an author is asked to withdraw his opinions because they do not suit what is clearly a prearranged and predetermined view, this is censorship in the service of ideology, and as such it should be abhorrent to any fair-minded person.

Fortunately, at the request of Senator Claiborne Pell, the Office of Technology Assessment (OTA), which advises the U.S. Congress on technology, held a workshop soon after publication of the NRC report. Here, with OTA officials chairing the meeting and preparing an account of the proceedings for Congress, the authors of the NRC parapsychology paper were part of a nine-person discussion group which included two parapsychologists, John Palmer and Charles Honorton. The far more balanced appraisal which came out of this meeting supplants the NRC report and should certainly have a greater influence on U.S. government bodies than the ill-fated NRC document.

Auto-ganzfeld research

In June 1990 Charles Honorton and six co-authors reported a series of 11 sub-experiments which, in total, consisted of 355 ganzfeld test sessions involving 241 different receivers. The experimental procedures were specifically designed after review of all critical articles on ganzfeld research to date — computer control of selection and presentation of target pictures, fully soundproofed rooms, blind judging, and automated data storage. It is doubtful whether any set of experiments in psychology, let alone parapsychology, has ever been conducted with such expertise and control. To his credit, Hyman has acknowledged that the flaw count in these auto-ganzfeld experiments is as close to zero as any human being can manage. Of the 355 sessions, with a chance average of 25%, Honorton and his group recorded a hit rate of 34%. This is not significantly different from the 38% estimate of the true effect size obtained from the previous metanalysis. The odds against chance for this finding are 20,000 to 1. Differences in the results obtained by the eight experimenters, which included Honorton himself, were trivial; there was no evidence of any experimenter

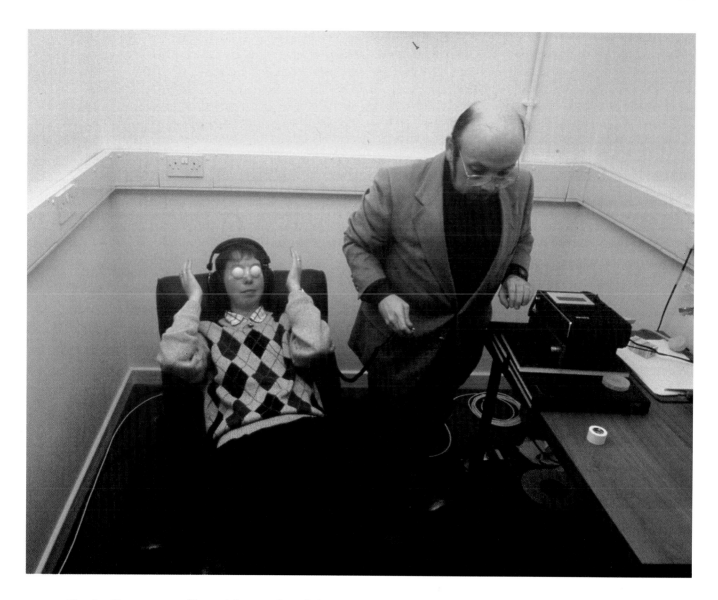

Charles Honorton conducting one of the auto-ganzfeld experiments that finally torpedoed the statistical and methodological criticisms of Ray Hyman.

effects. The results of this epic body of research are absolutely clear-cut. Hyman has implicitly accepted the findings. At least, to date his only comment has been that he wishes to see more evidence of this type. He has not stated what additional evidence would persuade him to accept the psi hypothesis.

Honorton's auto-ganzfeld research is as close to conclusive as we're ever likely to get. This immaculately conducted set of experiments gave results which were statistically significant and also showed an effect size very close to that predicted by metanalysis of all previous experiments. This is very, very powerful evidence indeed.

'Rhetoric Over Substance'?

The *Comitato Italiano per il Controllo delle Affirmazione sul Paranormale* is an Italian organization with similar goals to those of CSICOP, but with a rather better sense of balance. In 1992 it invited three parapsychologists and three skeptics to write articles for its publication. Each skeptic would write a critique of the three parapsychologists, and each parapsychologist would write a criticism of the skeptics. This is the kind of debate we badly need more of!

Ray Hyman's paper is of especial interest. Asked to write approximately ten pages, he managed just four. Abandoning any reference to his statistical or methodological criticisms of the past decade, he came up with an entirely new line of criticism: parapsychology is not a science because it is not *progressive*. He asserted that each generation of psi researchers does not build on knowledge which has been earlier learned, but switches to new fads and fashions in research. Claims for paranormal phenomena flit from one area to another, with no true growth of knowledge.

This claim is simply absurd. Noise-reduction models, as we have seen, have sought to integrate laboratory findings with ancient meditational texts, with nineteenth- and twentieth-century surveys of spontaneous psi experiences, and with the effects of personality variables on psi established during the 1940s and in later work. These models have been used to develop new experimental techniques which offer more complete control and manipulation of the kinds of 'noise' that may inhibit ESP. They clearly constitute a progressive, growing line of research. To be sure, 'noise' models require further work and development since they are too simplistic as they stand — and they will be further refined and developed, of that we have no doubt. This is no fad or passing fashion.

Indeed, the fact that Hyman had so little to say after a decade of engaging with frontier research in parapsychology is very telling. Honorton's contribution to the Italian symposium was entitled 'Rhetoric Over Substance: the impoverished state of skepticism'. It is a polemical title, but we invite any scientist to read Hyman's embarrassingly brief contribution and Honorton's extensively documented summary paper and judge the relative qualities for themselves.

To allow the reader some direct insight into this claimed 'impoverished state of skepticism', let us eavesdrop on a verbatim transcript of the OTA workshop we referred to earlier. Hyman begins the exchange by claiming that parapsychology is plagued with experimenter effects — that many experimenters cannot reproduce the results obtained by a handful of successful ones — and that this is a problem which is unique to, and a major problem for, parapsychology. The italic emphases are ours.

HYMAN: '...it's clear that some experimenters consistently get better results than other experimenters within the field. *That is different from any other field of science* that I know of, for all practical purposes.'

HONORTON: 'What about placebo research?'

HYMAN: 'What's that?'

HONORTON: 'What about medical placebo research?'

HYMAN: 'I don't know much about medical placebo research. But how about physics and...'

HONORTON: 'Must we compare ourselves to physics?'

HYMAN: 'Well, does placebo research get an experimenter effect there too?'

HONORTON: 'Very strongly.'

HYMAN: 'Okay. But when we get experimenter effects in those fields it's considered an artifact, right?'

HONORTON: 'A Rosenthal effect.' [a genuine, established effect in psychology]

HYMAN: 'Yes, in parapsychology, the experimenter effect is not...'

HONORTON: 'But certainly placebo is interpreted as something one wants to get rid of. But that really...if you look at it a little bit more deeply, it's begging the question. What is it about the way one physician administers a symbolic treatment that has an effect on alleviating pain that doesn't occur when another physician in the same study, using the same language, administers the same set?'

HYMAN: 'Okay. *Well, then, it exists in other fields.*'

If one were more mischievous than we are, all one would really want to say after this little exchange is 'Thankyou and goodnight, Dr. Hyman'.

Parapsychology as science

Notwithstanding the evidence quoted above, Ray Hyman has performed a service for science which historians of science will surely wish to analyze in detail (some have already begun to do so). Hyman has had the integrity to roll up his sleeves and *look* at the evidence which so many skeptics lackadaisically dismiss out of hand. That he has been forced to abandon standard skeptical arguments, and eventually resorted to a claim which even other skeptics have greeted with incredulity, is an important advance for parapsychology. His criticisms have obliged parapsychologists to defend and buttress their findings. As metanalyses of old bodies of evidence accumulate almost by the month, with the aid of 'outside' scientists who have been surprised by the merits of the data and findings, parapsychology is approaching a point of breakthrough. Some metanalyses reveal hitherto unexpected strengths in old experiments. We will give one example.

When Charles Honorton, Diane Ferrari, and Daryl Bem conducted a metanalysis of the relationship between ESP and extraversion, the results startled one of us (Sargent), some of whose free-response experiments had measured this personality trait. It was found that, for the four different experimenters involved, the average correlation was very similar and the effect size homogeneous. Sargent conducted most of the experiments and, at the time did not think the results were terribly important (most were not individually statistically different from chance). He was therefore astonished to learn that the average correlation for all of his own work was virtually identical to the average for the other three experimenters. Taken together, Sargent's results and those of the other three experimenters were highly significant and not due to chance!

Further, in their auto-ganzfeld experiments, all conducted subsequently, Honorton and his team replicated the earlier results with a similar effect size. Metanalysis revealed an order and similarity in old evidence that was stronger than anyone had realized and new experiments replicated the results of the old. This is startling. Without doubt, this is progress. This shows a lawful effect operating consistently across results from five independent researchers working across different decades (from the 1940s to the 1980s) and within very different cultures (America, Britain, South Africa). Such repeatability of effect is not easily come by in conventional psychology.

We consider that parapsychology is a science. If the epithet 'pseudo-scientific' is to be thrown about, it deserves to be aimed at the less informed critics of the field. Parapsychology is a science because it shows development of theory and method. It shows the *progressive problem shifts* which the philosopher of science Imre Lakatos has persuasively argued are the hallmark of scientific thought. It is a science which may hold deep implications for other sciences, from physics to psychology — only time will tell. It is a science which deserves better support from government funding agencies than it has received in the past. Above all, it needs the involvement of open-minded young scientists who are willing to address the evidence, and the issues, and conduct research of their own. And it is a science which addresses matters of importance — a great deal of essentially trivial research is funded in scientific laboratories around the world, but parapsychology is a science whose findings have implications for everyone. Those implications are practical (why else would Sony have established a large parapsychology laboratory in Japan recently?), and may one day profoundly change the way in which we think of ourselves and our lives.

We do not 'believe in psi'. Psi is not a matter of belief. It is a question of finding worthwhile evidence of human capacities and skills which we understand very poorly. We judge that parapsychology has certainly found some of that evidence.

We close with a justification of our assertion that parapsychology is reaching a point of breakthrough. There is a standard textbook of psychology (*Introduction to Psychology*), very widely used in the United States and other countries, which is known simply as

Hilgard & Atkinson after the original authors (many editions and generations of student readers later, it now has additional authors). When a skeptical psychologist ignorant of psi research was asked under what circumstances he would accept psi as a real effect, he replied: 'When I see it in Hilgard & Atkinson.'

The 1990 edition of this Bible of psychology contains a seven-page section on parapsychological research, reviewing both skeptical and parapsychological arguments and evidence. It concludes: '...much of the skepticism of psychologists toward psi is well-founded. But some of it is not. As we noted earlier, some scientists declare psi to be an impossibility and reject the legitimacy of parapsychology, *a priori* judgements that we believe to be out of place in science. Only 4 per cent of the college professors in the survey (cited earlier) declared psi to be an impossibility — but 34 per cent of the psychologists did so. Two hundred years ago, those same skeptics would have been equally certain that God does not hurl stones at us from heaven.'

Parapsychology is rapidly coming of age. Despite chronic financial undernourishment, its future as we head into a new century is exciting. It is time that more scientists took its findings seriously, and looked at the evidence on offer, because the best of it compares with the very best in any area they might be working in.

Bibliography

Some of the major research findings we have quoted in this book repose in specialist journals. Because few libraries stock the major psi journals, we have kept such references to a minimum, but for readers who want to get at original research work, tracking down these journals is the only way to do it.

Chapter 1

Richard Broughton's *Parapsychology: The Controversial Science* (Ballantine Books, 1991) is a useful book on the science of parapsychology, with many references for further reading. The British Society for Psychical Research (SPR) has a centenary volume, *Psychical Research: a guide to its history, principles and practices* (ed. I. Grattan-Guinness, Aquarian Press, 1982), which covers a wide range of topics, scientific and observational. The quality of articles is uneven, but as a general guide it is most helpful. Louisa Rhine's *ESP in Life and Lab.* (Macmillan, 1967) is a fine all-round survey of Rhine's early years and subsequent development, well written and enjoyable. Her later *The Invisible Picture: a study of psychic experiences* (McFarland, 1981) is excellent for those most interested in spontaneous psi. For heavyweight reviews of where parapsychology is going as a science, the six volumes of *Advances in Parapsychological Research* (vols. 1–3 from Plenum Books, 4–6 from McFarland, series editor Stanley Krippner) are the place to go.

Chapter 2

For a long original account of D.D. Home, see Earl of Dunraven, 'Experiences in Spiritualism with D.D. Home', *Proceedings of the Society for Psychical Research*, 1924, vol. 35, pages 1–285. As a general, highly readable account of Home's life *The Shadow and the Light* by Elizabeth Jenkins (Hamish Hamilton, 1981) is excellent. For a typical skeptical analysis, see T.H. Hall, *The Enigma of Daniel Home* (Prometheus, 1984). On Crookes's experiments, see R.G. Medhurst et al. (eds.), *Crookes and the Spirit World* (Taplinger, 1972). On Stepanek, see J.G. Pratt's article in *Proceedings of the American Society for Psychical Research*, 1973, vol. 30, pages 1–78. A shorter summary can be found in Pratt's chapter in J. Beloff (ed.), *New Directions in Parapsychology* (Paul Elek, 1974). Gardner's book is *How Not to Test a Psychic* (Prometheus, 1989); check also the review of this by Jurgen Keil, *Journal of Parapsychology*, 1990, vol. 54, pages 151–167.

Chapter 3

Schmidt's simplest REG system is described in his article 'Anomalous prediction of quantum processes by some human subjects', Boeing Scientific Research Laboratories Document DI.82.0821. Schmidt has published many articles in *Journal of Parapsychology* (his first report appeared in 1969, vol. 33, pages 99–108) and *Journal of the American Society for Psychical Research* in the last 25 years. The research of the Jahn group is summarized in R.G. Jahn and B.J. Dunne, *Margins of Reality* (Harcourt Brace Jovanovich, 1987). The technical bulletins of the PEAR group are not easily available, but this book gives abundant detail. Dean Radin and Jessica Utts' paper is in *Journal of Scientific Exploration* (1989, vol. 1, pages 65–79).

Chapter 4

John Palmer's chapter on belief and psi (in B.B. Wolman [ed.], *Handbook of Parapsychology*, Van Nostrand Reinhold, 1977) is dated, but still an excellent example of how to analyze this effect. On extraversion, see Sargent's article in the journal *Personality and Individual Differences*, 1981, vol. 2, pages 137–143. On anxiety/neuroticism, see Palmer's chapter (see above). Cultural factors are considered in A. Angoff and D. Barth (eds.), *Parapsychology and Anthropology* (Parapsychology Foundation, 1974).

Chapter 5

M. Ullman, S. Krippner, and A. Vaughan's book *Dream Telepathy* (Turnstone, 1973) remains a classic. Honorton's older papers on altered states are summarized in B.B. Wolman (ed.), *Handbook of Parapsychology* (Van Nostrand Reinhold, 1977). References for Chapter 11 include many others on ganzfeld ESP.

Chapter 6

Honorton's chapter in *Handbook of Parapsychology* (see above) covers hypnosis studies, relaxation, and meditation, and Honorton and Krippner's formal review of hypnosis studies is in *Journal of the American Society for Psychical Research*, 1969, vol. 63, pages 214–252. See also E. Schechter on hypnosis studies in *Journal of the American Society for Psychical Research*, 1984, vol. 78, pages 1–27. William Braud reviewed autonomic nervous system activity and ESP in *Journal of the American Society for Psychical Research*, 1981, vol. 75, pages 1–35, suggesting a curvilinear relationship not unlike that noted elsewhere for motivational effects on psi (see Chapter 8).

Chapter 7

A scholarly, outstanding study of poltergeists is A.O. Gauld and A.D. Cornell's *Poltergeists* (Routledge & Kegan Paul, 1981). On metal-bending, see J.B. Hasted's *The Metal Benders* (RKP, 1980) and Richard Broughton's update of general trends in Chapter 6 of his *Parapsychology: the controversial science* (Ballantine, 1991). A general survey of recent PK research is given by Gertrude Schmeidler in *Advances in Parapsychological Research*, vol. 6 (McFarland, 1990, pages 11–53) and some papers in earlier volumes in this series are helpful also. William Braud's bio-PK research is summarized in his paper with Marilyn Schlitz in the journal *Subtle Energies*, 1990, vol. 2, pages 1–46; the hemolysis experiments are described in detail by Braud in *Journal of the American Society for Psychical Research*, 1990, vol. 81, pages 1–25.

Chapter 8

Stanford's most recent description and evaluation is in *Advances in Parapsychological Research*, Vol. 6 (McFarland, 1990, pages 54–167). Cogently argued and self-critical, this review is an excellent summary of all relevant PMIR research to date.

Chapter 9

An early debating ground for physics models are the papers in A. Puharich (ed.), *The Iceland Papers* (Essentia Associates, 1979). Physicist David Bohm explores mind-matter interactions in an article in *Journal of the American Society for Psychical Research*, 1986, vol. 80, pages 113–135. Walker's theory is presented in *Psychoenergetic Systems*, 1979, vol. 3, pages 259–299. He also has two later articles in *Journal of Parapsychology* (1984, vol. 48, pages 227–332) and *Journal of the American Society for Psychical Research* (1987, vol. 81, pages 333–369) which amplify aspects of his QM model and reply to criticisms. Be warned: these are heavy going!

Chapter 10

On OBEs, see S.J. Blackmore, *Beyond the Body* (Heinemann, 1982). On NDEs, see R.A. Moody Jnr., *Life After Life* (Mockingbird, 1975) and especially M. Sabom's excellent *Recollections of Death: a medical investigation* (Harper & Row, 1982). Two articles by A.O. Gauld (chapter in B.B. Wolman [ed.], *Handbook of Parapsychology*, Van Nostrand Reinhold, 1977, and in *Proceedings of the Society for Psychical Research*, 1971, vol. 55, pages 273–340) consider mediumship. On reincarnation, see I. Stevenson, 'Twenty cases suggestive of reincarnation', (*Proceedings of the American Society for Psychical Research*, 1966, vol. 26, pages 1–362) and his four-volume *Cases of the Reincarnation Type* (University of Virginia Press, 1975, 1977, 1980, 1983). Mills' two-part paper is in *Journal of Scientific Exploration*, 1990, vol. 4, pages 171–188 and 189–202; Keil's is in the same journal, 1991, vol. 5, pages 27–59.

Chapter 11

Rawlins' exposé is in *Fate*, October 1981. Issues 9, 10, and 11 of *Zetetic Scholar* (1982–1983) contain articles by Curry, Kammann, Hoebens, and others on the 'Starbaby' scandal. Kammann's devastating critique is in issue 10, 1982. The 'reappraisal' of the KZA Mars research is in *Skeptical Inquirer*, Spring 1982, pages 77–82. For an overview of CSICOP in later years see G.P. Hansen's article in *Journal of the American Society for Psychical Research*, 1992, vol. 86, pages 21–63. Shneour's article criticizing Randi's behavior in the Benveniste affair is in *Skeptical Inquirer*, 1989, vol. 14, 91–95.

The Hyman/Honorton debate is in *Journal of Parapsychology*, 1985, vol. 49, pages 3–49 (Hyman) and 51–91 (Honorton), and the joint communiqué is in *Journal of Parapsychology*, 1986, vol. 50, pages 351–364. Our metanalysis data were taken from an as-yet-unpublished paper by Charles Honorton. The NRC report is D. Druckman and J.A. Swets (eds.), *Enhancing Human Performance* (National Academy Press, 1987); the critique is by J.A. Palmer, C. Honorton, and J. Utts, *Journal of the American Society for Psychical Research*, 1989, vol. 83, pages 31–49. The OTA workshop is summarized in *Journal of the American Society for Psychical Research*, 1989, volume 83, pages 316–339 (we also have a verbatim transcript of the workshop from which the Hyman-Honorton dialogue is taken). For further spirited exchanges on ganzfeld research, see papers by S.J. Blackmore, C.L. Sargent, and T.A. Harley and G.R. Matthews in *Journal of the Society for Psychical Research*, 1987, vol. 84, July 1987, and the Hyman-Honorton Italian exchange (unfortunately we do not have a certain statement of where these papers will appear). The extraversion metanalysis is taken from an as-yet-unpublished paper by C. Honorton, D.C. Ferrari, and D.J. Bem. On metanalysis in parapsychology generally, see J. Utts, *Statistical Science*, 1991, vol. 6, pages 363–403 (including commentaries). Further examples of metanalysis in psi research, which we have not had the space to quote in our chapter, include: precognition experiments (C. Honorton and D.C. Ferrari, *Journal of Parapsychology*, 1989, vol. 53, pages 281–308) and PK work with REGs (D.I. Radin and R.D. Nelson, *Foundations of Physics*, 1989, volume 19, pages 1499–1514).

Index

Picture credits